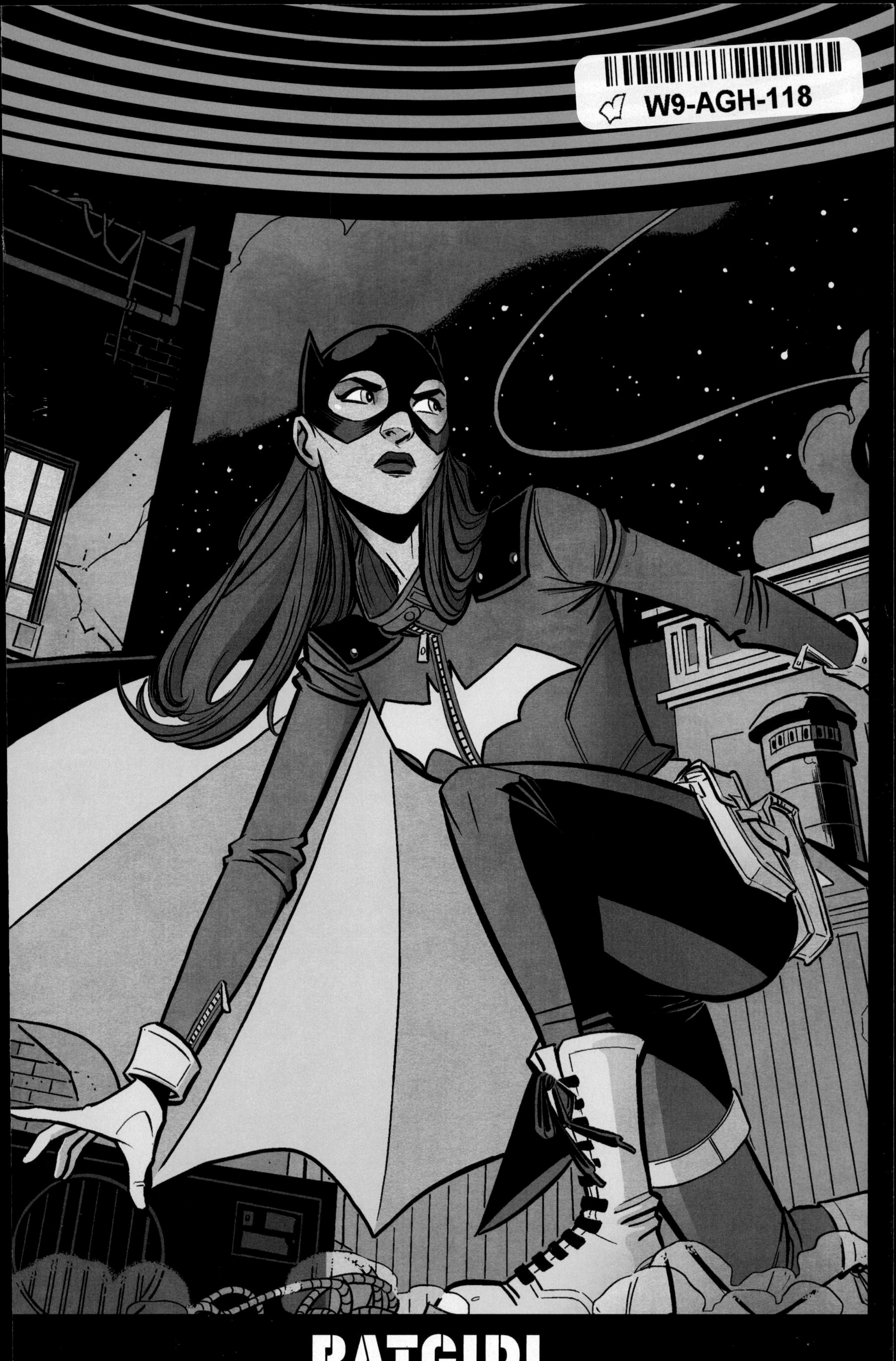

BATGIRL

VOL.3 SUMMER OF LIES

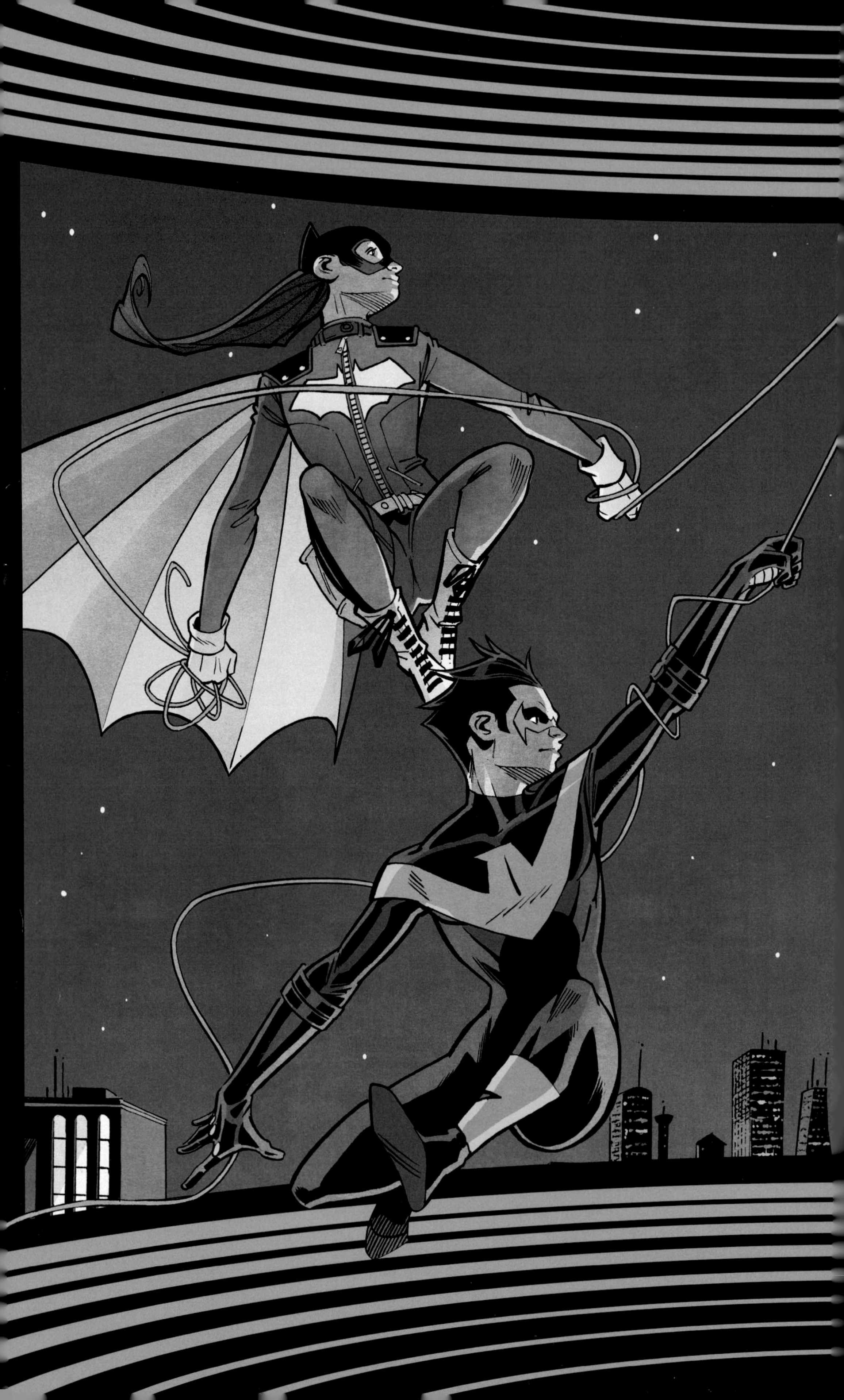

BATGIRL

VOL.3 SUMMER OF LIES

HOPE LARSON
writer

CHRIS WILDGOOSE
JOSE MARZAN JR.
ELEONORA CARLINI
INAKI MIRANDA
ANDY OWENS
artists

MAT LOPES
CRIS PETER
EVA DE LA CRUZ
colorists

DERON BENNETT
letterer

DAN MORA
collection cover artist

BATMAN created by **BOB KANE** with **BILL FINGER**

REBECCA TAYLOR CHRIS CONROY Editors - Original Series
BRITTANY HOLZHERR Associate Editor - Original Series
JEB WOODARD Group Editor - Collected Editions ✳ **ROBIN WILDMAN** Editor - Collected Edition
STEVE COOK Design Director - Books ✳ **SHANNON STEWART** Publication Design

BOB HARRAS Senior VP - Editor-in-Chief, DC Comics
PAT McCALLUM Executive Editor, DC Comics

DIANE NELSON President ✳ **DAN DiDIO** Publisher ✳ **JIM LEE** Publisher ✳ **GEOFF JOHNS** President & Chief Creative Officer
AMIT DESAI Executive VP - Business & Marketing Strategy, Direct to Consumer & Global Franchise Management
SAM ADES Senior VP & General Manager, Digital Services ✳ **BOBBIE CHASE** VP & Executive Editor, Young Reader & Talent Development
MARK CHIARELLO Senior VP - Art, Design & Collected Editions ✳ **JOHN CUNNINGHAM** Senior VP - Sales & Trade Marketing
ANNE DePIES Senior VP - Business Strategy, Finance & Administration ✳ **DON FALLETTI** VP - Manufacturing Operations
LAWRENCE GANEM VP - Editorial Administration & Talent Relations ✳ **ALISON GILL** Senior VP - Manufacturing & Operations
HANK KANALZ Senior VP - Editorial Strategy & Administration ✳ **JAY KOGAN** VP - Legal Affairs ✳ **JACK MAHAN** VP - Business Affairs
NICK J. NAPOLITANO VP - Manufacturing Administration ✳ **EDDIE SCANNELL** VP - Consumer Marketing
COURTNEY SIMMONS Senior VP - Publicity & Communications ✳ **JIM (SKI) SOKOLOWSKI** VP - Comic Book Specialty Sales & Trade Marketing
NANCY SPEARS VP - Mass, Book, Digital Sales & Trade Marketing ✳ **MICHELE R. WELLS** VP - Content Strategy

BATGIRL VOL. 3: SUMMER OF LIES

DC Comics, 2900 West Alameda Ave., Burbank, CA 91505
Printed by LSC Communications, Kendallville, IN, USA. 2/23/18. First Printing.
ISBN: 978-1-4012-7890-8

Library of Congress Cataloging-in-Publication Data is available.

PEFC Certified

Printed on paper from
sustainably managed
forests, controlled
sources

PEFC/29-31-337   www.pefc.org

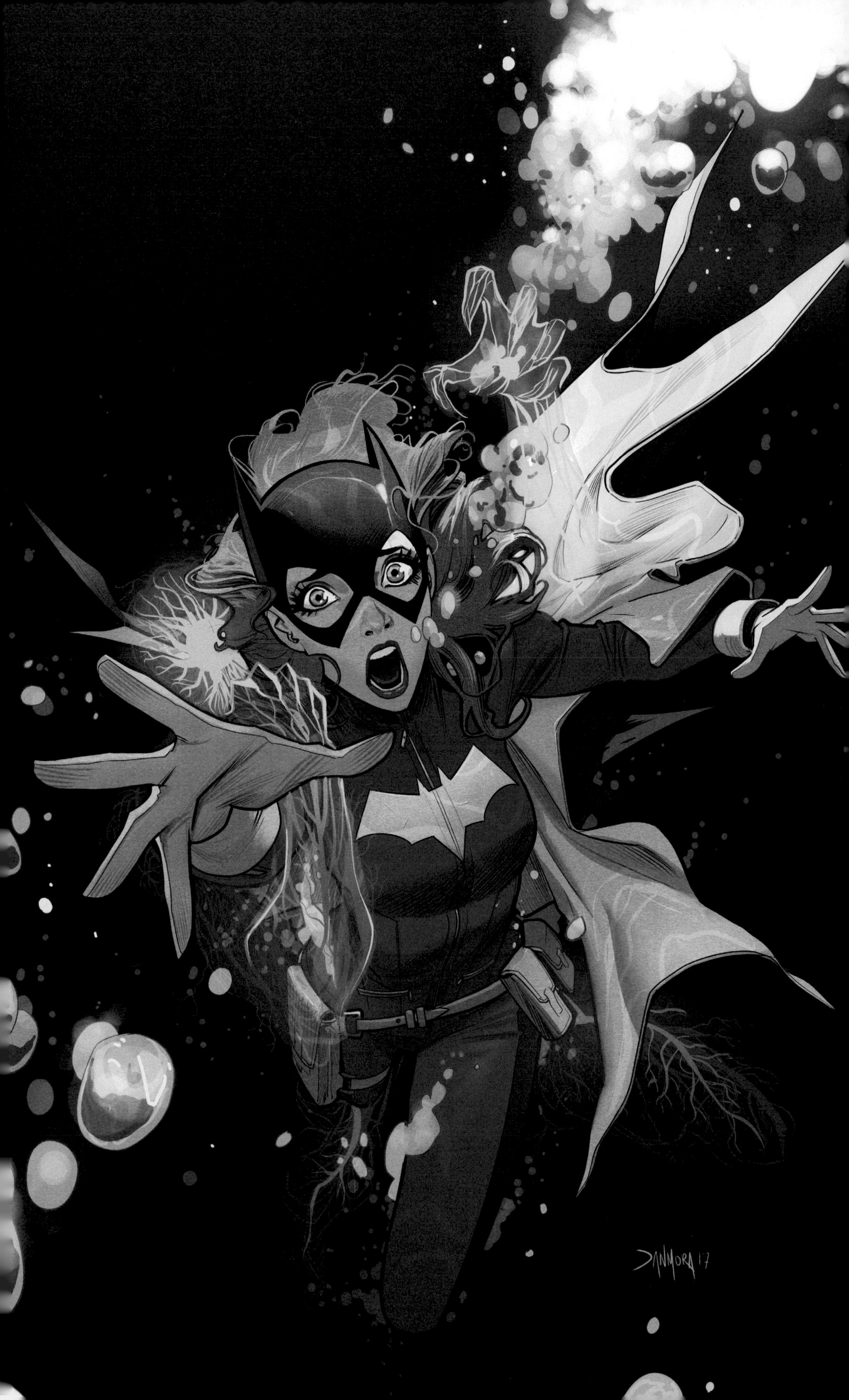
DANMORA '17

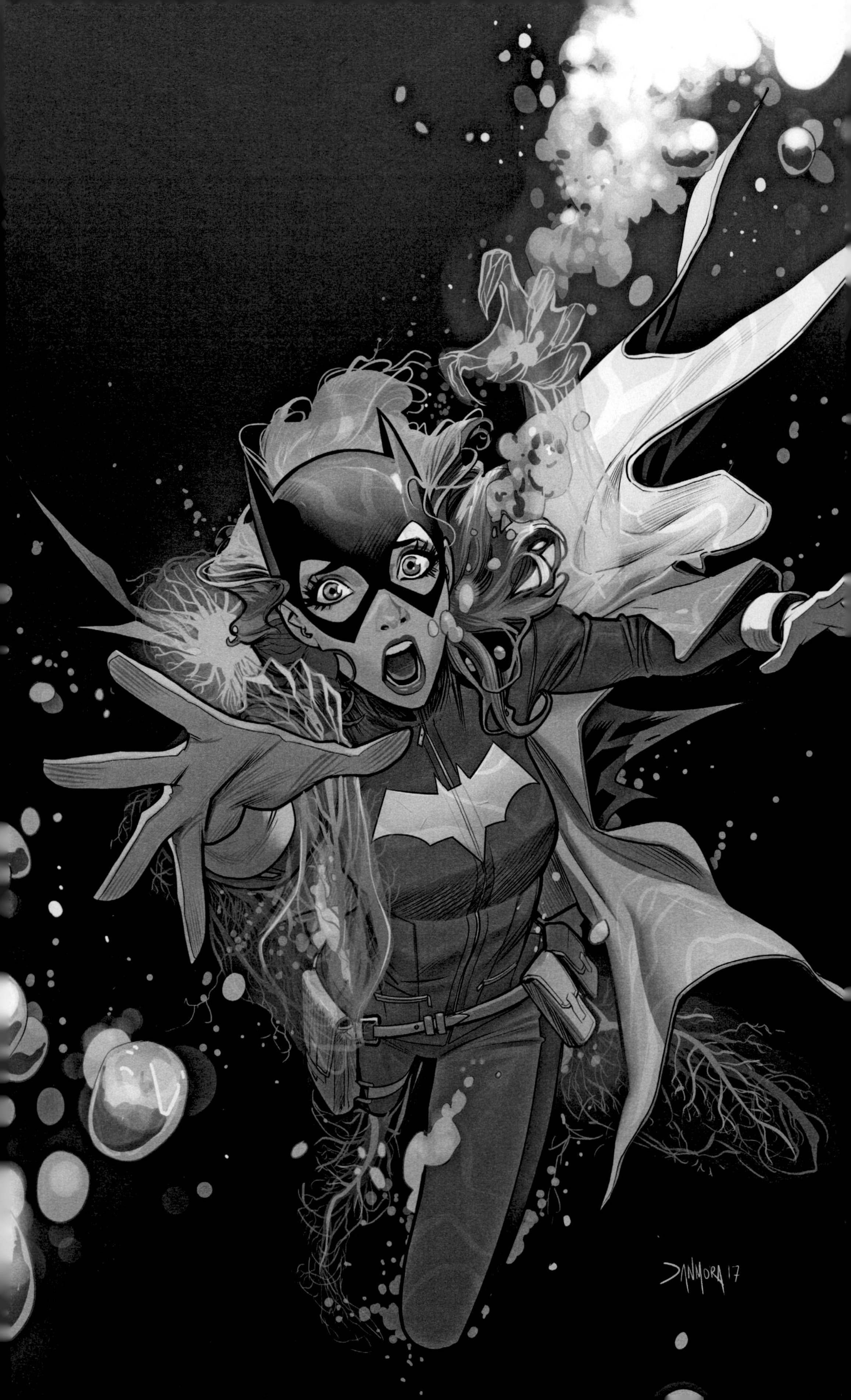

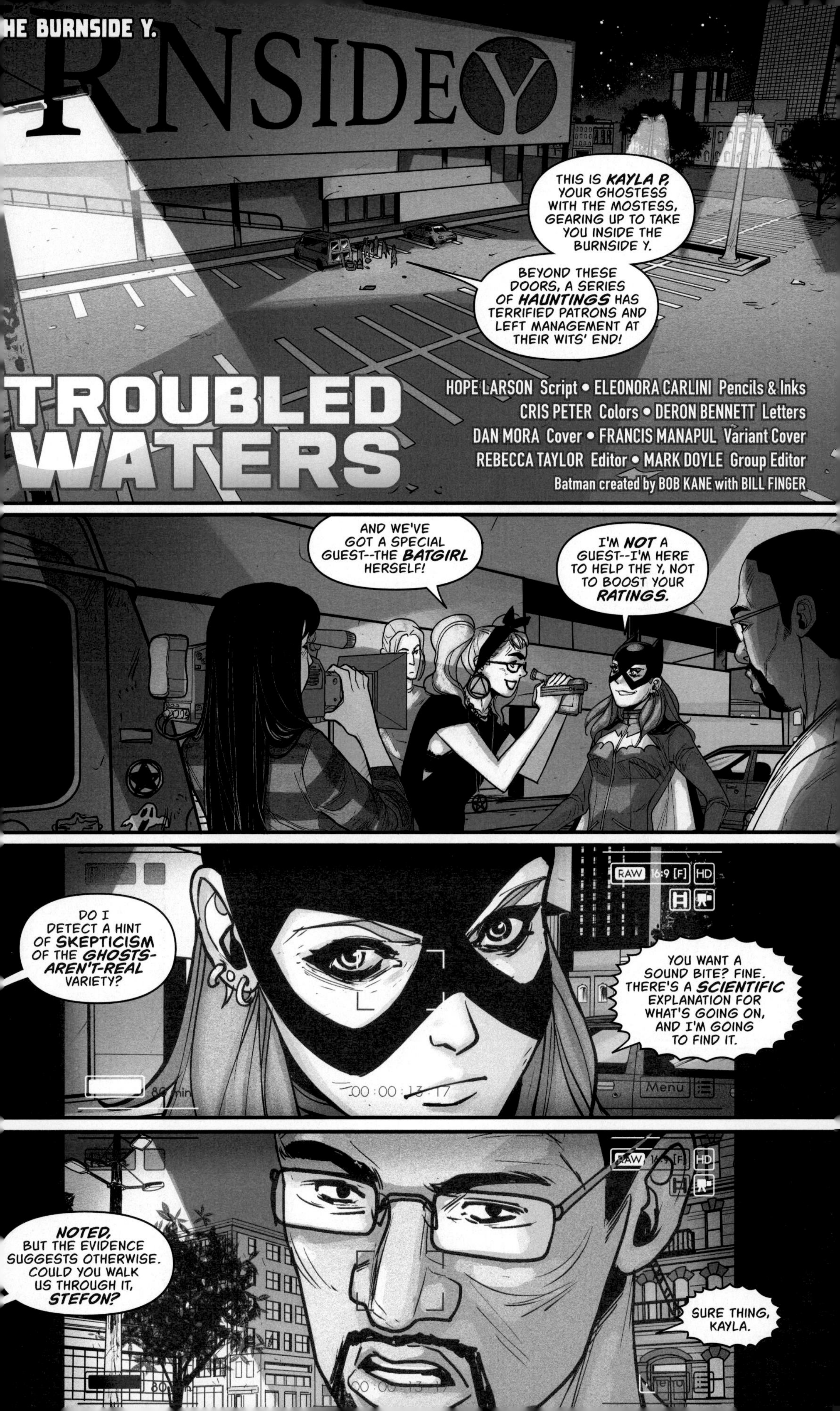

HE BURNSIDE Y.
RNSIDE Y
THIS IS KAYLA P., YOUR GHOSTESS WITH THE MOSTESS, GEARING UP TO TAKE YOU INSIDE THE BURNSIDE Y.
BEYOND THESE DOORS, A SERIES OF HAUNTINGS HAS TERRIFIED PATRONS AND LEFT MANAGEMENT AT THEIR WITS' END!
TROUBLED WATERS
HOPE LARSON Script • ELEONORA CARLINI Pencils & Inks
CRIS PETER Colors • DERON BENNETT Letters
DAN MORA Cover • FRANCIS MANAPUL Variant Cover
REBECCA TAYLOR Editor • MARK DOYLE Group Editor
Batman created by BOB KANE with BILL FINGER
AND WE'VE GOT A SPECIAL GUEST--THE BATGIRL HERSELF!
I'M NOT A GUEST--I'M HERE TO HELP THE Y, NOT TO BOOST YOUR RATINGS.
RAW 16:9 [F] HD
DO I DETECT A HINT OF SKEPTICISM OF THE GHOSTS-AREN'T-REAL VARIETY?
YOU WANT A SOUND BITE? FINE. THERE'S A SCIENTIFIC EXPLANATION FOR WHAT'S GOING ON, AND I'M GOING TO FIND IT.
Menu
NOTED, BUT THE EVIDENCE SUGGESTS OTHERWISE. COULD YOU WALK US THROUGH IT, STEFON?
SURE THING, KAYLA.

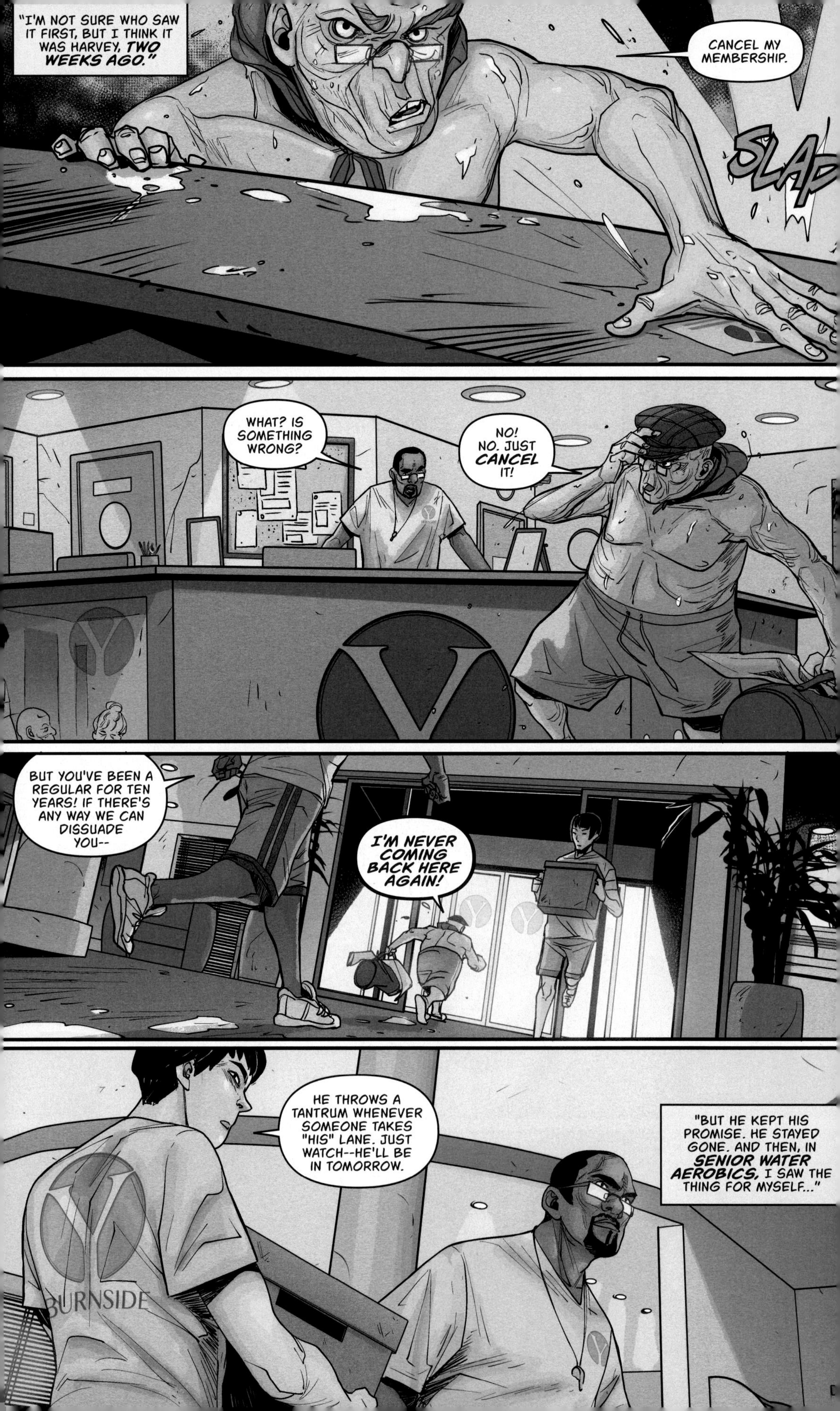
"I'M NOT SURE WHO SAW IT FIRST, BUT I THINK IT WAS HARVEY, TWO WEEKS AGO."
CANCEL MY MEMBERSHIP.
SLAP
WHAT? IS SOMETHING WRONG?
NO! NO. JUST CANCEL IT!
BUT YOU'VE BEEN A REGULAR FOR TEN YEARS! IF THERE'S ANY WAY WE CAN DISSUADE YOU--
I'M NEVER COMING BACK HERE AGAIN!
HE THROWS A TANTRUM WHENEVER SOMEONE TAKES "HIS" LANE. JUST WATCH--HE'LL BE IN TOMORROW.
"BUT HE KEPT HIS PROMISE. HE STAYED GONE. AND THEN, IN SENIOR WATER AEROBICS, I SAW THE THING FOR MYSELF..."
BURNSIDE

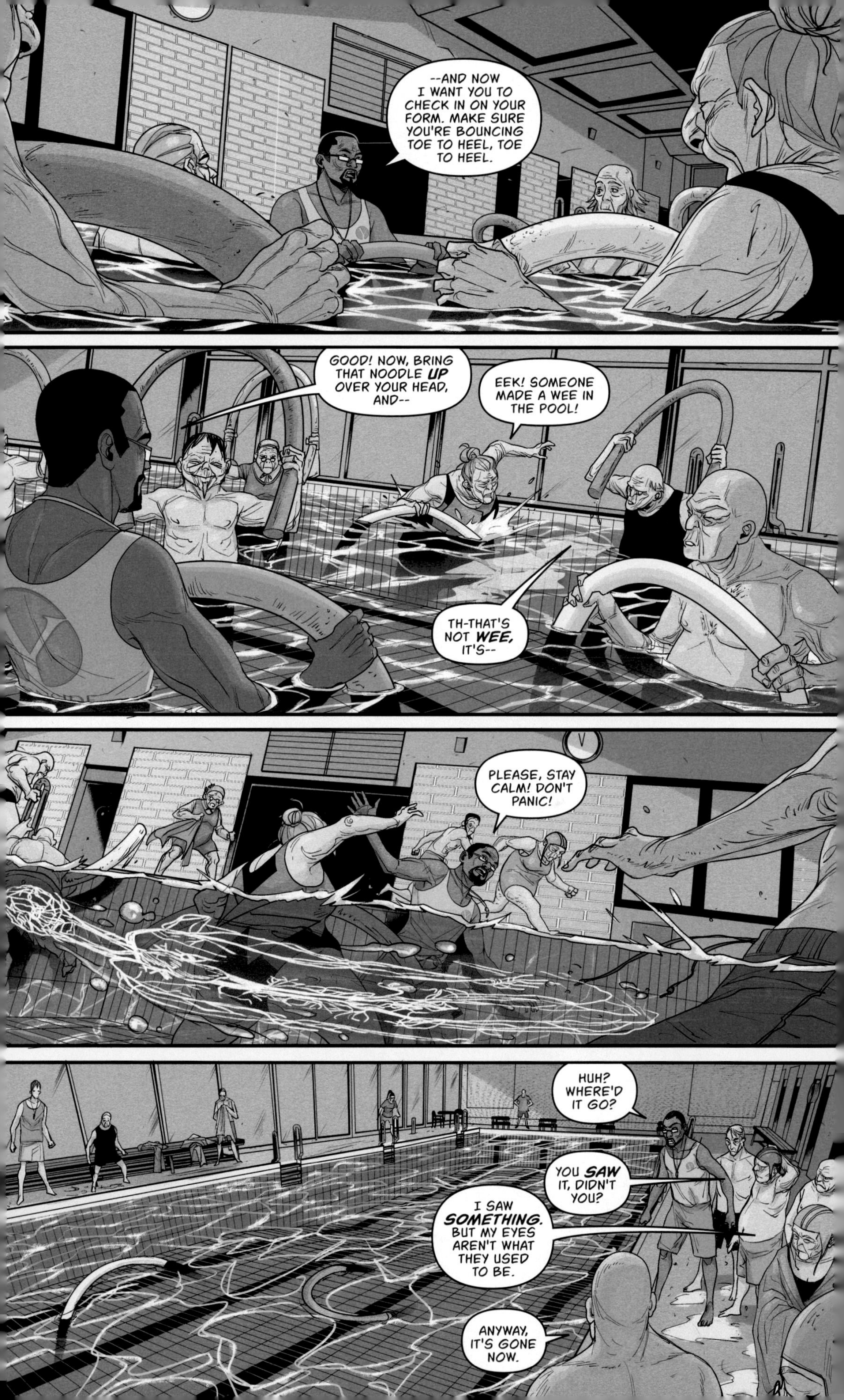
--AND NOW I WANT YOU TO CHECK IN ON YOUR FORM. MAKE SURE YOU'RE BOUNCING TOE TO HEEL, TOE TO HEEL.
GOOD! NOW, BRING THAT NOODLE UP OVER YOUR HEAD, AND--
EEK! SOMEONE MADE A WEE IN THE POOL!
TH-THAT'S NOT WEE, IT'S--
PLEASE, STAY CALM! DON'T PANIC!
HUH? WHERE'D IT GO?
YOU SAW IT, DIDN'T YOU?
I SAW SOMETHING. BUT MY EYES AREN'T WHAT THEY USED TO BE.
ANYWAY, IT'S GONE NOW.

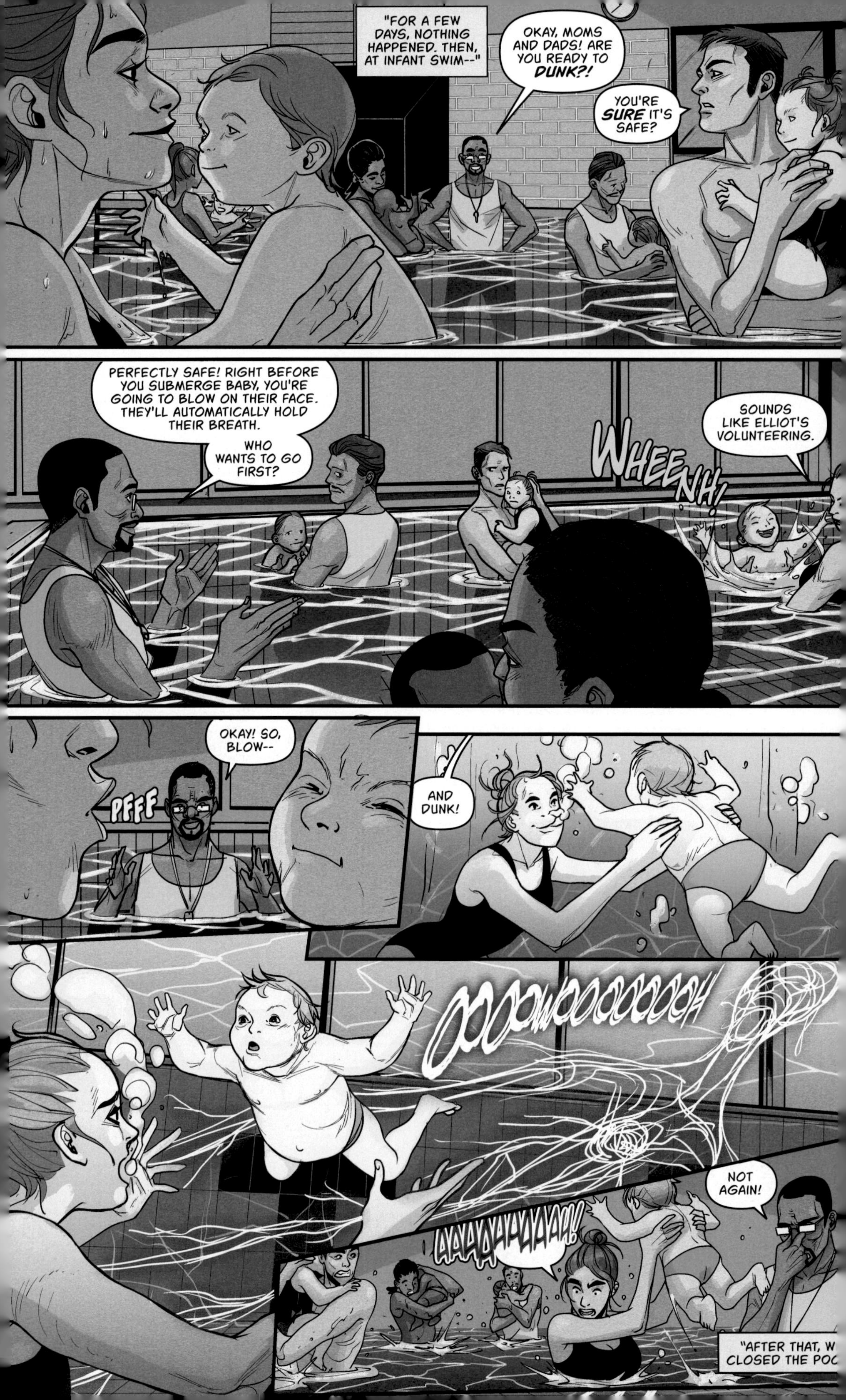
"FOR A FEW DAYS, NOTHING HAPPENED. THEN, AT INFANT SWIM--"
OKAY, MOMS AND DADS! ARE YOU READY TO DUNK?!
YOU'RE SURE IT'S SAFE?
PERFECTLY SAFE! RIGHT BEFORE YOU SUBMERGE BABY, YOU'RE GOING TO BLOW ON THEIR FACE. THEY'LL AUTOMATICALLY HOLD THEIR BREATH.
WHO WANTS TO GO FIRST?
WHEENH!
SOUNDS LIKE ELLIOT'S VOLUNTEERING.
OKAY! SO, BLOW--
PFFF
AND DUNK!
OOOOWOOOOOOOH
NOT AGAIN!
AAAAAAAAAAAH!
"AFTER THAT, W
CLOSED THE POO

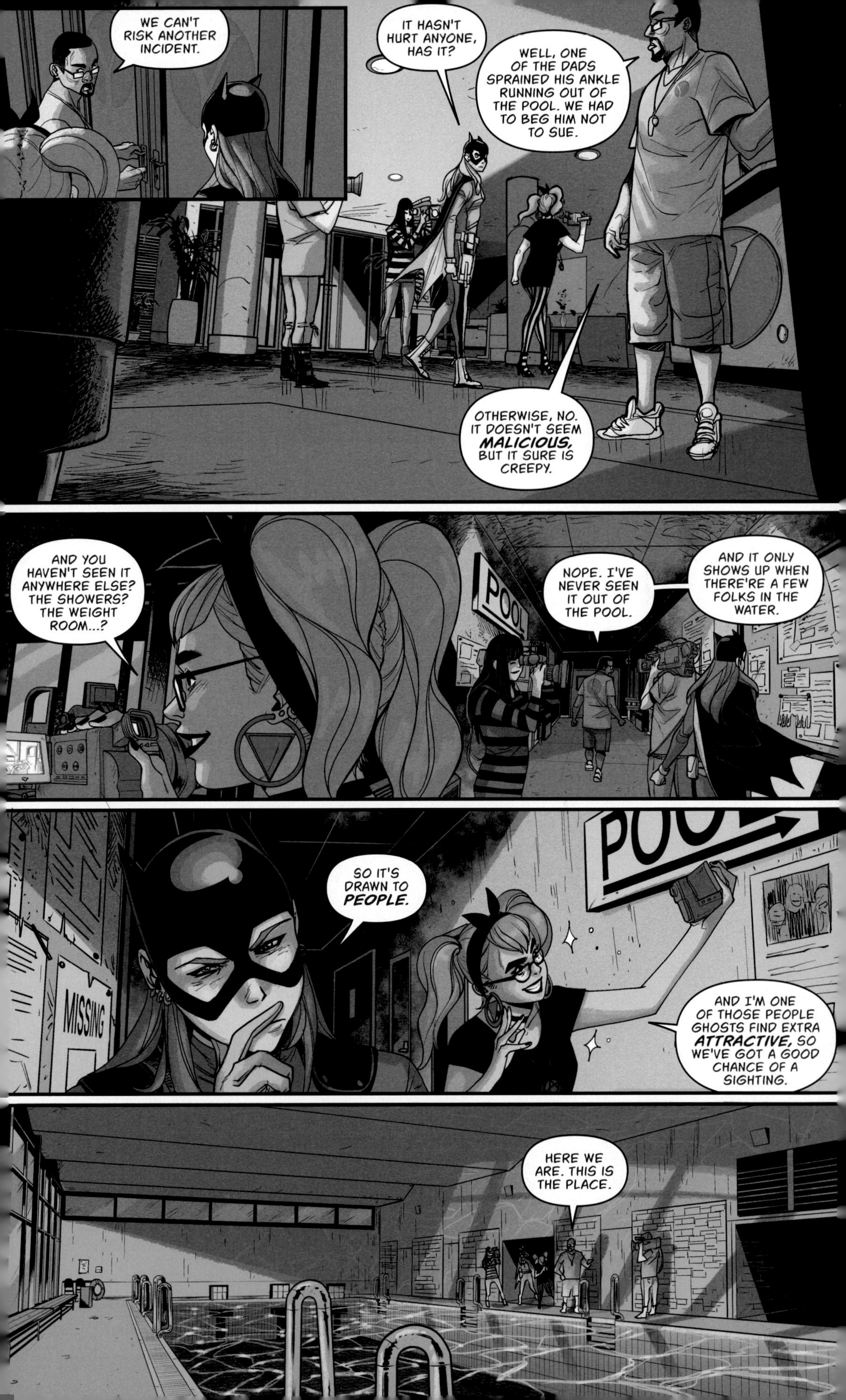
WE CAN'T RISK ANOTHER INCIDENT.
IT HASN'T HURT ANYONE, HAS IT?
WELL, ONE OF THE DADS SPRAINED HIS ANKLE RUNNING OUT OF THE POOL. WE HAD TO BEG HIM NOT TO SUE.
OTHERWISE, NO. IT DOESN'T SEEM MALICIOUS, BUT IT SURE IS CREEPY.
AND YOU HAVEN'T SEEN IT ANYWHERE ELSE? THE SHOWERS? THE WEIGHT ROOM...?
POOL
NOPE. I'VE NEVER SEEN IT OUT OF THE POOL.
AND IT ONLY SHOWS UP WHEN THERE'RE A FEW FOLKS IN THE WATER.
MISSING
SO IT'S DRAWN TO PEOPLE.
AND I'M ONE OF THOSE PEOPLE GHOSTS FIND EXTRA ATTRACTIVE, SO WE'VE GOT A GOOD CHANCE OF A SIGHTING.
HERE WE ARE. THIS IS THE PLACE.

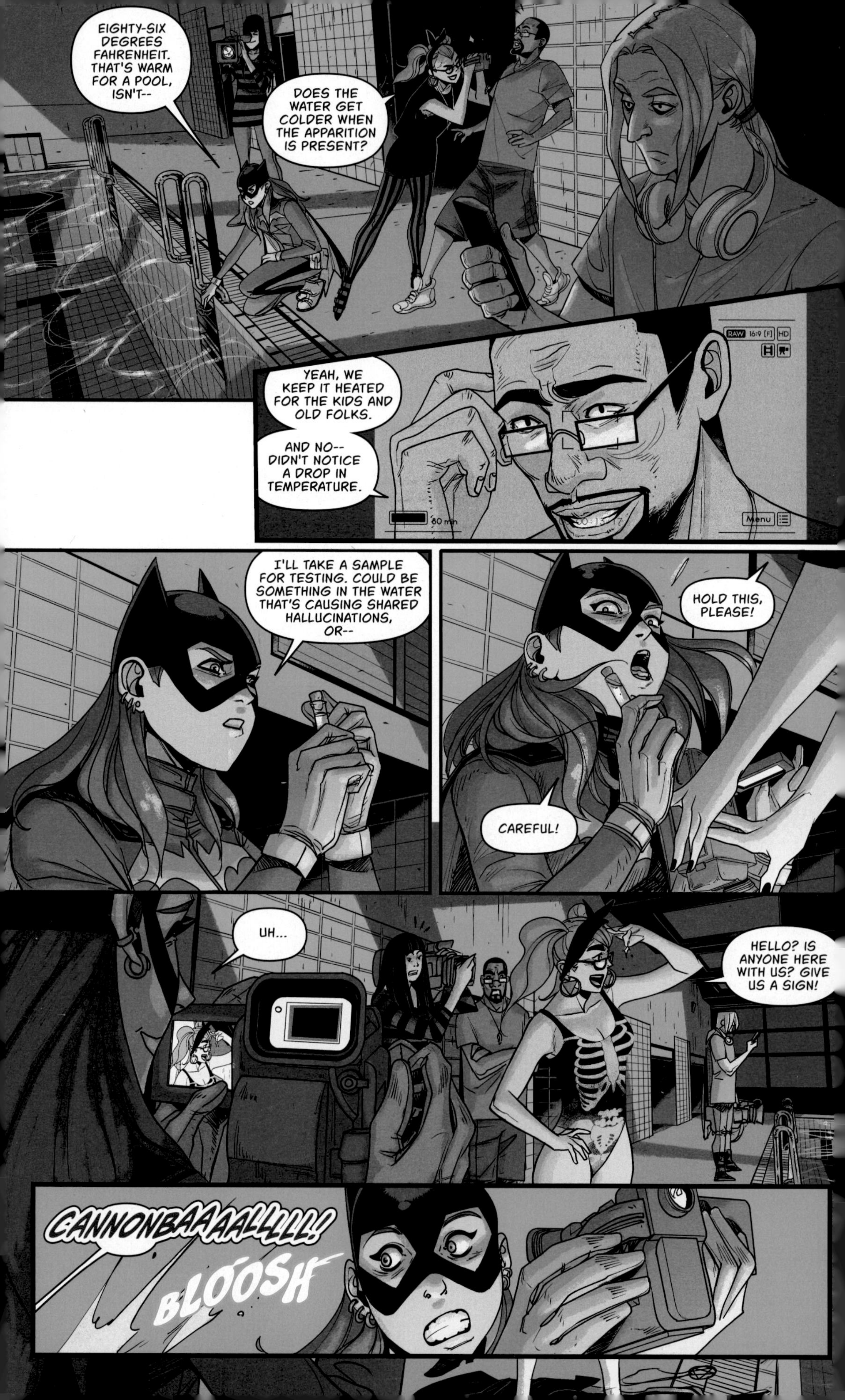
EIGHTY-SIX DEGREES FAHRENHEIT. THAT'S WARM FOR A POOL, ISN'T--
DOES THE WATER GET COLDER WHEN THE APPARITION IS PRESENT?
RAW 16:9 [F] HD
YEAH, WE KEEP IT HEATED FOR THE KIDS AND OLD FOLKS.
AND NO-- DIDN'T NOTICE A DROP IN TEMPERATURE.
80 min
Menu
I'LL TAKE A SAMPLE FOR TESTING. COULD BE SOMETHING IN THE WATER THAT'S CAUSING SHARED HALLUCINATIONS, OR--
HOLD THIS, PLEASE!
CAREFUL!
UH...
HELLO? IS ANYONE HERE WITH US? GIVE US A SIGN!
CANNONBAAAAALLLLL!
BLOOSH

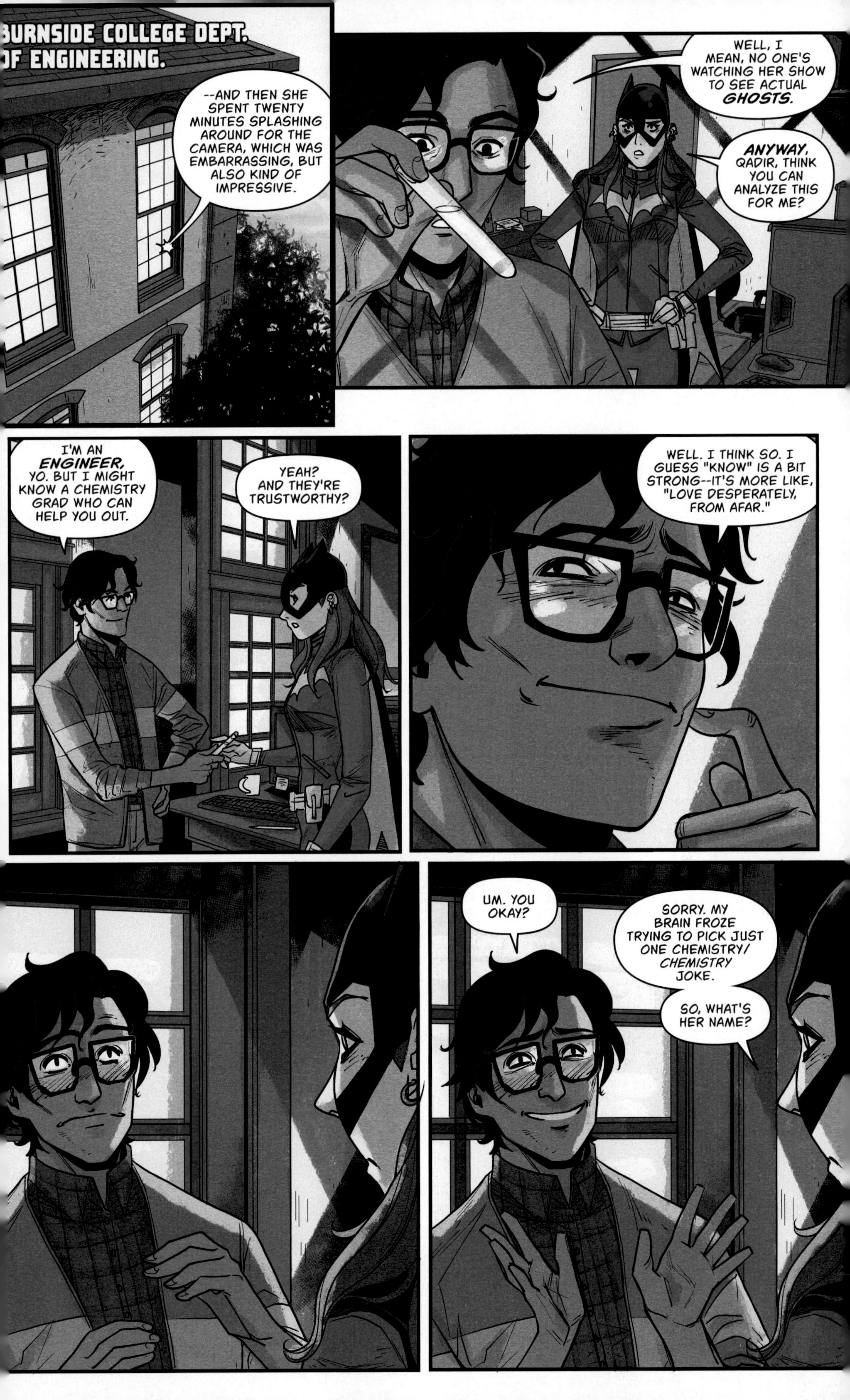
BURNSIDE COLLEGE DEPT. OF ENGINEERING.
--AND THEN SHE SPENT TWENTY MINUTES SPLASHING AROUND FOR THE CAMERA, WHICH WAS EMBARRASSING, BUT ALSO KIND OF IMPRESSIVE.
WELL, I MEAN, NO ONE'S WATCHING HER SHOW TO SEE ACTUAL GHOSTS.
ANYWAY, QADIR, THINK YOU CAN ANALYZE THIS FOR ME?
I'M AN ENGINEER, YO. BUT I MIGHT KNOW A CHEMISTRY GRAD WHO CAN HELP YOU OUT.
YEAH? AND THEY'RE TRUSTWORTHY?
WELL. I THINK SO. I GUESS "KNOW" IS A BIT STRONG--IT'S MORE LIKE, "LOVE DESPERATELY, FROM AFAR."
UM. YOU OKAY?
SORRY. MY BRAIN FROZE TRYING TO PICK JUST ONE CHEMISTRY/ CHEMISTRY JOKE.
SO, WHAT'S HER NAME?

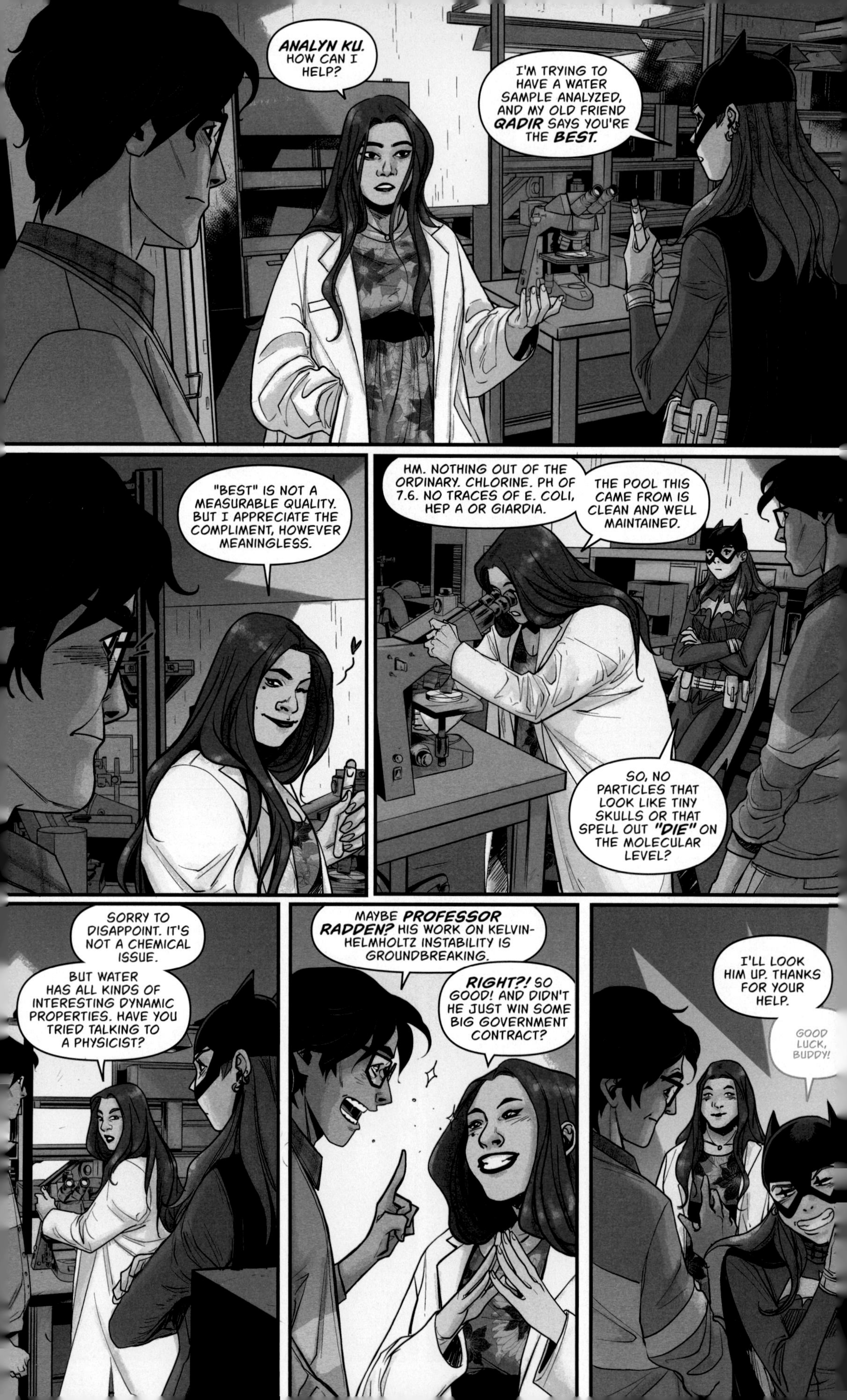
ANALYN KU. HOW CAN I HELP?
I'M TRYING TO HAVE A WATER SAMPLE ANALYZED, AND MY OLD FRIEND QADIR SAYS YOU'RE THE BEST.
"BEST" IS NOT A MEASURABLE QUALITY. BUT I APPRECIATE THE COMPLIMENT, HOWEVER MEANINGLESS.
HM. NOTHING OUT OF THE ORDINARY. CHLORINE. PH OF 7.6. NO TRACES OF E. COLI, HEP A OR GIARDIA.
THE POOL THIS CAME FROM IS CLEAN AND WELL MAINTAINED.
SO, NO PARTICLES THAT LOOK LIKE TINY SKULLS OR THAT SPELL OUT "DIE" ON THE MOLECULAR LEVEL?
SORRY TO DISAPPOINT. IT'S NOT A CHEMICAL ISSUE.
BUT WATER HAS ALL KINDS OF INTERESTING DYNAMIC PROPERTIES. HAVE YOU TRIED TALKING TO A PHYSICIST?
MAYBE PROFESSOR RADDEN? HIS WORK ON KELVIN-HELMHOLTZ INSTABILITY IS GROUNDBREAKING.
RIGHT?! SO GOOD! AND DIDN'T HE JUST WIN SOME BIG GOVERNMENT CONTRACT?
I'LL LOOK HIM UP. THANKS FOR YOUR HELP.
GOOD LUCK, BUDDY!

I'VE HEARD OF RADDEN.

WHEN I LAUNCHED **GORDON CLEAN ENERGY,** HE WROTE ME A LONG, POMPOUS LETTER WELCOMING ME INTO THE SCIENTIFIC COMMUNITY AND OFFERING TO "MENTOR" ME.

SEEMED LIKE A COME-ON. I SHREDDED IT.

LIBRARY

BURNSIDE COLLEGE SCIENCE LIBRARY.

I THINK I'LL **READ UP** ON HIM BEFORE I **REACH OUT.**

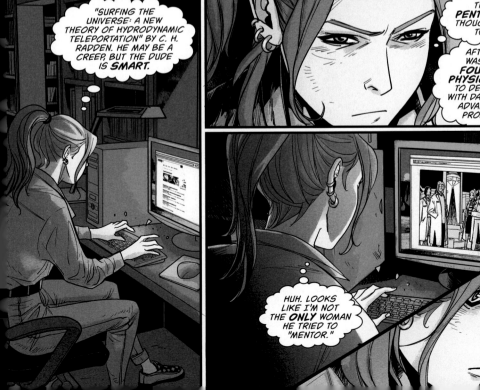

"SURFING THE UNIVERSE: A NEW THEORY OF HYDRODYNAMIC TELEPORTATION" BY C. H. RADDEN. HE MAY BE A CREEP, BUT THE DUDE IS **SMART.**

THE **PENTAGON** THOUGHT SO, TOO.

AFTER THIS PAPER WAS PUBLISHED IN **FOUNDATIONS OF PHYSICS,** HE WAS HIRED TO DEVELOP THIS TECH WITH DARPA--THE DEFENSE ADVANCED RESEARCH PROJECTS AGENCY.

HUH. LOOKS LIKE I'M NOT THE **ONLY** WOMAN HE TRIED TO "MENTOR."

AND ISN'T THAT--?

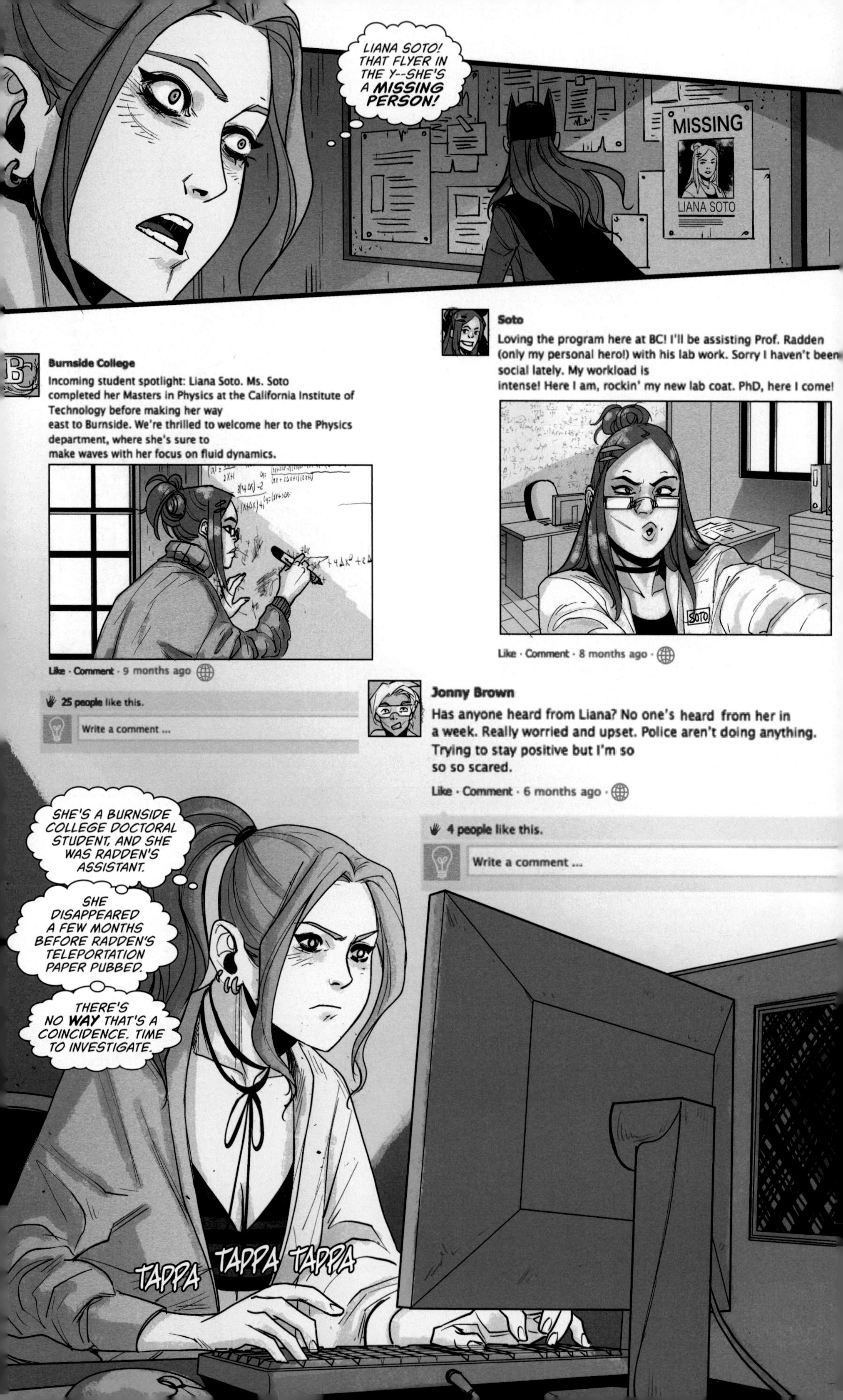
LIANA SOTO! THAT FLYER IN THE Y--SHE'S A MISSING PERSON!
MISSING
LIANA SOTO
Burnside College
Incoming student spotlight: Liana Soto. Ms. Soto completed her Masters in Physics at the California Institute of Technology before making her way east to Burnside. We're thrilled to welcome her to the Physics department, where she's sure to make waves with her focus on fluid dynamics.
Like · Comment · 9 months ago
25 people like this.
Write a comment ...
Soto
Loving the program here at BC! I'll be assisting Prof. Radden (only my personal hero!) with his lab work. Sorry I haven't been social lately. My workload is intense! Here I am, rockin' my new lab coat. PhD, here I come!
SOTO
Like · Comment · 8 months ago
Jonny Brown
Has anyone heard from Liana? No one's heard from her in a week. Really worried and upset. Police aren't doing anything. Trying to stay positive but I'm so so so scared.
Like · Comment · 6 months ago
4 people like this.
Write a comment ...
SHE'S A BURNSIDE COLLEGE DOCTORAL STUDENT, AND SHE WAS RADDEN'S ASSISTANT.
SHE DISAPPEARED A FEW MONTHS BEFORE RADDEN'S TELEPORTATION PAPER PUBBED.
THERE'S NO WAY THAT'S A COINCIDENCE. TIME TO INVESTIGATE.
TAPPA TAPPA TAPPA

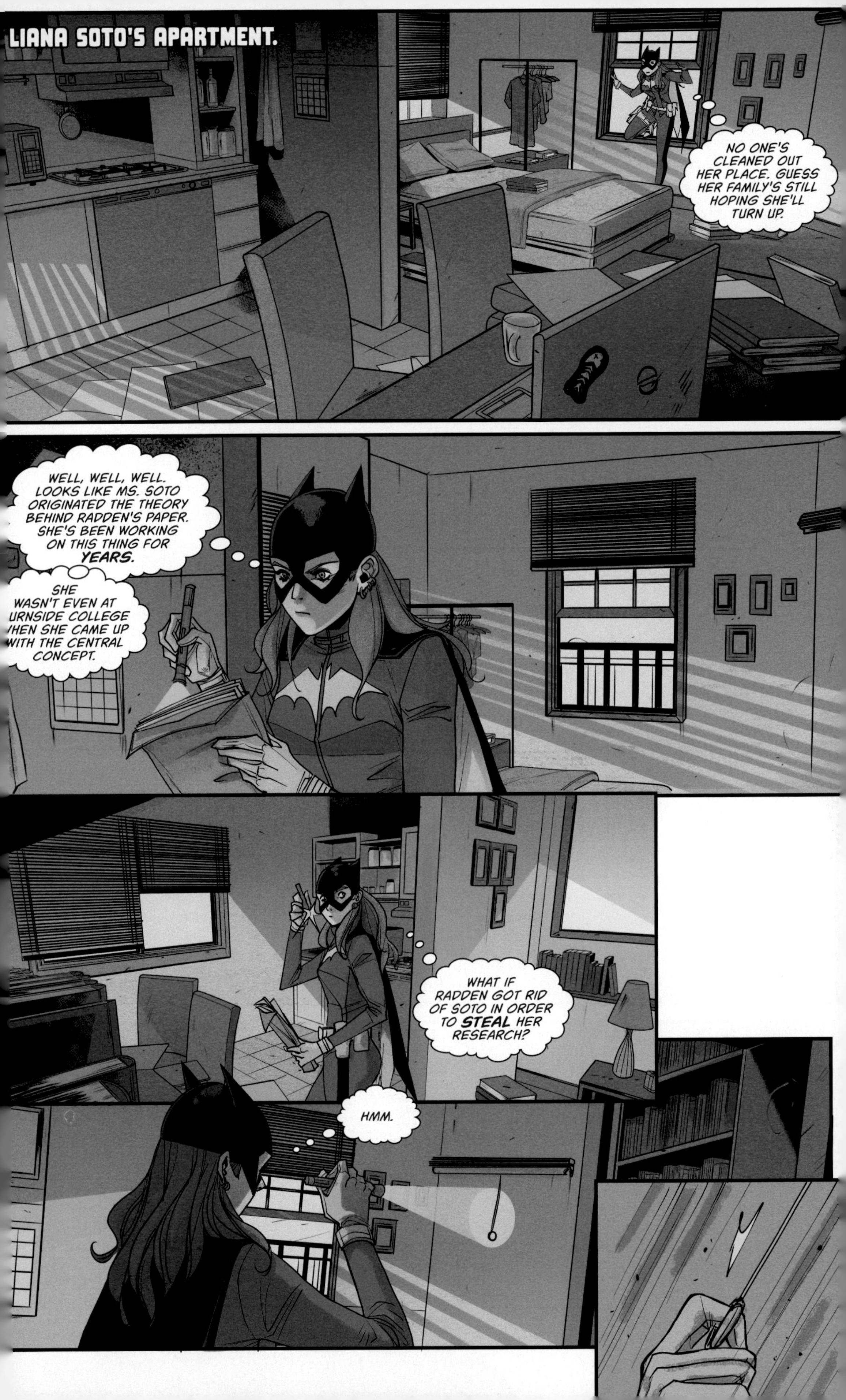
LIANA SOTO'S APARTMENT.
NO ONE'S CLEANED OUT HER PLACE. GUESS HER FAMILY'S STILL HOPING SHE'LL TURN UP.
WELL, WELL, WELL. LOOKS LIKE MS. SOTO ORIGINATED THE THEORY BEHIND RADDEN'S PAPER. SHE'S BEEN WORKING ON THIS THING FOR YEARS.
SHE WASN'T EVEN AT URNSIDE COLLEGE WHEN SHE CAME UP WITH THE CENTRAL CONCEPT.
WHAT IF RADDEN GOT RID OF SOTO IN ORDER TO STEAL HER RESEARCH?
HMM.

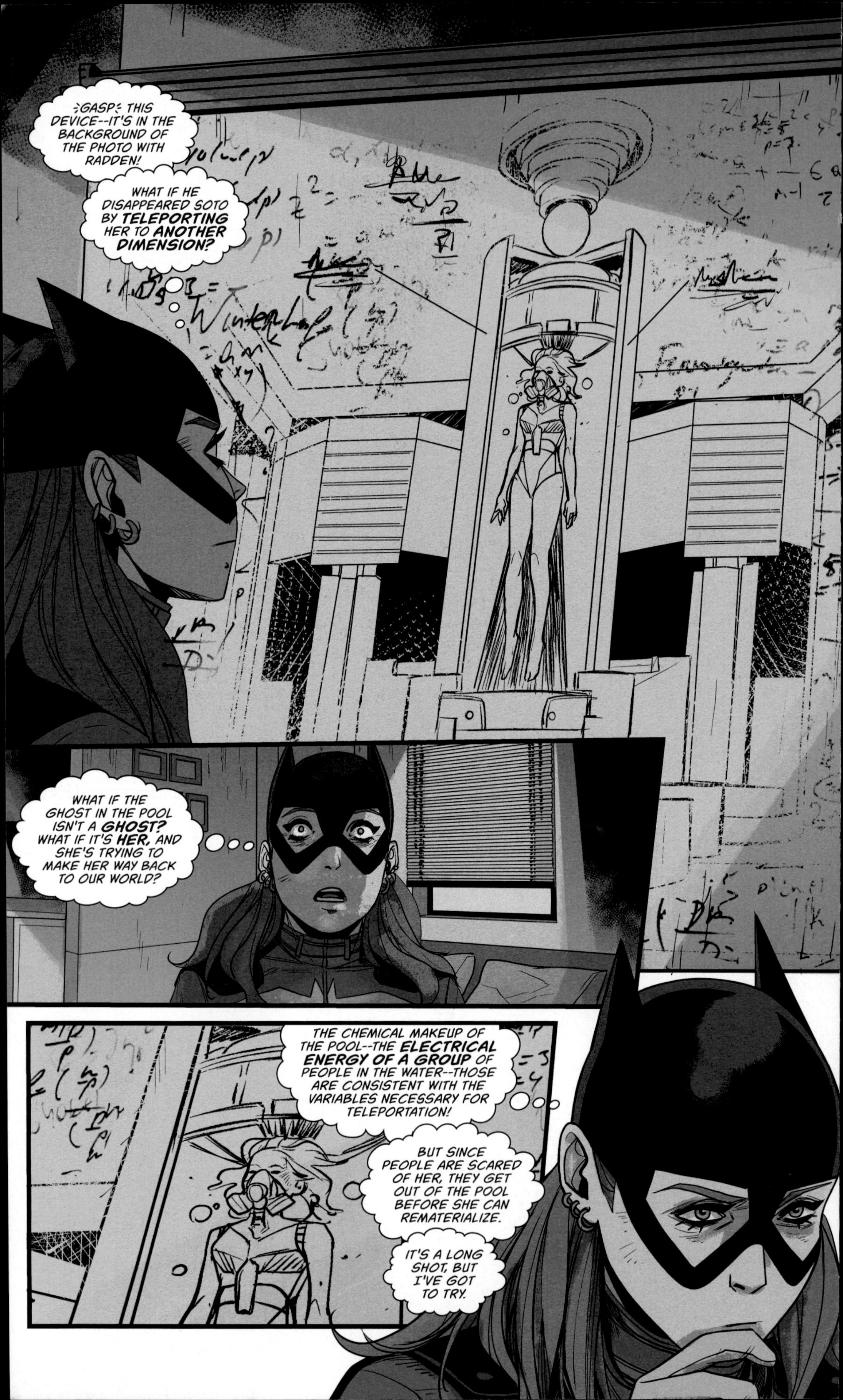

GASP THIS DEVICE--IT'S IN THE BACKGROUND OF THE PHOTO WITH RADDEN!
WHAT IF HE DISAPPEARED SOTO BY TELEPORTING HER TO ANOTHER DIMENSION?
WHAT IF THE GHOST IN THE POOL ISN'T A GHOST? WHAT IF IT'S HER, AND SHE'S TRYING TO MAKE HER WAY BACK TO OUR WORLD?
THE CHEMICAL MAKEUP OF THE POOL--THE ELECTRICAL ENERGY OF A GROUP OF PEOPLE IN THE WATER--THOSE ARE CONSISTENT WITH THE VARIABLES NECESSARY FOR TELEPORTATION!
BUT SINCE PEOPLE ARE SCARED OF HER, THEY GET OUT OF THE POOL BEFORE SHE CAN REMATERIALIZE.
IT'S A LONG SHOT, BUT I'VE GOT TO TRY.

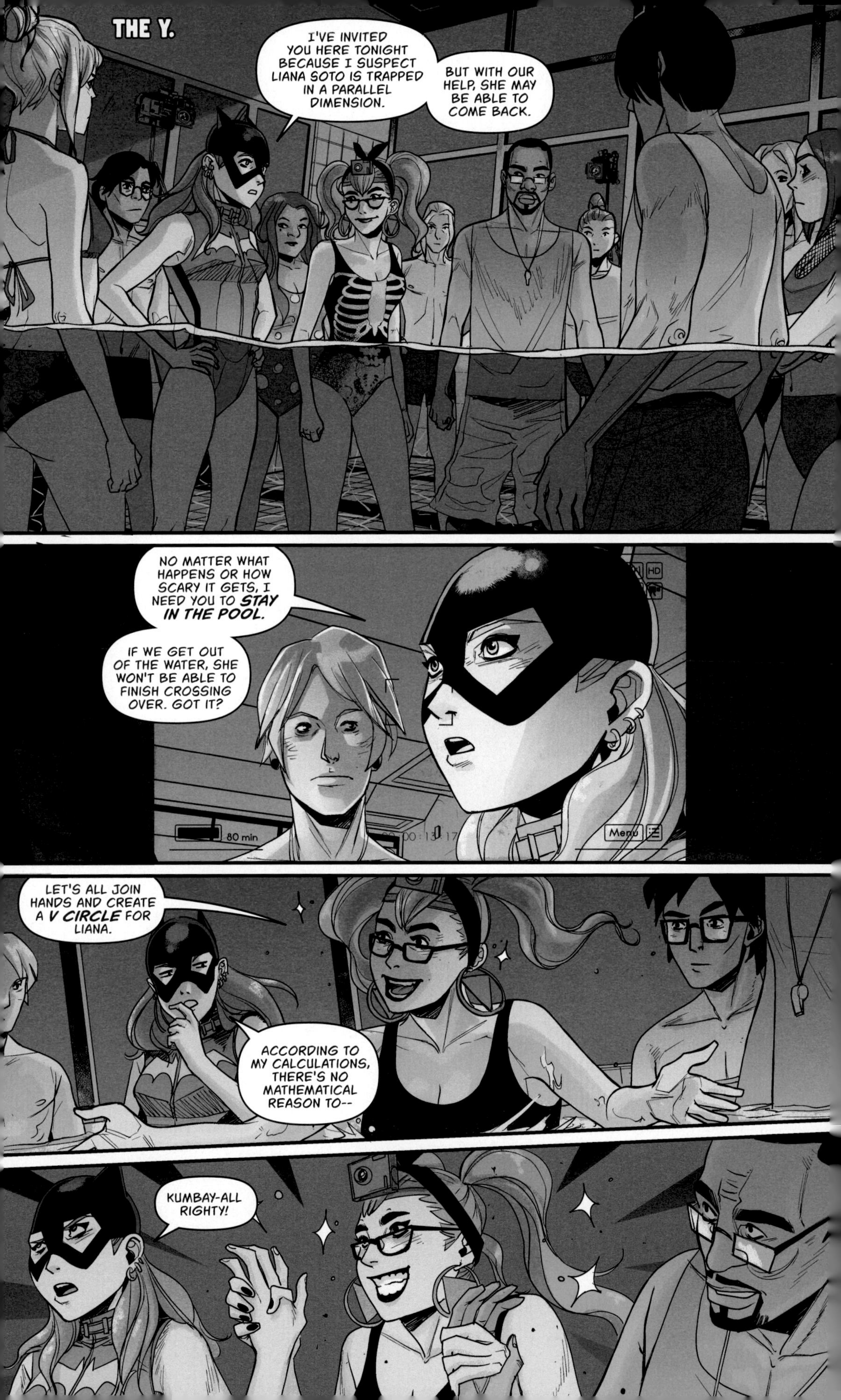
THE Y.
I'VE INVITED YOU HERE TONIGHT BECAUSE I SUSPECT LIANA SOTO IS TRAPPED IN A PARALLEL DIMENSION.
BUT WITH OUR HELP, SHE MAY BE ABLE TO COME BACK.
NO MATTER WHAT HAPPENS OR HOW SCARY IT GETS, I NEED YOU TO STAY IN THE POOL.
IF WE GET OUT OF THE WATER, SHE WON'T BE ABLE TO FINISH CROSSING OVER. GOT IT?
HD
80 min
Menu
LET'S ALL JOIN HANDS AND CREATE A V CIRCLE FOR LIANA.
ACCORDING TO MY CALCULATIONS, THERE'S NO MATHEMATICAL REASON TO--
KUMBAY-ALL RIGHTY!

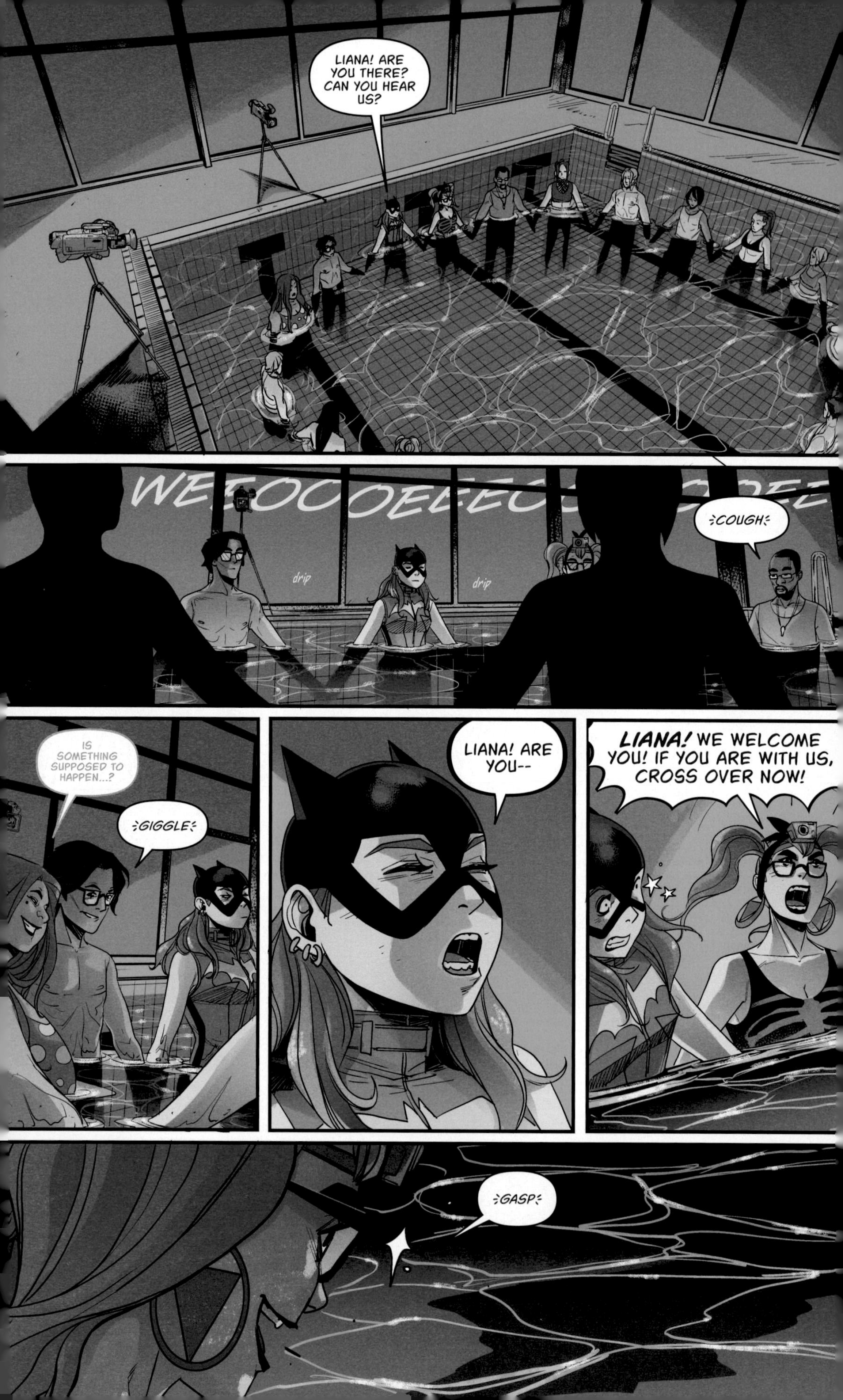
LIANA! ARE YOU THERE? CAN YOU HEAR US?
WEEOOOEEEEOOOEEE
COUGH
drip
drip
IS SOMETHING SUPPOSED TO HAPPEN...?
GIGGLE
LIANA! ARE YOU--
LIANA! WE WELCOME YOU! IF YOU ARE WITH US, CROSS OVER NOW!
GASP

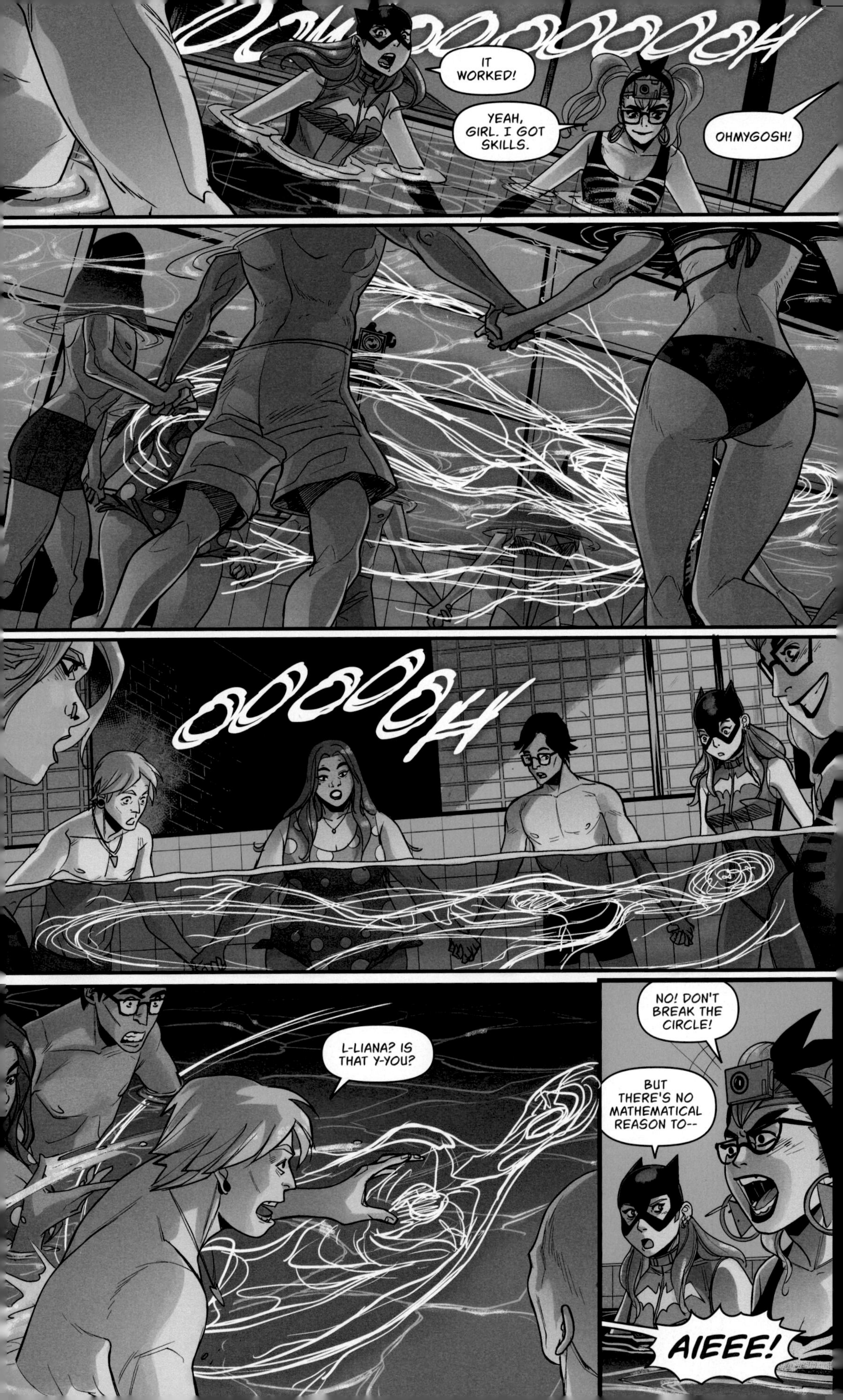
OOWOOOOOOOOOH
IT WORKED!
YEAH, GIRL. I GOT SKILLS.
OHMYGOSH!
OOOOOH
L-LIANA? IS THAT Y-YOU?
NO! DON'T BREAK THE CIRCLE!
BUT THERE'S NO MATHEMATICAL REASON TO--
AIEEE!

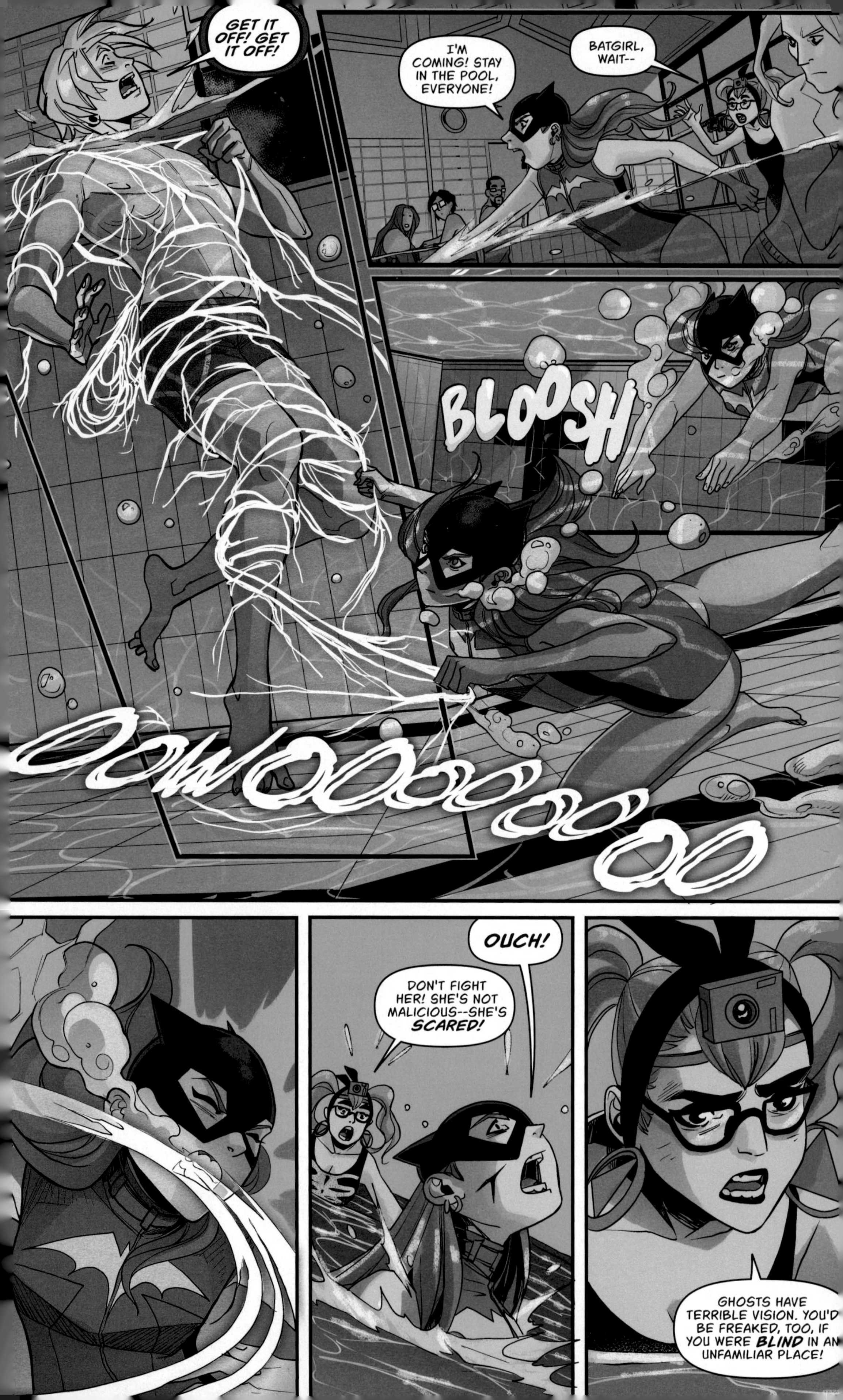
GET IT OFF! GET IT OFF!
I'M COMING! STAY IN THE POOL, EVERYONE!
BATGIRL, WAIT--
BLOOSH
OOWOOOOOOOOO
OUCH!
DON'T FIGHT HER! SHE'S NOT MALICIOUS--SHE'S SCARED!
GHOSTS HAVE TERRIBLE VISION. YOU'D BE FREAKED, TOO, IF YOU WERE BLIND IN AN UNFAMILIAR PLACE!

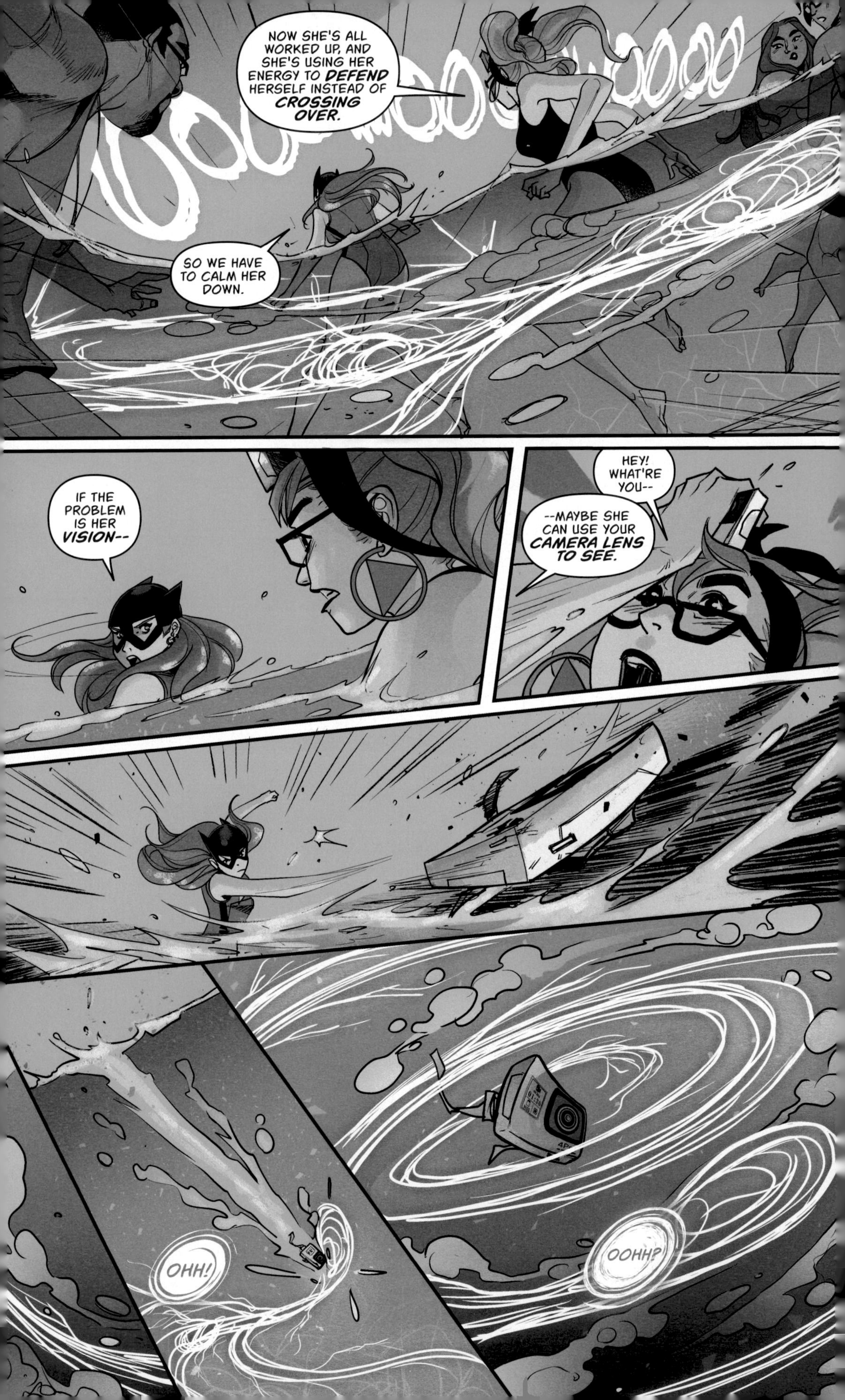
NOW SHE'S ALL WORKED UP, AND SHE'S USING HER ENERGY TO DEFEND HERSELF INSTEAD OF CROSSING OVER.
SO WE HAVE TO CALM HER DOWN.
IF THE PROBLEM IS HER VISION--
HEY! WHAT'RE YOU--
--MAYBE SHE CAN USE YOUR CAMERA LENS TO SEE.
OHH!
OOHH?

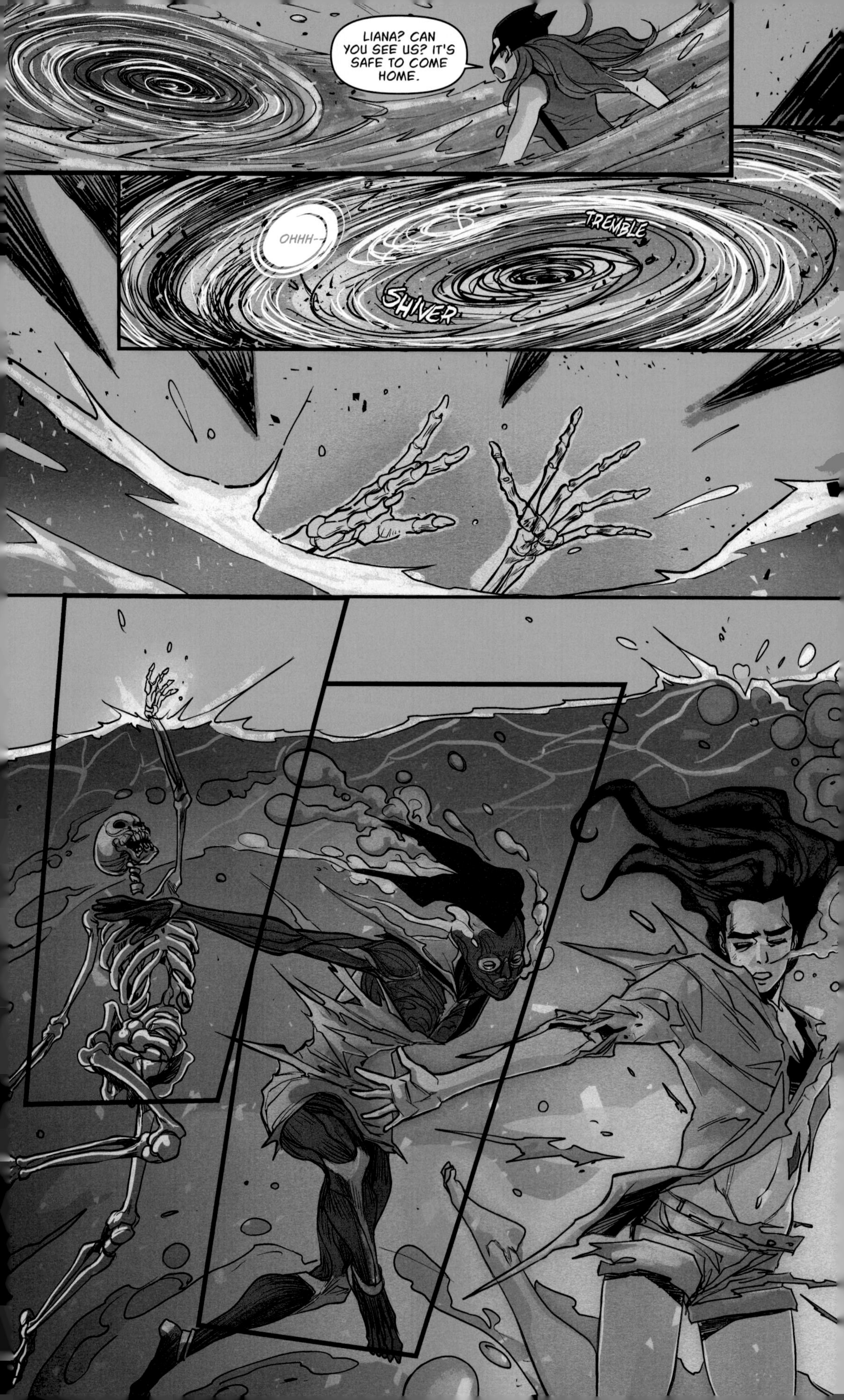
LIANA? CAN YOU SEE US? IT'S SAFE TO COME HOME.
OHHH--
TREMBLE
SHIVER

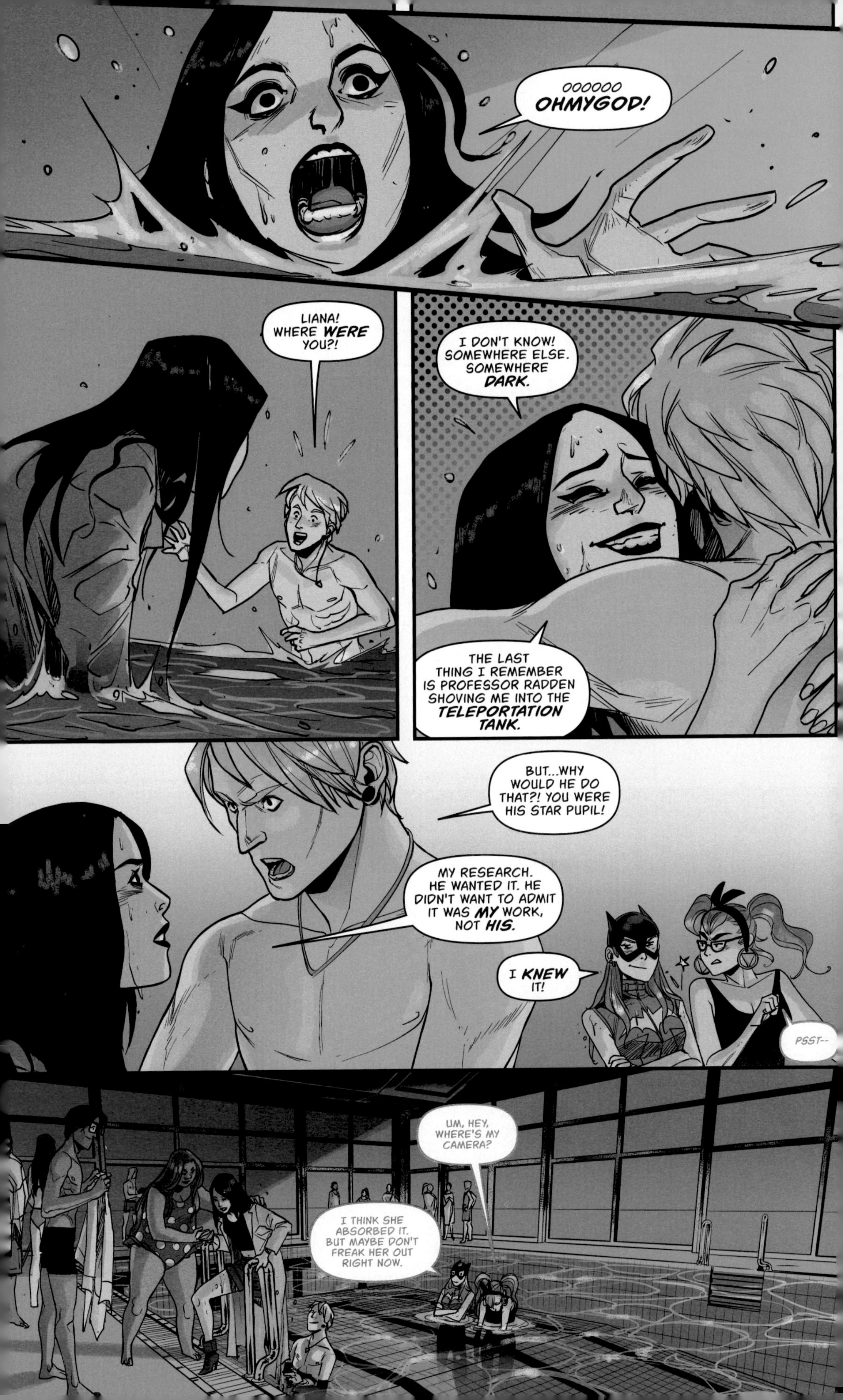
OOOOOO OHMYGOD!
LIANA! WHERE WERE YOU?!
I DON'T KNOW! SOMEWHERE ELSE. SOMEWHERE DARK.
THE LAST THING I REMEMBER IS PROFESSOR RADDEN SHOVING ME INTO THE TELEPORTATION TANK.
BUT...WHY WOULD HE DO THAT?! YOU WERE HIS STAR PUPIL!
MY RESEARCH. HE WANTED IT. HE DIDN'T WANT TO ADMIT IT WAS MY WORK, NOT HIS.
I KNEW IT!
PSST--
UM, HEY, WHERE'S MY CAMERA?
I THINK SHE ABSORBED IT. BUT MAYBE DON'T FREAK HER OUT RIGHT NOW.

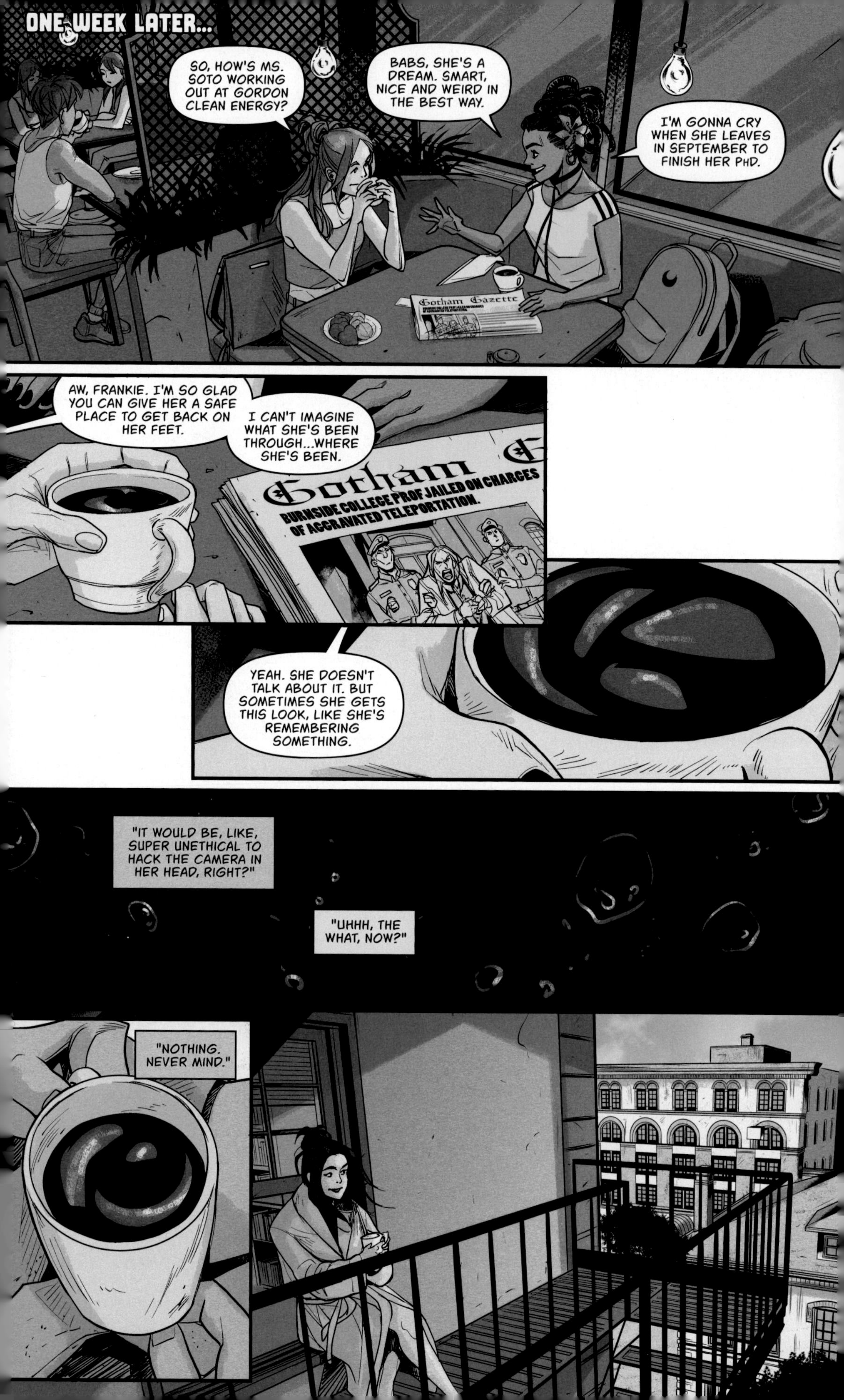
ONE WEEK LATER...
SO, HOW'S MS. SOTO WORKING OUT AT GORDON CLEAN ENERGY?
BABS, SHE'S A DREAM. SMART, NICE AND WEIRD IN THE BEST WAY.
I'M GONNA CRY WHEN SHE LEAVES IN SEPTEMBER TO FINISH HER PhD.
Gotham Gazette
AW, FRANKIE. I'M SO GLAD YOU CAN GIVE HER A SAFE PLACE TO GET BACK ON HER FEET.
I CAN'T IMAGINE WHAT SHE'S BEEN THROUGH...WHERE SHE'S BEEN.
Gotham
BURNSIDE COLLEGE PROF JAILED ON CHARGES OF AGGRAVATED TELEPORTATION.
YEAH. SHE DOESN'T TALK ABOUT IT. BUT SOMETIMES SHE GETS THIS LOOK, LIKE SHE'S REMEMBERING SOMETHING.
"IT WOULD BE, LIKE, SUPER UNETHICAL TO HACK THE CAMERA IN HER HEAD, RIGHT?"
"UHHH, THE WHAT, NOW?"
"NOTHING. NEVER MIND."

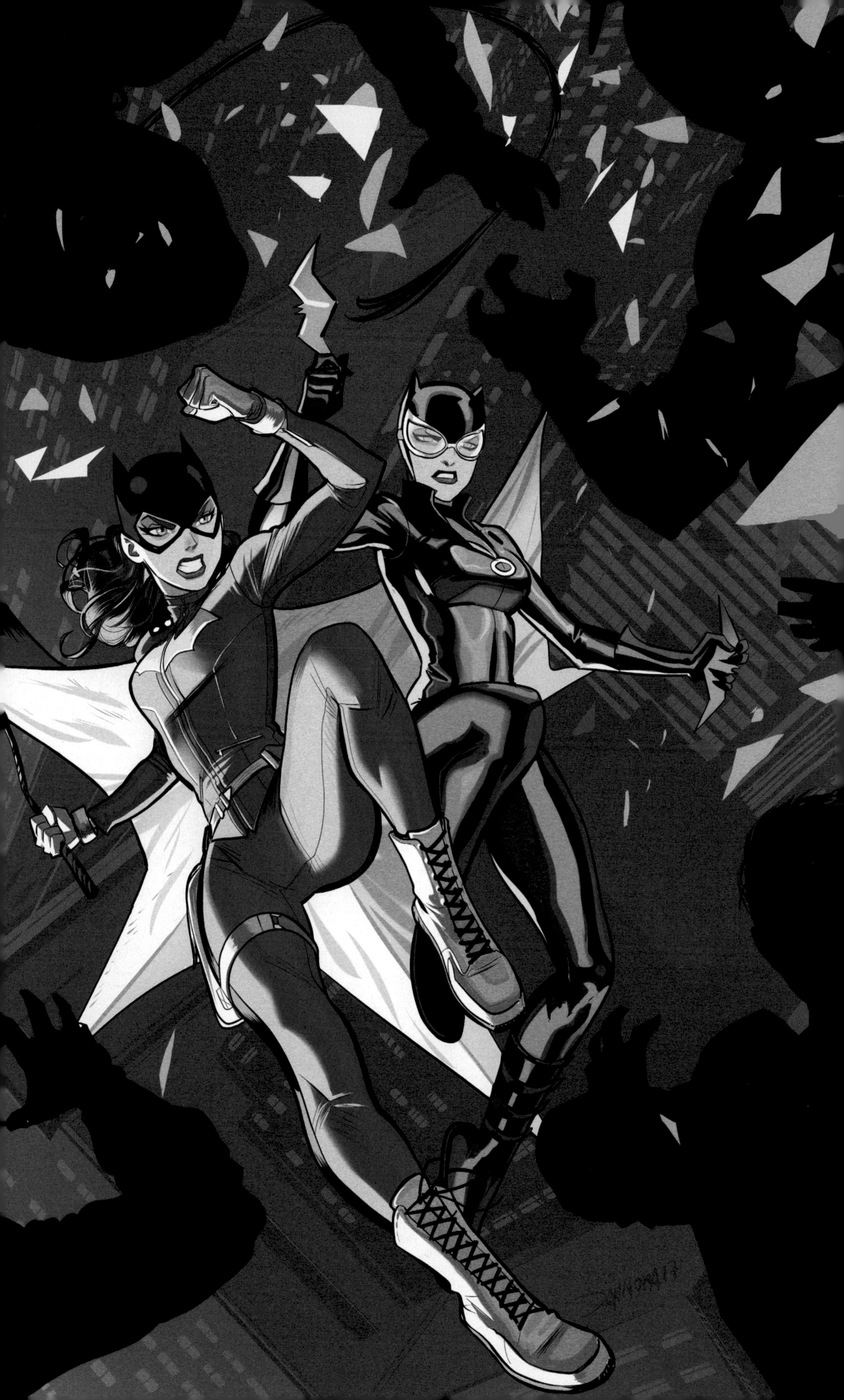

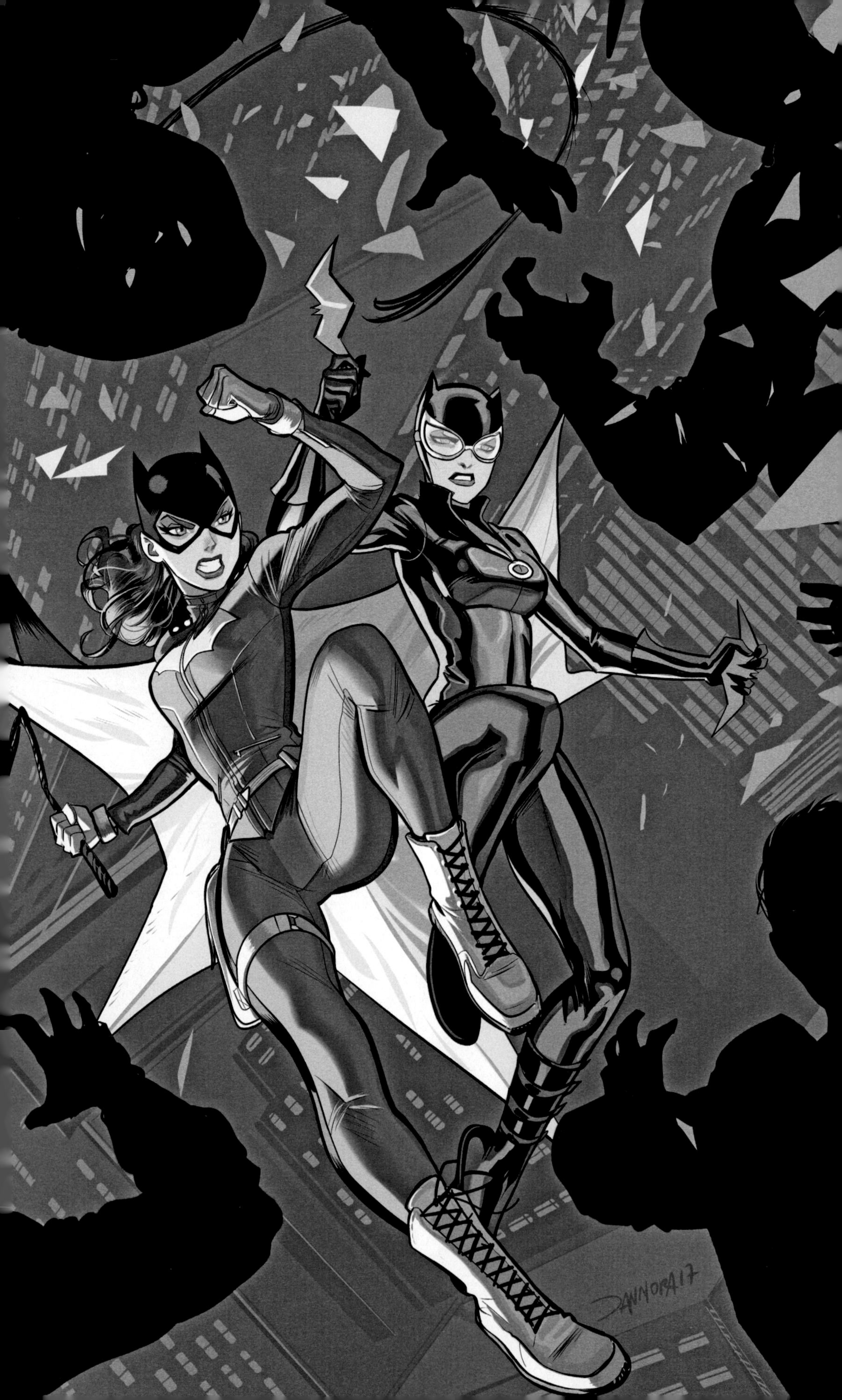

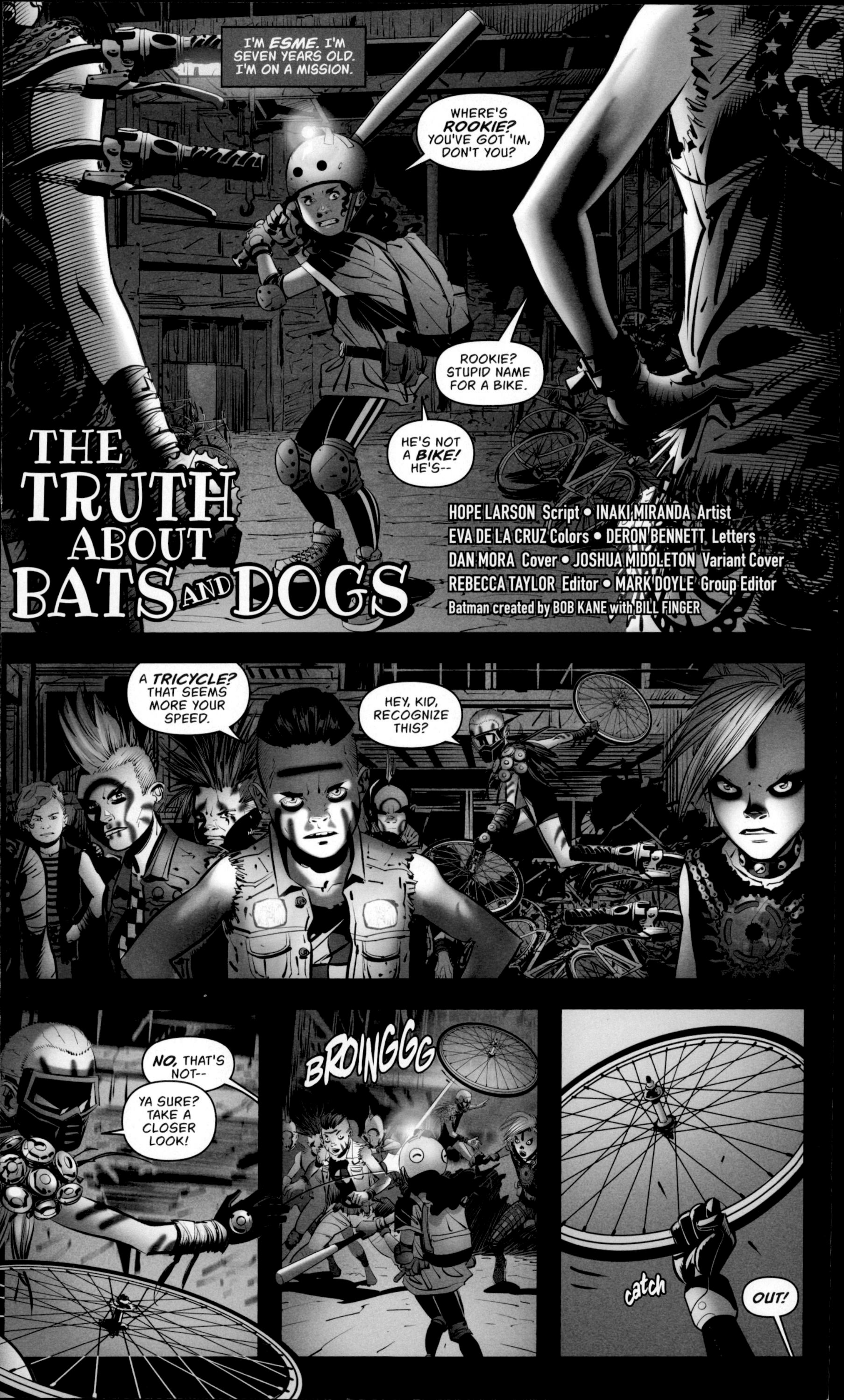

I'M ESME. I'M SEVEN YEARS OLD. I'M ON A MISSION.
WHERE'S ROOKIE? YOU'VE GOT 'IM, DON'T YOU?
ROOKIE? STUPID NAME FOR A BIKE.
HE'S NOT A BIKE! HE'S--
THE TRUTH ABOUT BATS AND DOGS
HOPE LARSON Script • INAKI MIRANDA Artist
EVA DE LA CRUZ Colors • DERON BENNETT Letters
DAN MORA Cover • JOSHUA MIDDLETON Variant Cover
REBECCA TAYLOR Editor • MARK DOYLE Group Editor
Batman created by BOB KANE with BILL FINGER
A TRICYCLE? THAT SEEMS MORE YOUR SPEED.
HEY, KID, RECOGNIZE THIS?
NO, THAT'S NOT--
YA SURE? TAKE A CLOSER LOOK!
BROINGGG
catch
OUT!

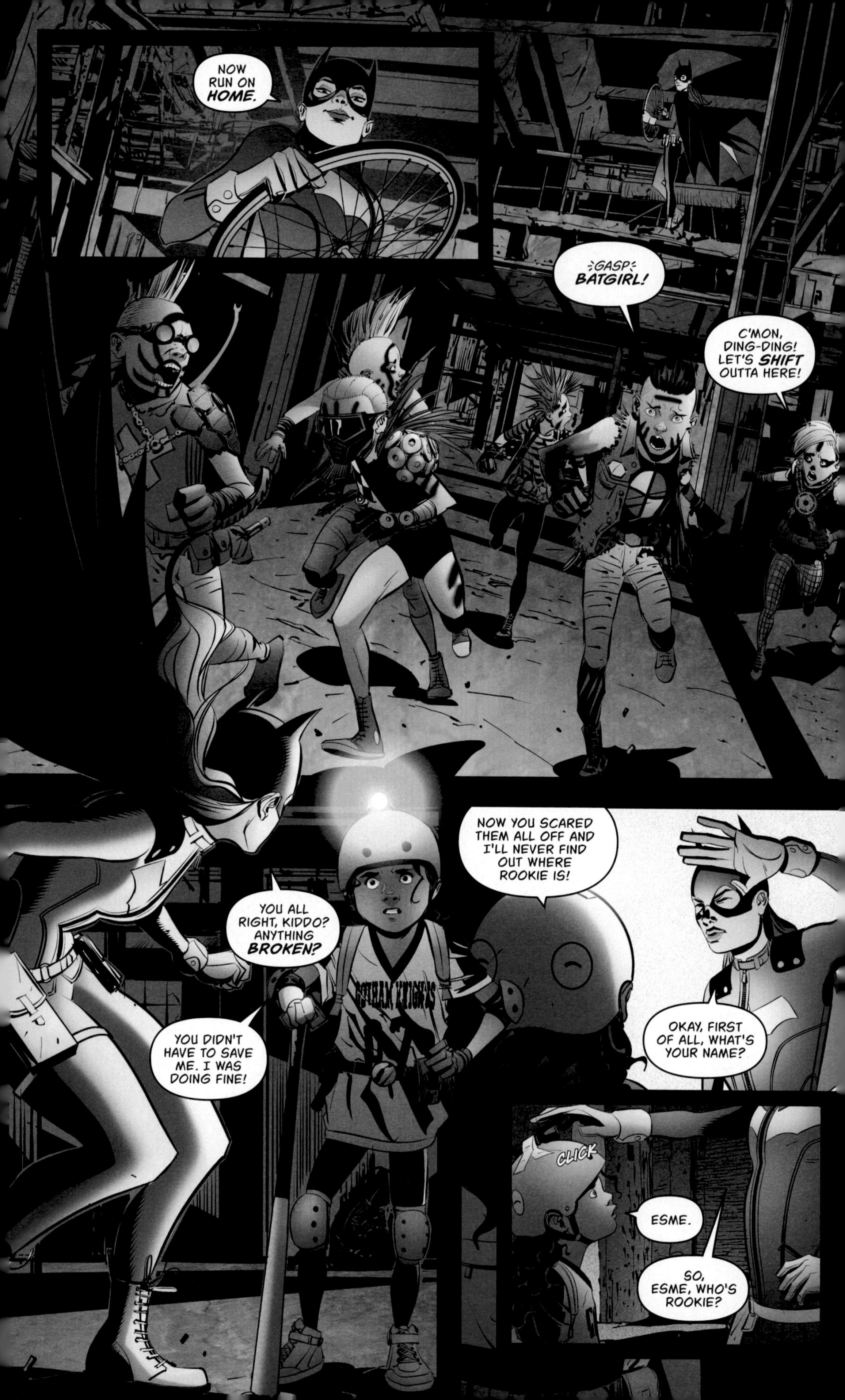
NOW RUN ON HOME.
GASP BATGIRL!
C'MON, DING-DING! LET'S SHIFT OUTTA HERE!
YOU ALL RIGHT, KIDDO? ANYTHING BROKEN?
YOU DIDN'T HAVE TO SAVE ME. I WAS DOING FINE!
NOW YOU SCARED THEM ALL OFF AND I'LL NEVER FIND OUT WHERE ROOKIE IS!
OKAY, FIRST OF ALL, WHAT'S YOUR NAME?
CLICK
ESME.
SO, ESME, WHO'S ROOKIE?

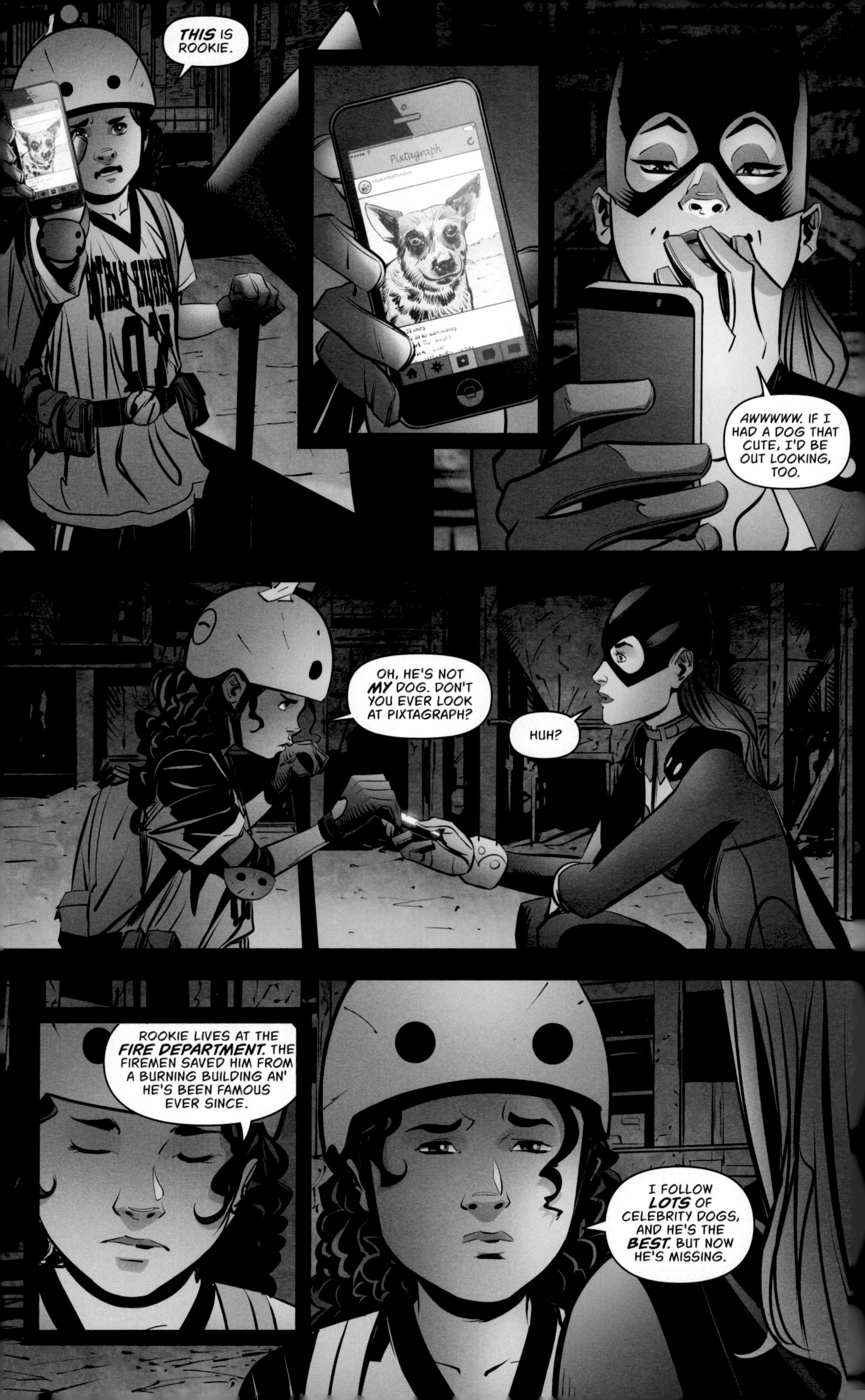
THIS IS ROOKIE.
Pixtagraph
AWWWWW. IF I HAD A DOG THAT CUTE, I'D BE OUT LOOKING, TOO.
OH, HE'S NOT MY DOG. DON'T YOU EVER LOOK AT PIXTAGRAPH?
HUH?
ROOKIE LIVES AT THE FIRE DEPARTMENT. THE FIREMEN SAVED HIM FROM A BURNING BUILDING AN' HE'S BEEN FAMOUS EVER SINCE.
I FOLLOW LOTS OF CELEBRITY DOGS, AND HE'S THE BEST. BUT NOW HE'S MISSING.

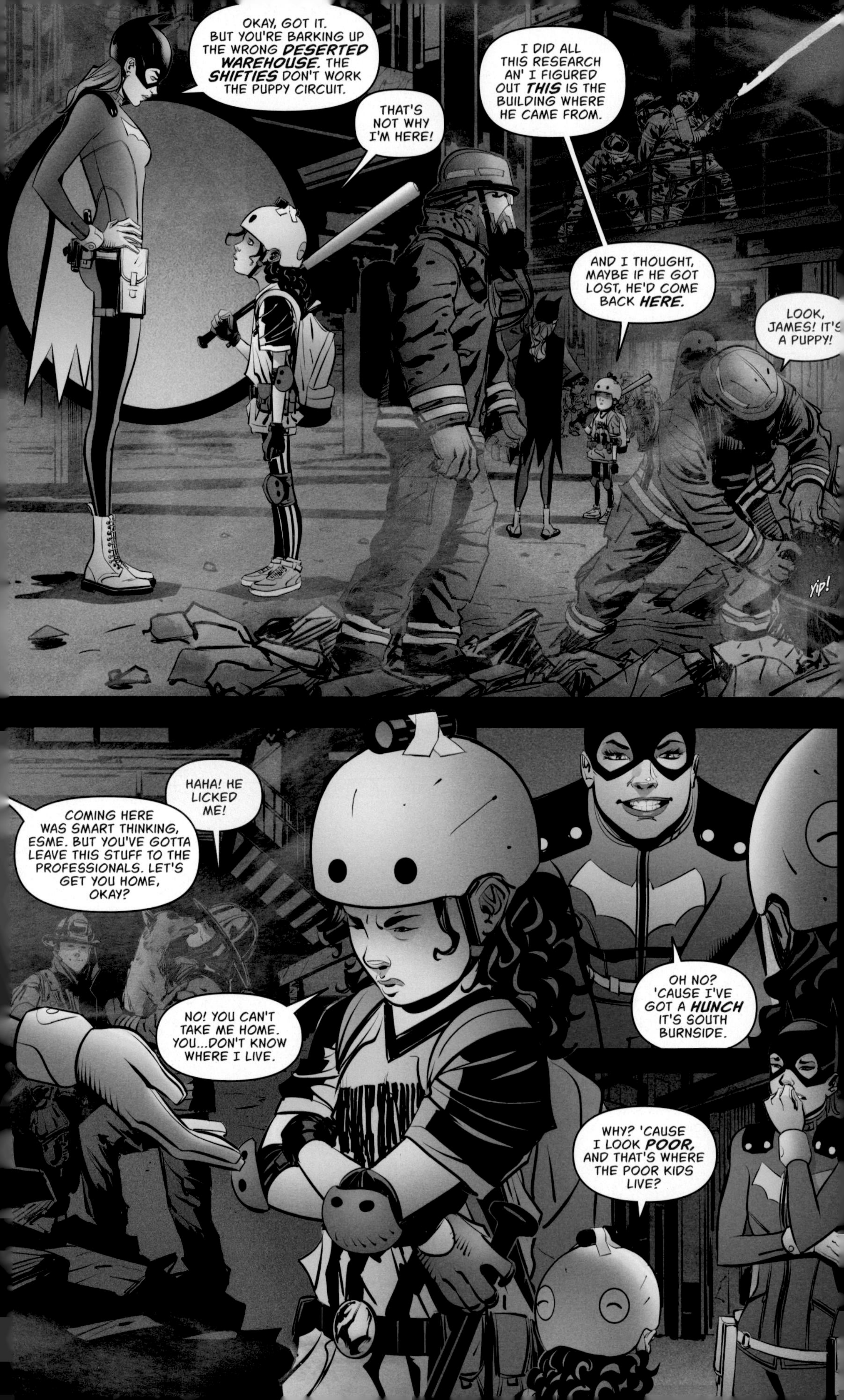

OKAY, GOT IT. BUT YOU'RE BARKING UP THE WRONG DESERTED WAREHOUSE. THE SHIFTIES DON'T WORK THE PUPPY CIRCUIT.
THAT'S NOT WHY I'M HERE!
I DID ALL THIS RESEARCH AN' I FIGURED OUT THIS IS THE BUILDING WHERE HE CAME FROM.
AND I THOUGHT, MAYBE IF HE GOT LOST, HE'D COME BACK HERE.
LOOK, JAMES! IT'S A PUPPY!
yip!
COMING HERE WAS SMART THINKING, ESME. BUT YOU'VE GOTTA LEAVE THIS STUFF TO THE PROFESSIONALS. LET'S GET YOU HOME, OKAY?
HAHA! HE LICKED ME!
NO! YOU CAN'T TAKE ME HOME. YOU...DON'T KNOW WHERE I LIVE.
OH NO? 'CAUSE I'VE GOT A HUNCH IT'S SOUTH BURNSIDE.
WHY? 'CAUSE I LOOK POOR, AND THAT'S WHERE THE POOR KIDS LIVE?

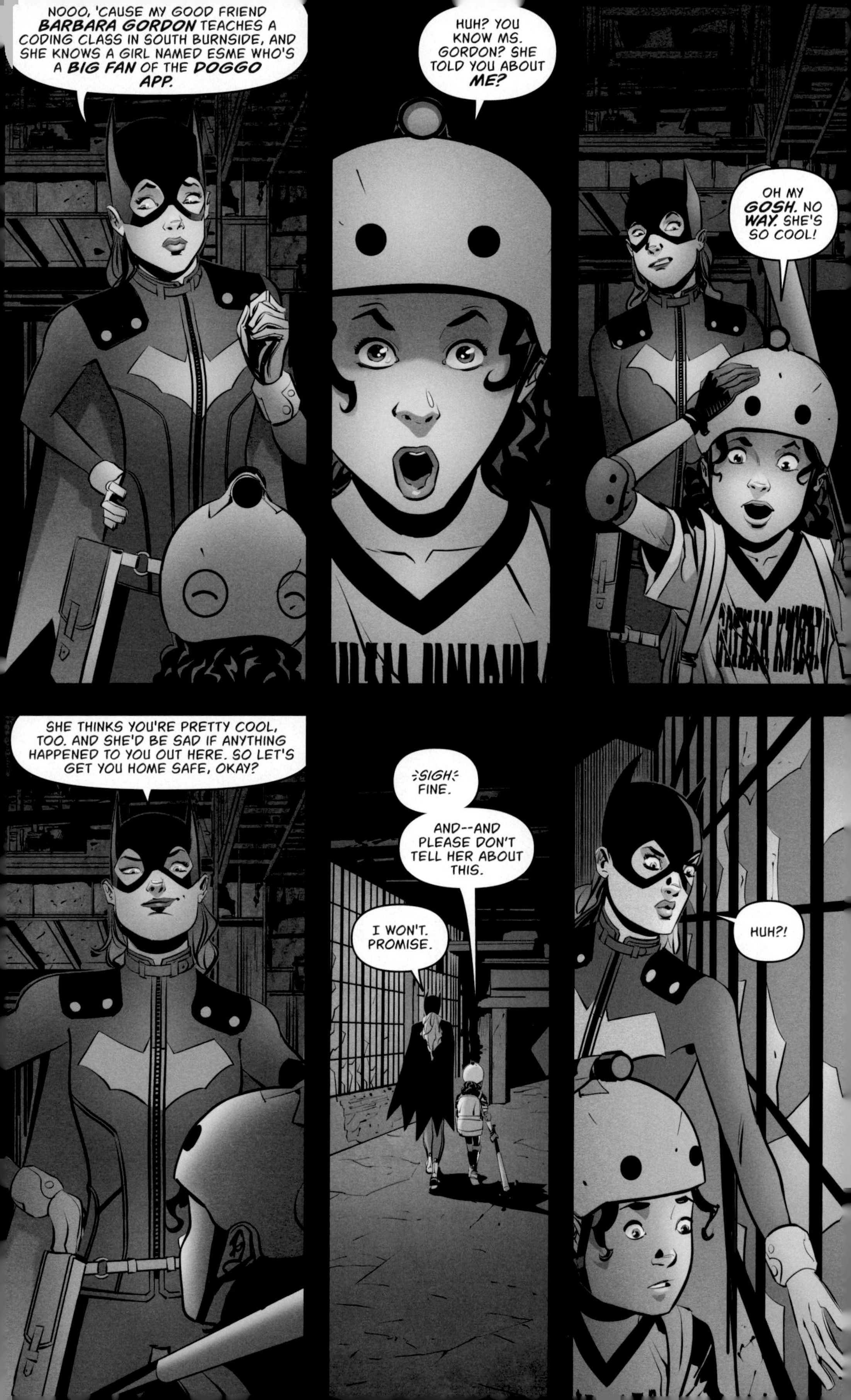
NOOO, 'CAUSE MY GOOD FRIEND BARBARA GORDON TEACHES A CODING CLASS IN SOUTH BURNSIDE, AND SHE KNOWS A GIRL NAMED ESME WHO'S A BIG FAN OF THE DOGGO APP.
HUH? YOU KNOW MS. GORDON? SHE TOLD YOU ABOUT ME?
OH MY GOSH. NO WAY. SHE'S SO COOL!
SHE THINKS YOU'RE PRETTY COOL, TOO. AND SHE'D BE SAD IF ANYTHING HAPPENED TO YOU OUT HERE. SO LET'S GET YOU HOME SAFE, OKAY?
SIGH FINE.
AND--AND PLEASE DON'T TELL HER ABOUT THIS.
I WON'T. PROMISE.
HUH?!

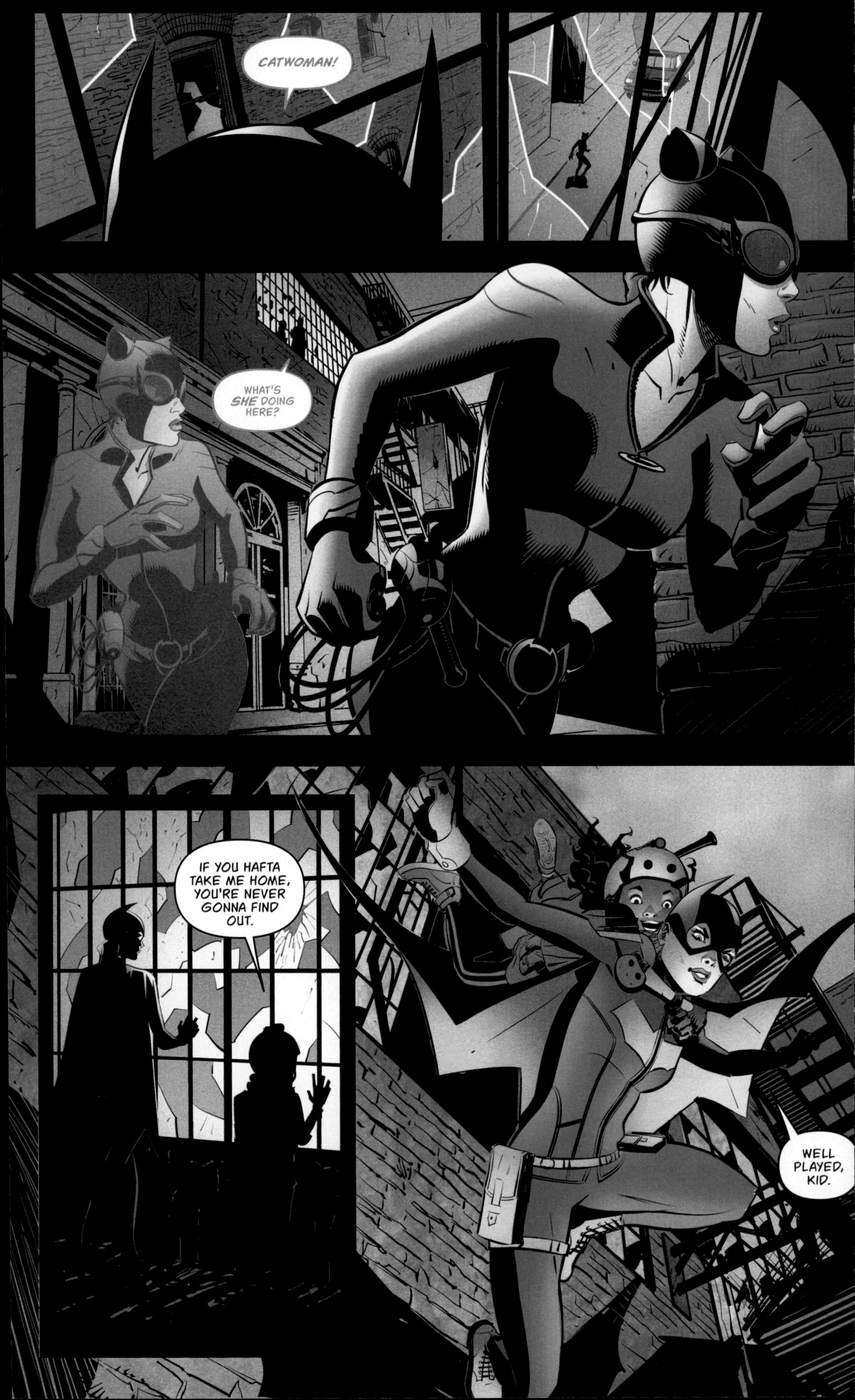
CATWOMAN!
WHAT'S SHE DOING HERE?
IF YOU HAFTA TAKE ME HOME, YOU'RE NEVER GONNA FIND OUT.
WELL PLAYED, KID.

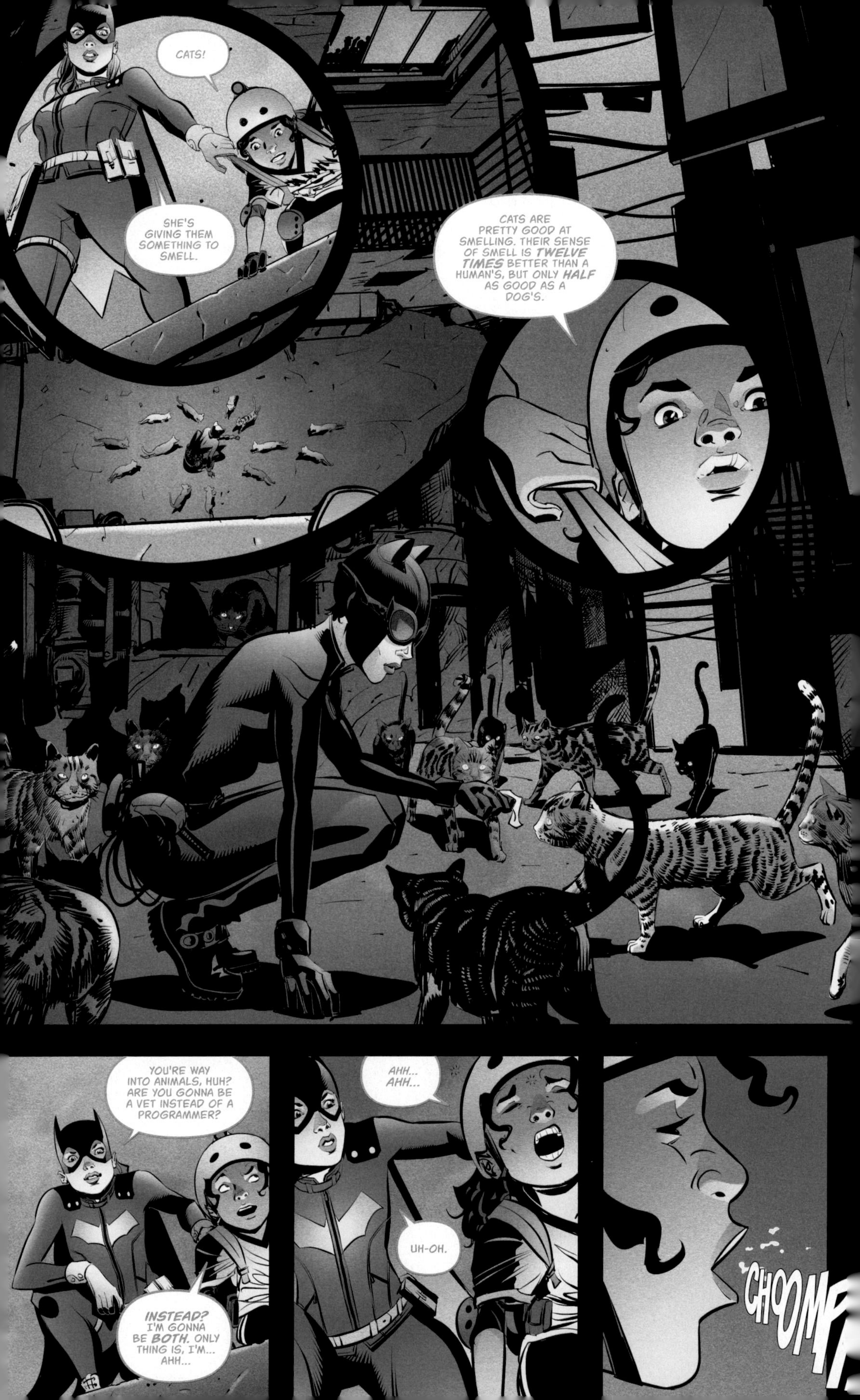

CATS!
SHE'S GIVING THEM SOMETHING TO SMELL.
CATS ARE PRETTY GOOD AT SMELLING. THEIR SENSE OF SMELL IS TWELVE TIMES BETTER THAN A HUMAN'S, BUT ONLY HALF AS GOOD AS A DOG'S.
YOU'RE WAY INTO ANIMALS, HUH? ARE YOU GONNA BE A VET INSTEAD OF A PROGRAMMER?
INSTEAD? I'M GONNA BE BOTH. ONLY THING IS, I'M... AHH...
AHH... AHH...
UH-OH.
CHOOMF!

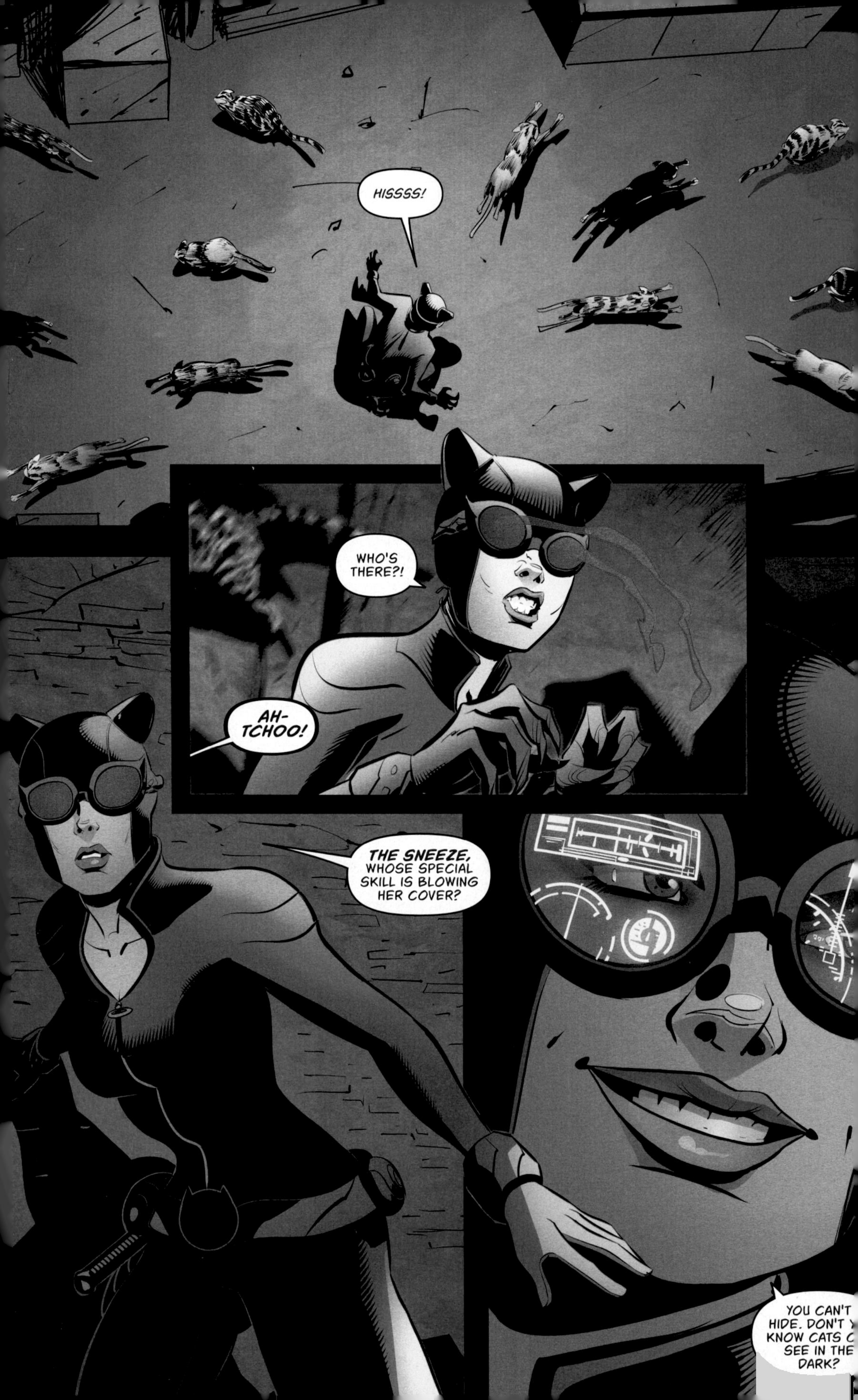

HISSSS!
WHO'S THERE?!
AH-TCHOO!
THE SNEEZE, WHOSE SPECIAL SKILL IS BLOWING HER COVER?
YOU CAN'T HIDE. DON'T Y KNOW CATS C SEE IN THE DARK?

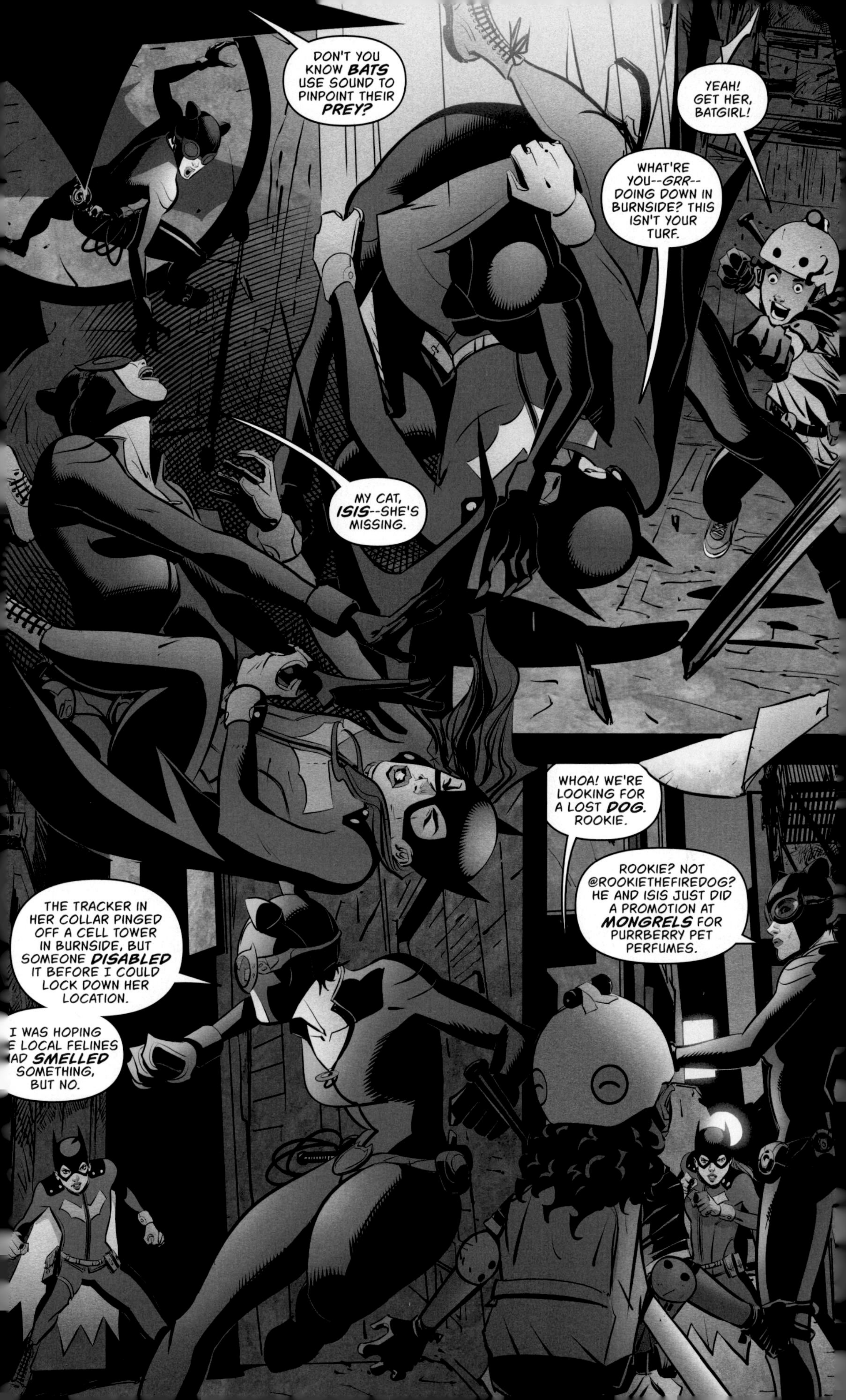
DON'T YOU KNOW BATS USE SOUND TO PINPOINT THEIR PREY?
YEAH! GET HER, BATGIRL!
WHAT'RE YOU--GRR-- DOING DOWN IN BURNSIDE? THIS ISN'T YOUR TURF.
MY CAT, ISIS--SHE'S MISSING.
WHOA! WE'RE LOOKING FOR A LOST DOG. ROOKIE.
ROOKIE? NOT @ROOKIETHEFIREDOG? HE AND ISIS JUST DID A PROMOTION AT MONGRELS FOR PURRBERRY PET PERFUMES.
THE TRACKER IN HER COLLAR PINGED OFF A CELL TOWER IN BURNSIDE, BUT SOMEONE DISABLED IT BEFORE I COULD LOCK DOWN HER LOCATION.
SMELLED SOMETHING, BUT NO.

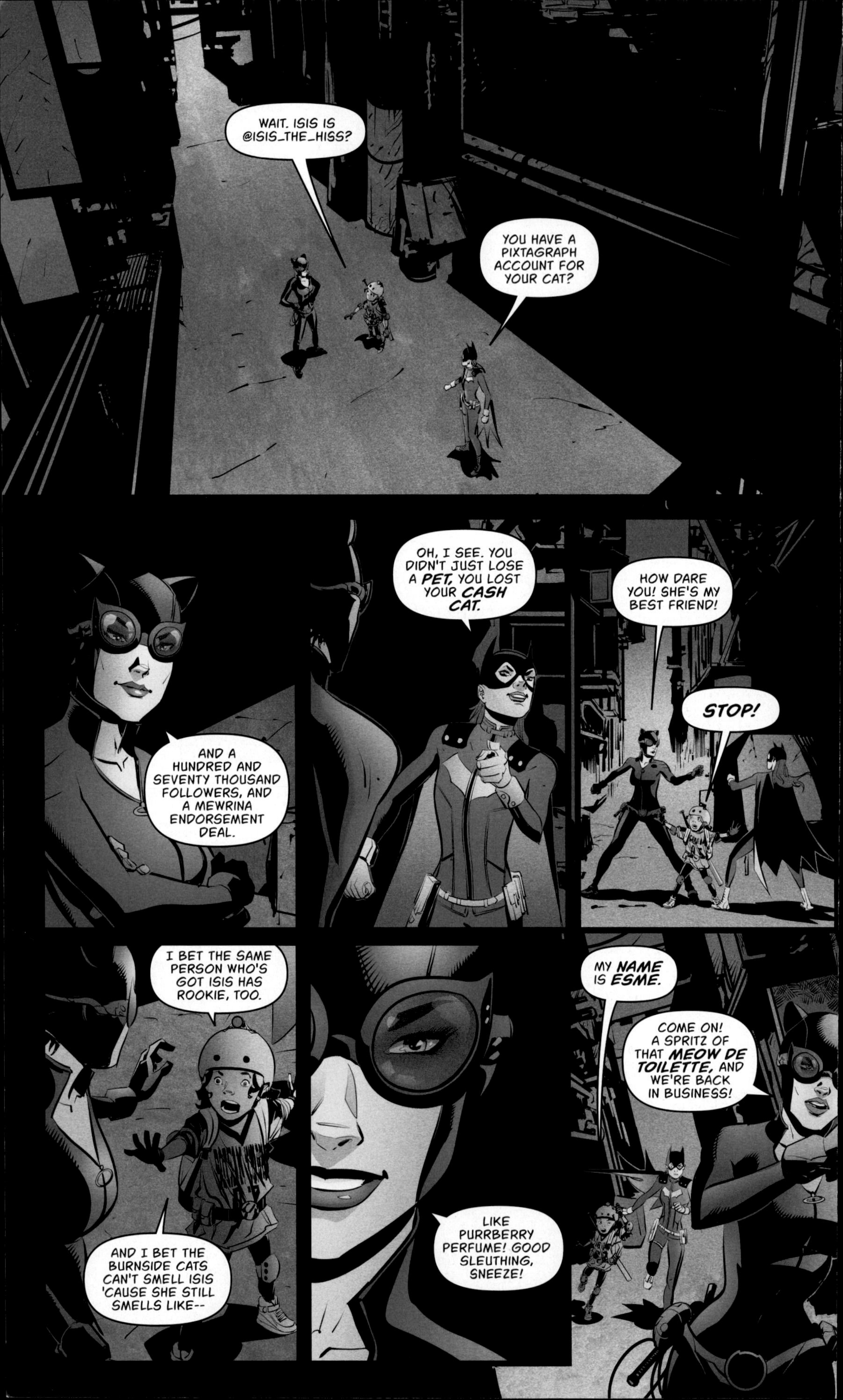

WAIT. ISIS IS @ISIS_THE_HISS?
YOU HAVE A PIXTAGRAPH ACCOUNT FOR YOUR CAT?
AND A HUNDRED AND SEVENTY THOUSAND FOLLOWERS, AND A MEWRINA ENDORSEMENT DEAL.
OH, I SEE. YOU DIDN'T JUST LOSE A PET, YOU LOST YOUR CASH CAT.
HOW DARE YOU! SHE'S MY BEST FRIEND!
STOP!
I BET THE SAME PERSON WHO'S GOT ISIS HAS ROOKIE, TOO.
AND I BET THE BURNSIDE CATS CAN'T SMELL ISIS 'CAUSE SHE STILL SMELLS LIKE--
LIKE PURRBERRY PERFUME! GOOD SLEUTHING, SNEEZE!
MY NAME IS ESME.
COME ON! A SPRITZ OF THAT MEOW DE TOILETTE, AND WE'RE BACK IN BUSINESS!

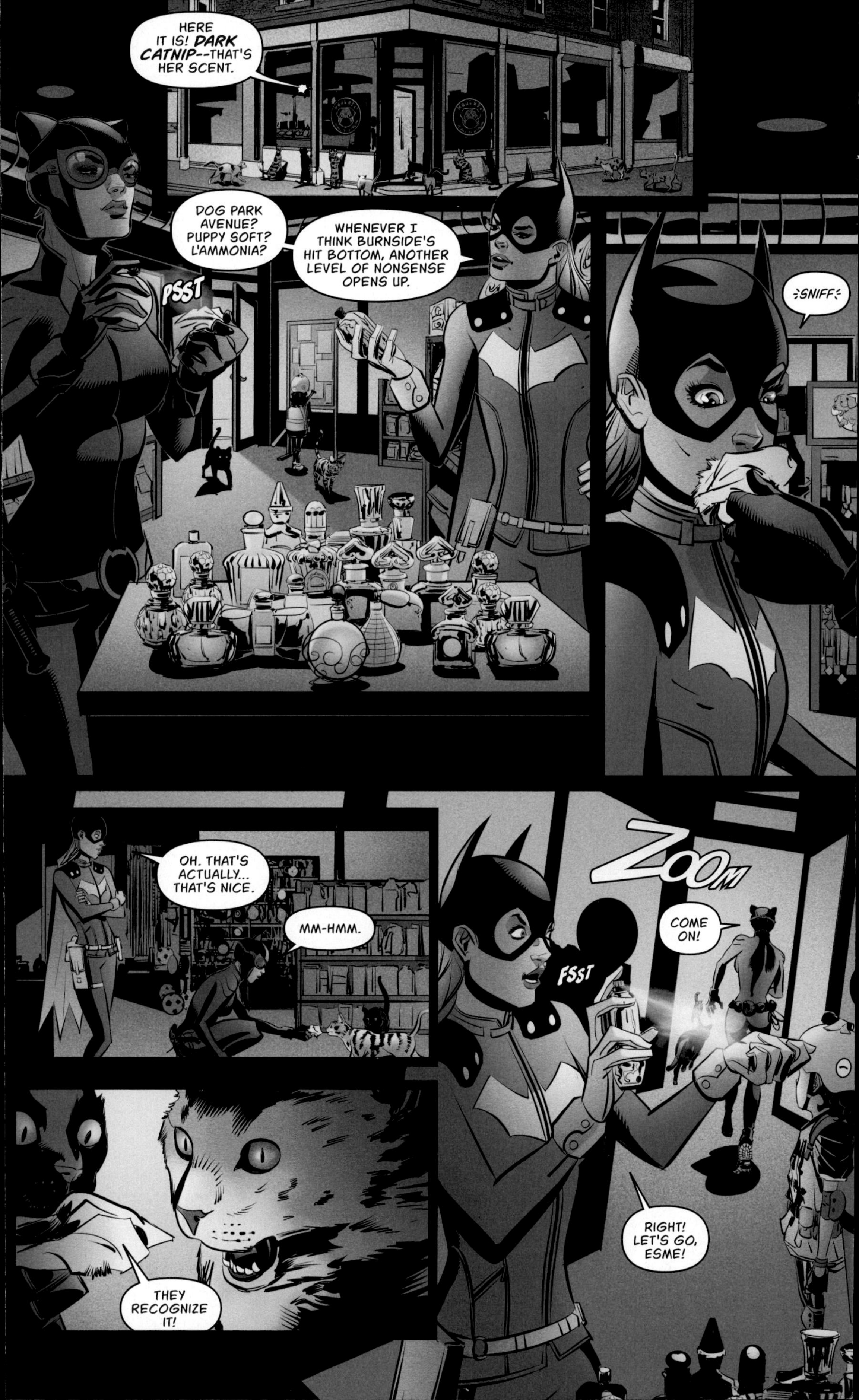
HERE IT IS! DARK CATNIP--THAT'S HER SCENT.
DOG PARK AVENUE? PUPPY SOFT? L'AMMONIA?
WHENEVER I THINK BURNSIDE'S HIT BOTTOM, ANOTHER LEVEL OF NONSENSE OPENS UP.
PSST
SNIFF
OH. THAT'S ACTUALLY... THAT'S NICE.
MM-HMM.
THEY RECOGNIZE IT!
ZOOM
COME ON!
FSST
RIGHT! LET'S GO, ESME!

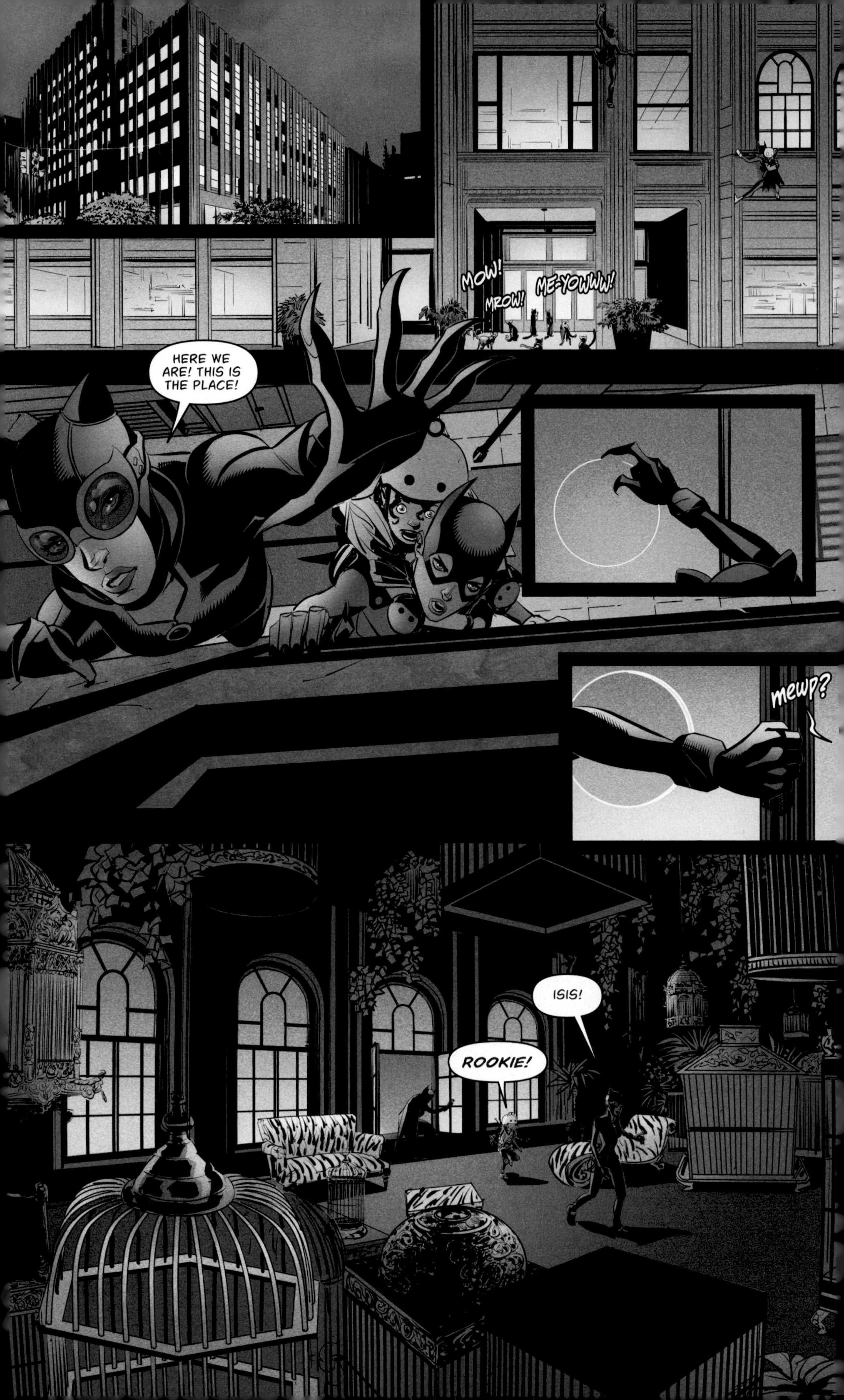
MOW!
MROW!
ME-YOWWW!
HERE WE ARE! THIS IS THE PLACE!
mewp?
ISIS!
ROOKIE!

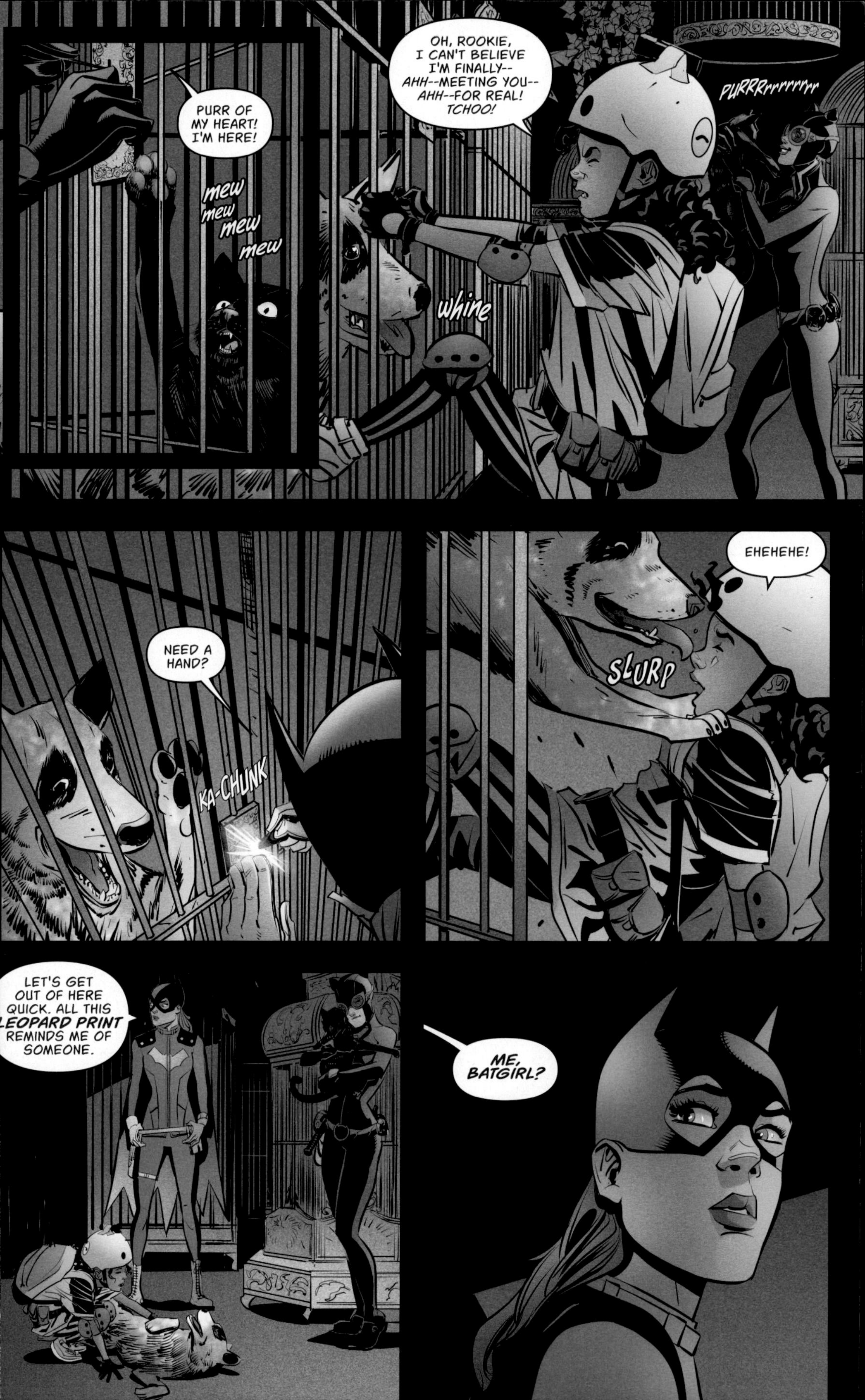
PURR OF MY HEART! I'M HERE!
mew mew mew mew
OH, ROOKIE, I CAN'T BELIEVE I'M FINALLY-- AHH--MEETING YOU-- AHH--FOR REAL! TCHOO!
PURRRrrrrrrrr
whine
NEED A HAND?
KA-CHUNK
EHEHEHE!
SLURP
LET'S GET OUT OF HERE QUICK. ALL THIS LEOPARD PRINT REMINDS ME OF SOMEONE.
ME, BATGIRL?

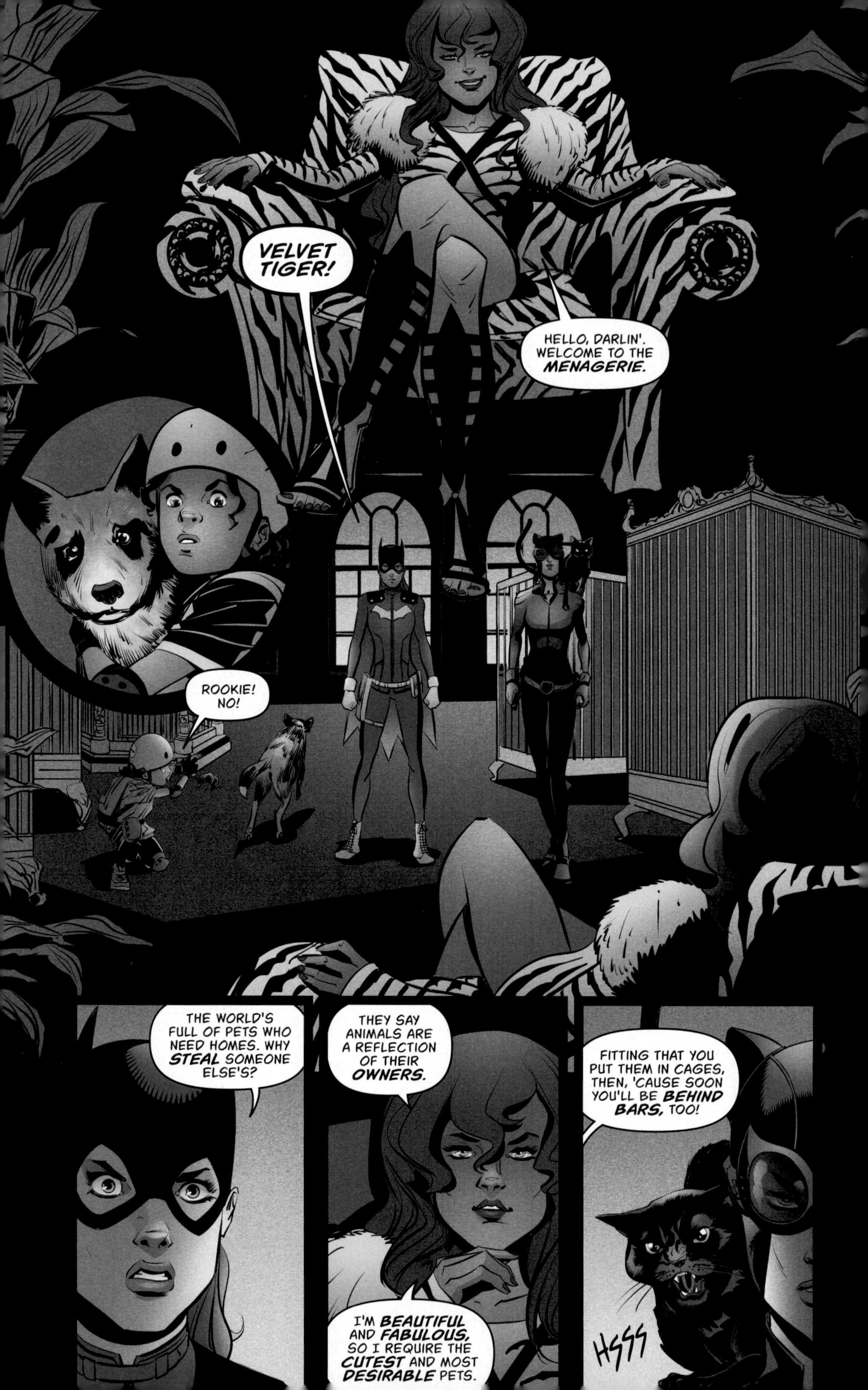
VELVET TIGER!
HELLO, DARLIN'. WELCOME TO THE MENAGERIE.
ROOKIE! NO!
THE WORLD'S FULL OF PETS WHO NEED HOMES. WHY STEAL SOMEONE ELSE'S?
THEY SAY ANIMALS ARE A REFLECTION OF THEIR OWNERS.
I'M BEAUTIFUL AND FABULOUS, SO I REQUIRE THE CUTEST AND MOST DESIRABLE PETS.
FITTING THAT YOU PUT THEM IN CAGES, THEN, 'CAUSE SOON YOU'LL BE BEHIND BARS, TOO!
HSSS

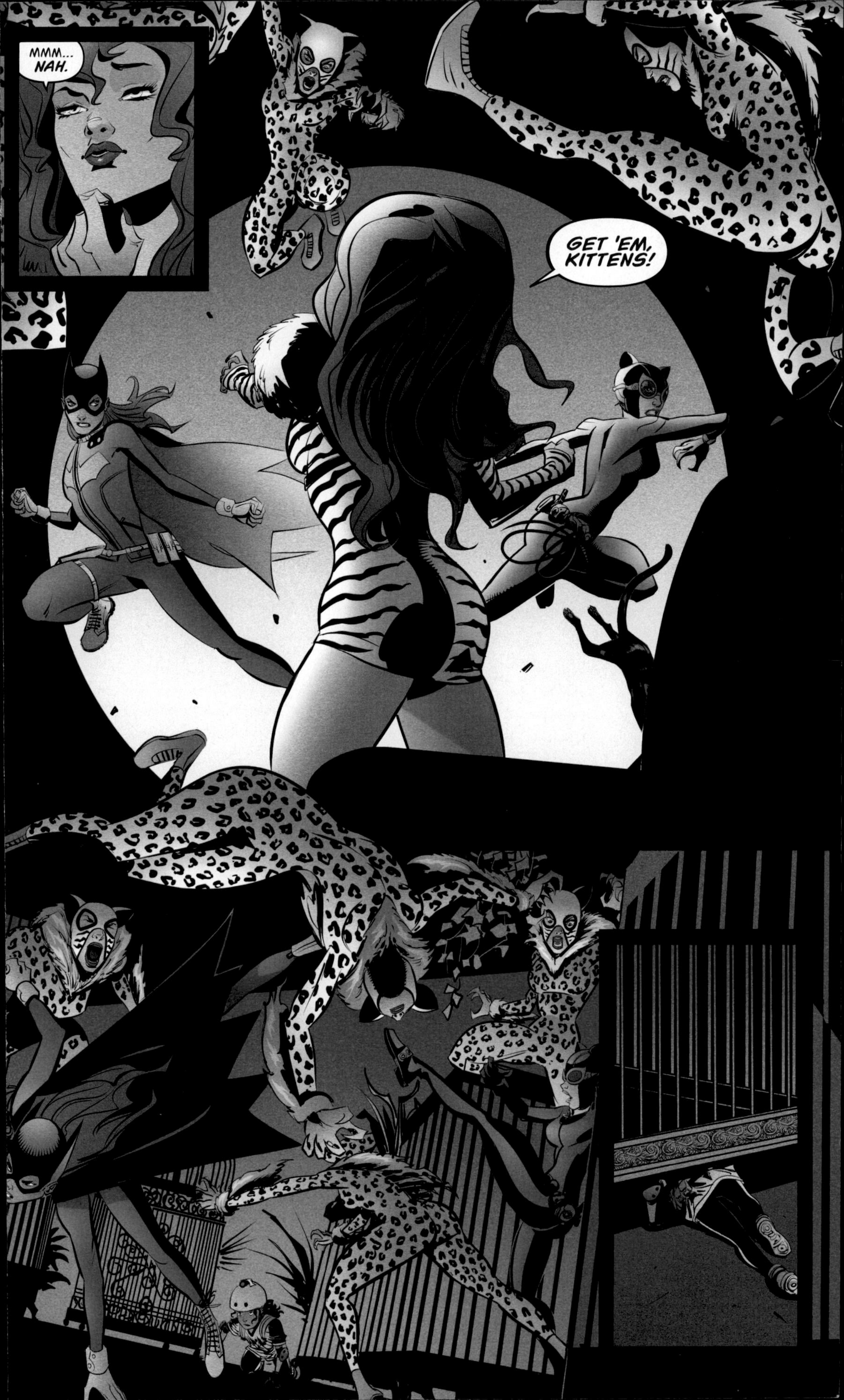

MMM... NAH.
GET 'EM, KITTENS!

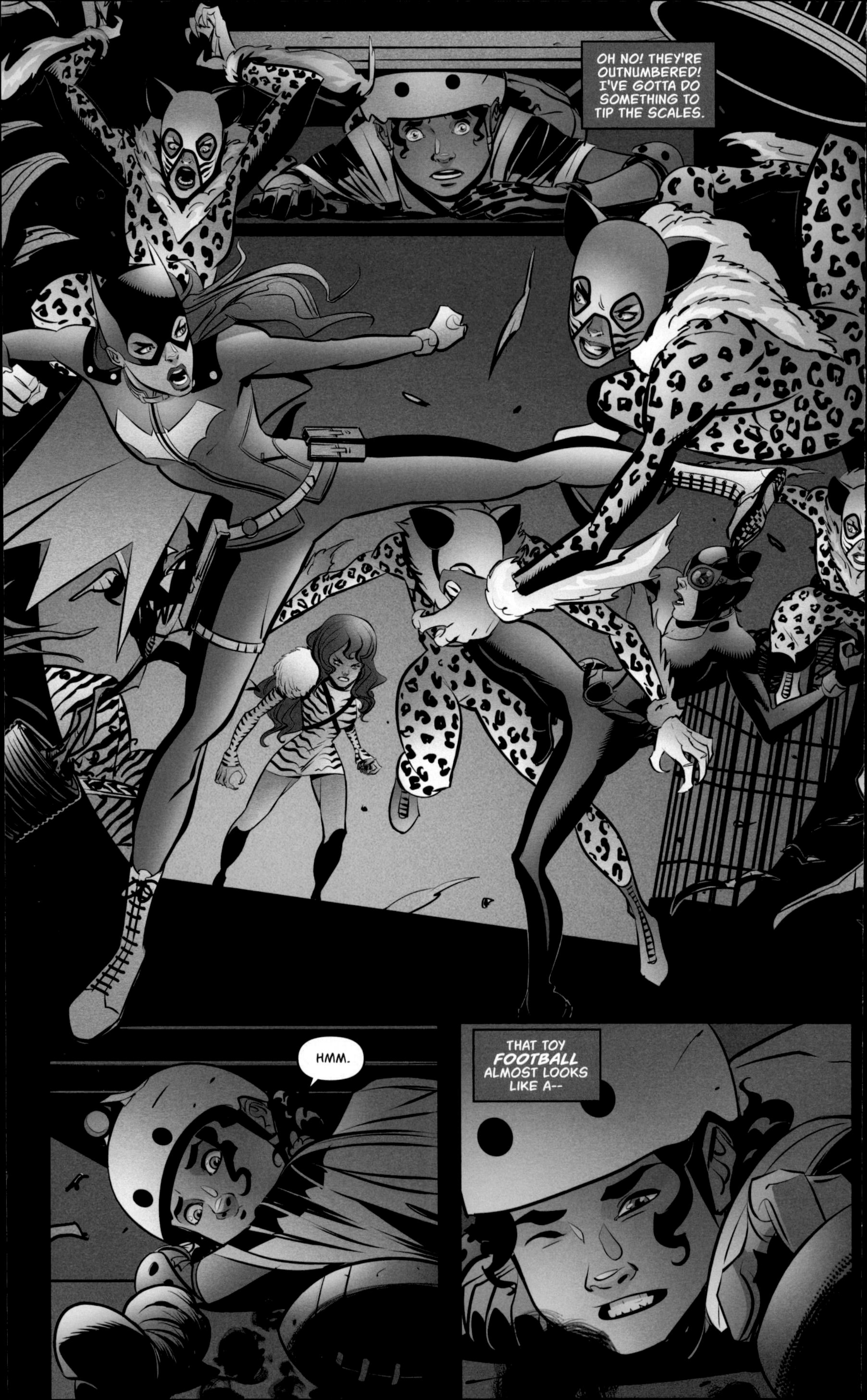

OH NO! THEY'RE OUTNUMBERED! I'VE GOTTA DO SOMETHING TO TIP THE SCALES.
HMM.
THAT TOY FOOTBALL ALMOST LOOKS LIKE A--

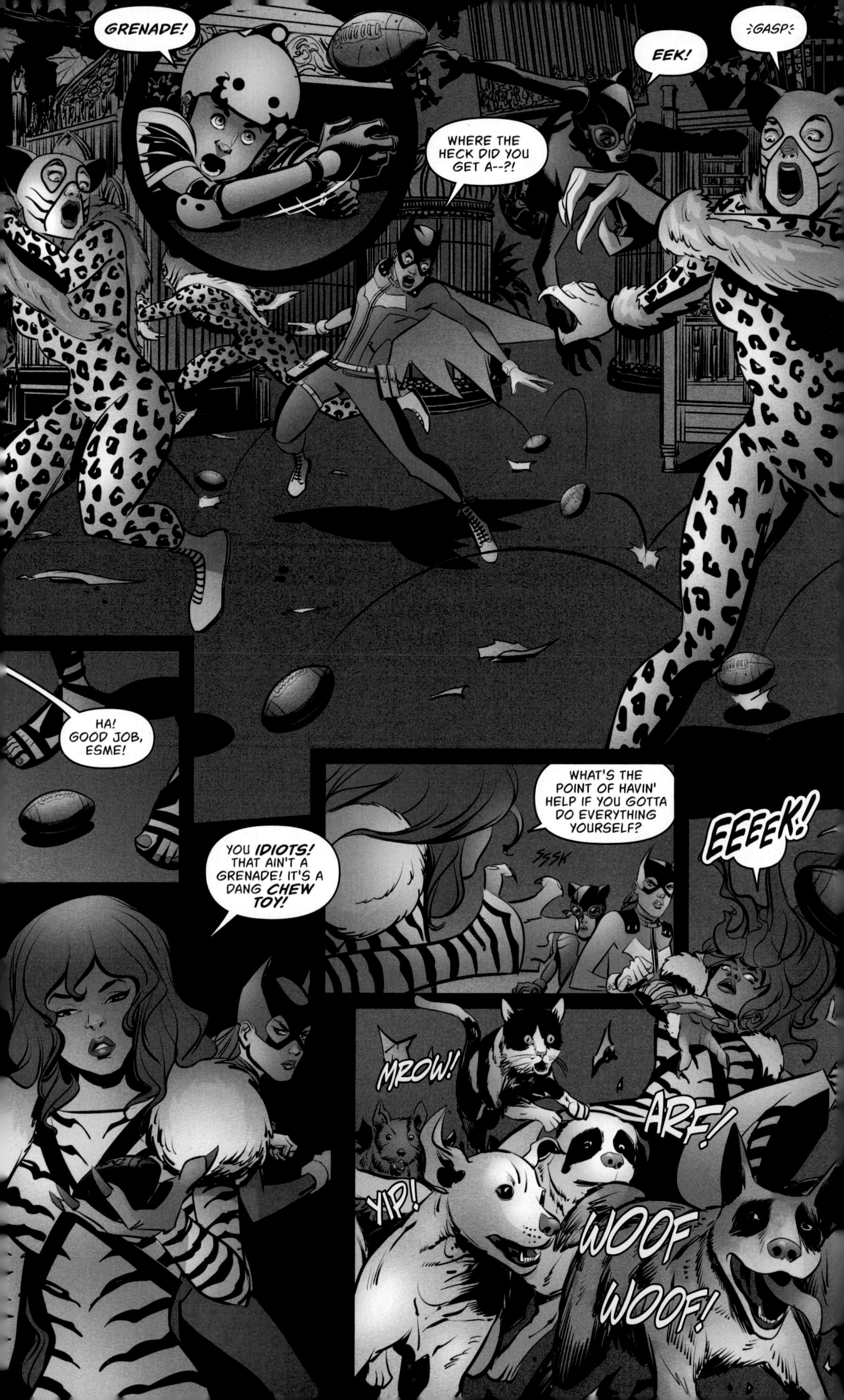

GRENADE!
EEK!
GASP
WHERE THE HECK DID YOU GET A--?!
HA! GOOD JOB, ESME!
YOU IDIOTS! THAT AIN'T A GRENADE! IT'S A DANG CHEW TOY!
WHAT'S THE POINT OF HAVIN' HELP IF YOU GOTTA DO EVERYTHING YOURSELF?
SSSK
EEEEK!
MROW!
ARF!
YIP!
WOOF WOOF!

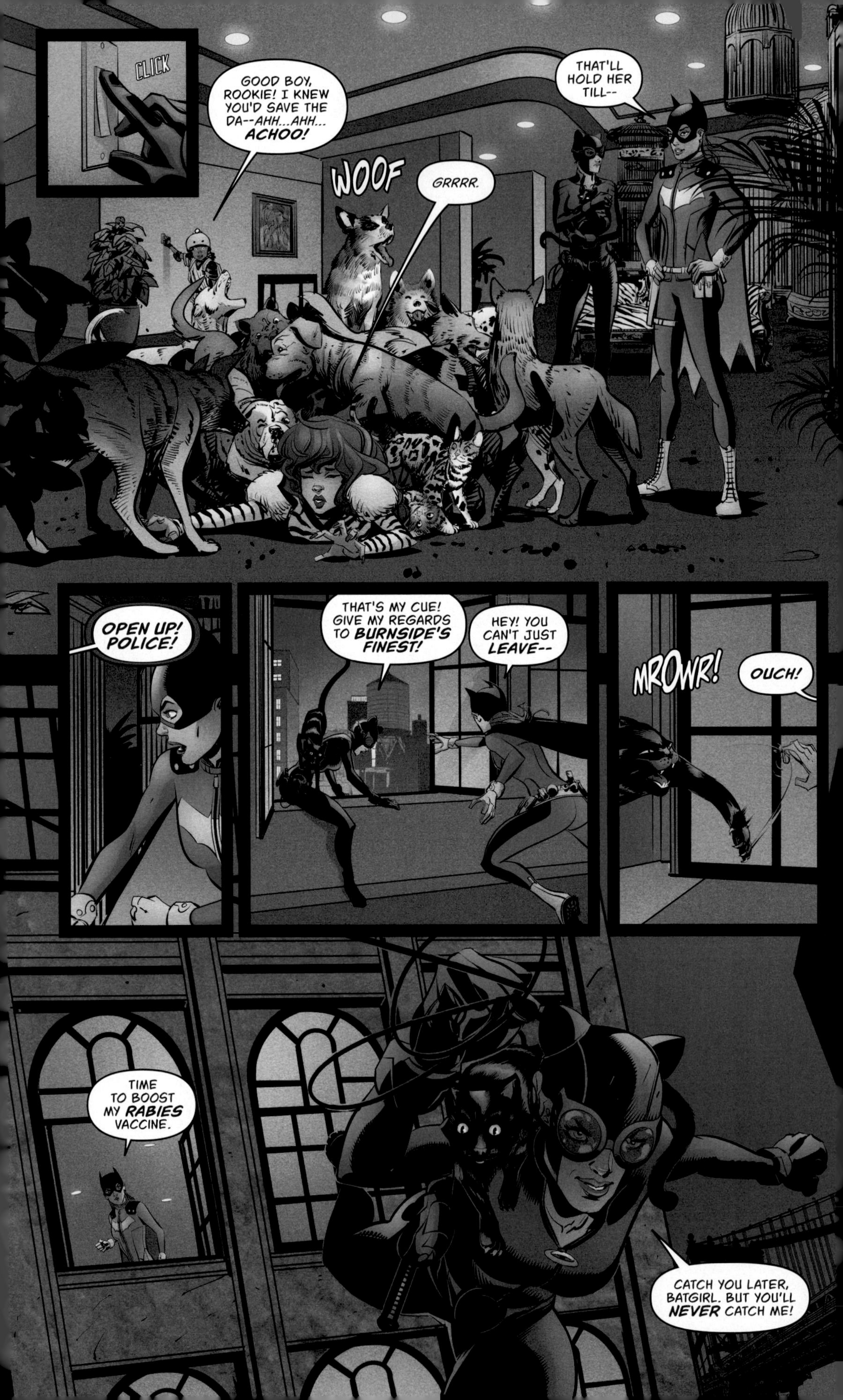
CLICK
GOOD BOY, ROOKIE! I KNEW YOU'D SAVE THE DA--AHH...AHH... ACHOO!
WOOF
GRRRR.
THAT'LL HOLD HER TILL--
OPEN UP! POLICE!
THAT'S MY CUE! GIVE MY REGARDS TO BURNSIDE'S FINEST!
HEY! YOU CAN'T JUST LEAVE--
MROWR!
OUCH!
TIME TO BOOST MY RABIES VACCINE.
CATCH YOU LATER, BATGIRL. BUT YOU'LL NEVER CATCH ME!

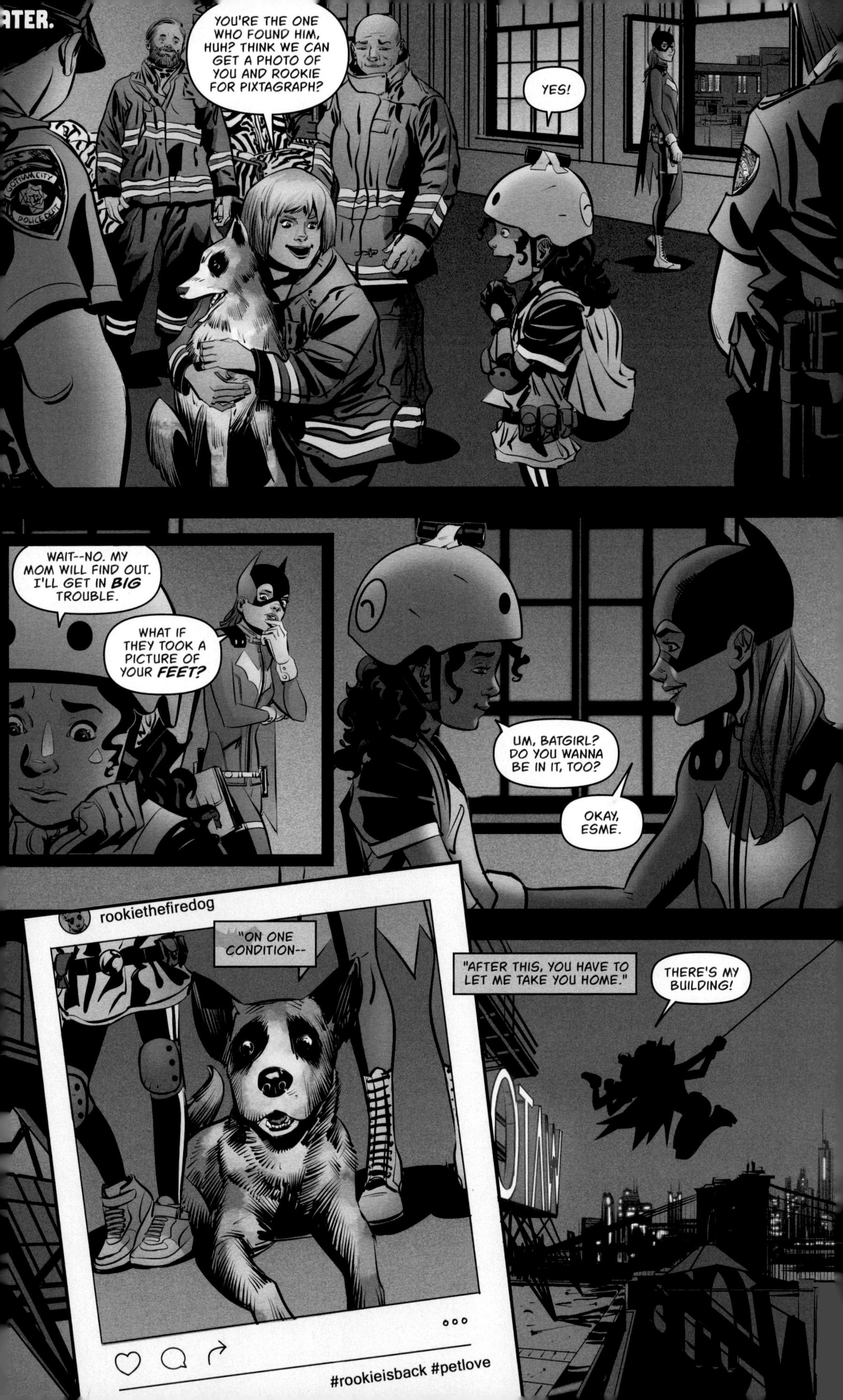
ATER.
YOU'RE THE ONE WHO FOUND HIM, HUH? THINK WE CAN GET A PHOTO OF YOU AND ROOKIE FOR PIXTAGRAPH?
YES!
WAIT--NO. MY MOM WILL FIND OUT. I'LL GET IN BIG TROUBLE.
WHAT IF THEY TOOK A PICTURE OF YOUR FEET?
UM, BATGIRL? DO YOU WANNA BE IN IT, TOO?
OKAY, ESME.
rookiethefiredog
"ON ONE CONDITION--
"AFTER THIS, YOU HAVE TO LET ME TAKE YOU HOME."
THERE'S MY BUILDING!
#rookieisback #petlove

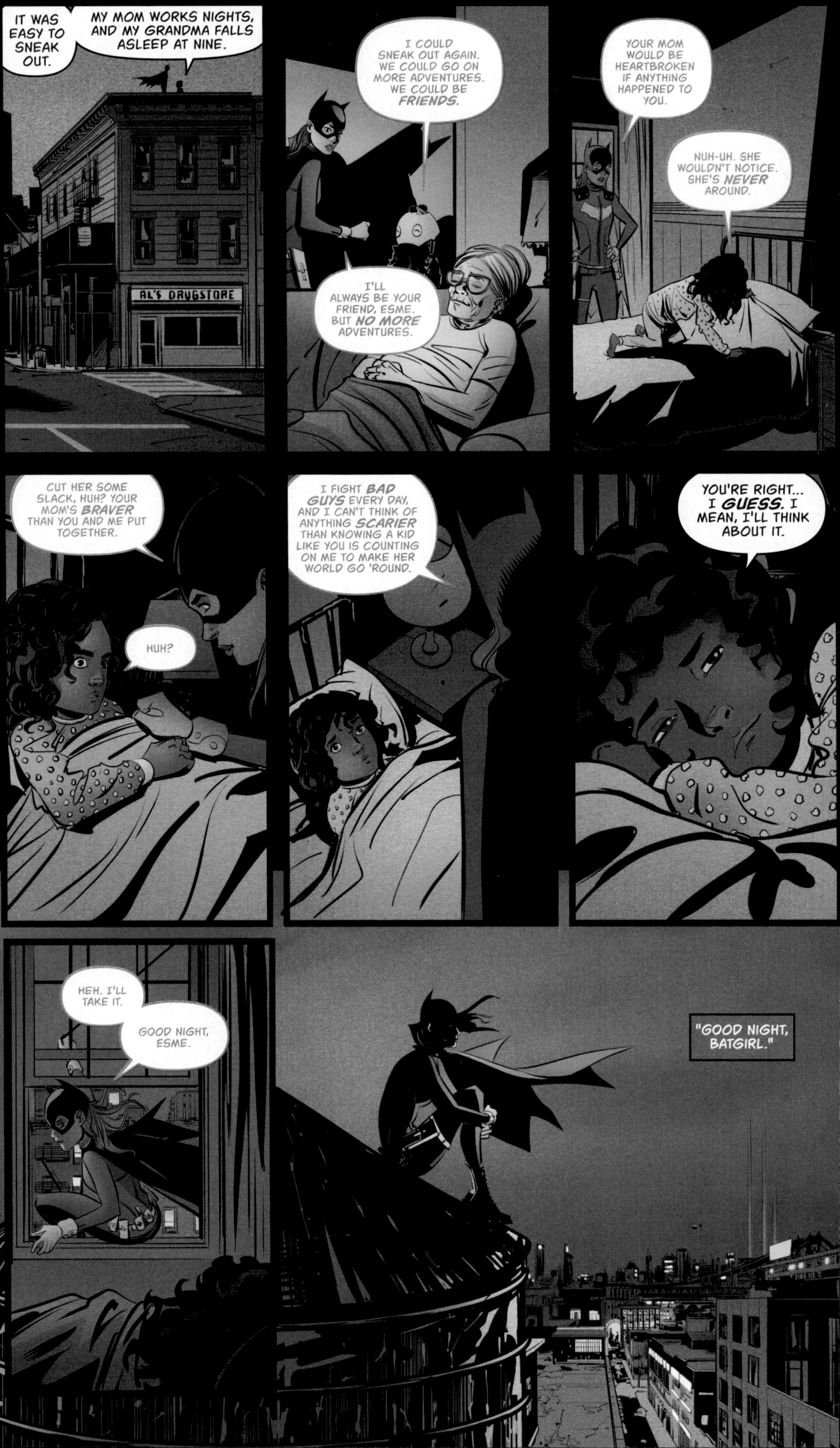
IT WAS EASY TO SNEAK OUT.
MY MOM WORKS NIGHTS, AND MY GRANDMA FALLS ASLEEP AT NINE.
AL'S DRUGSTORE
I COULD SNEAK OUT AGAIN. WE COULD GO ON MORE ADVENTURES. WE COULD BE FRIENDS.
I'LL ALWAYS BE YOUR FRIEND, ESME. BUT NO MORE ADVENTURES.
YOUR MOM WOULD BE HEARTBROKEN IF ANYTHING HAPPENED TO YOU.
NUH-UH. SHE WOULDN'T NOTICE. SHE'S NEVER AROUND.
CUT HER SOME SLACK, HUH? YOUR MOM'S BRAVER THAN YOU AND ME PUT TOGETHER.
HUH?
I FIGHT BAD GUYS EVERY DAY, AND I CAN'T THINK OF ANYTHING SCARIER THAN KNOWING A KID LIKE YOU IS COUNTING ON ME TO MAKE HER WORLD GO 'ROUND.
YOU'RE RIGHT... I GUESS. I MEAN, I'LL THINK ABOUT IT.
HEH. I'LL TAKE IT.
GOOD NIGHT, ESME.
"GOOD NIGHT, BATGIRL."

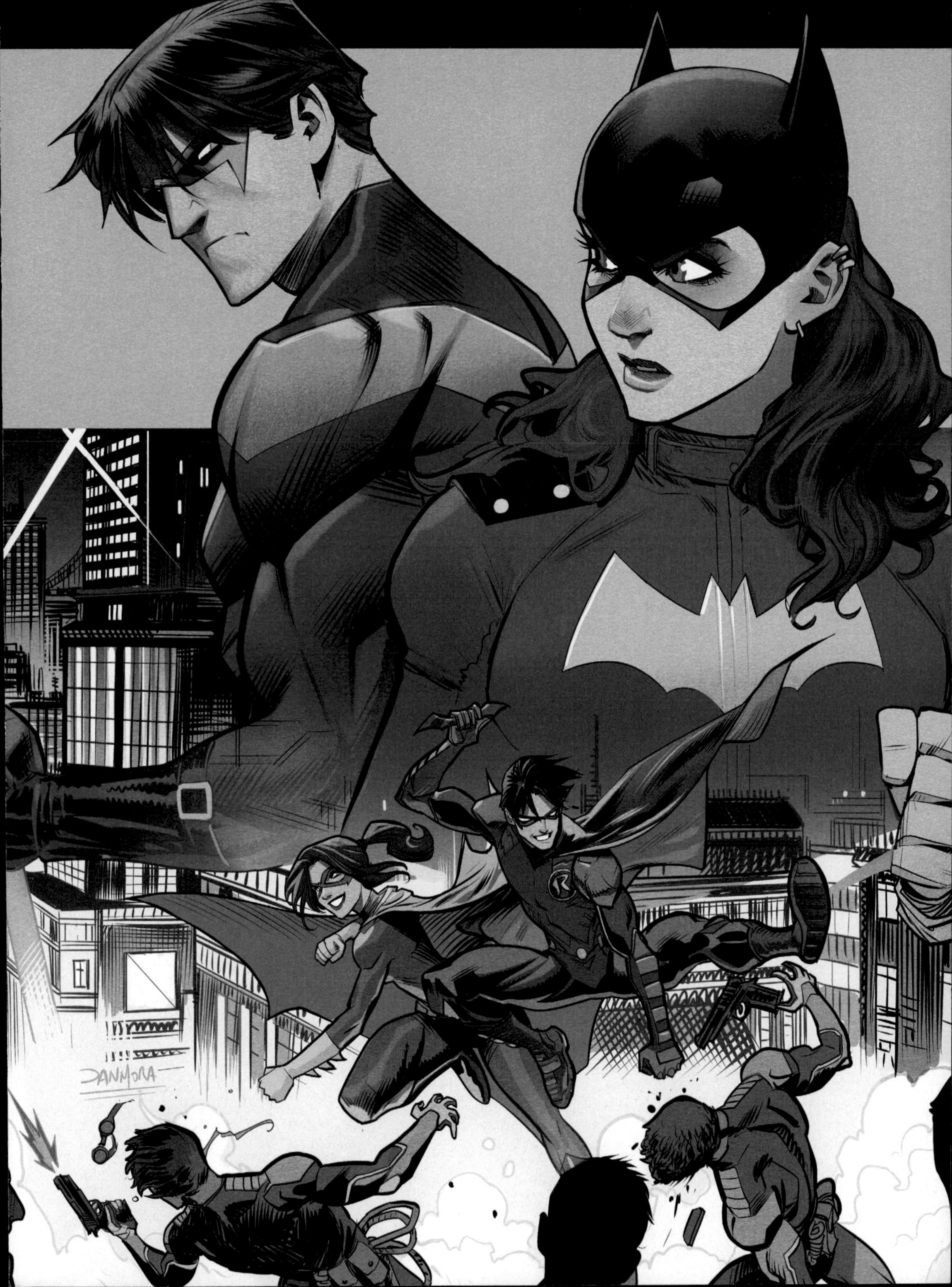
DANMORA

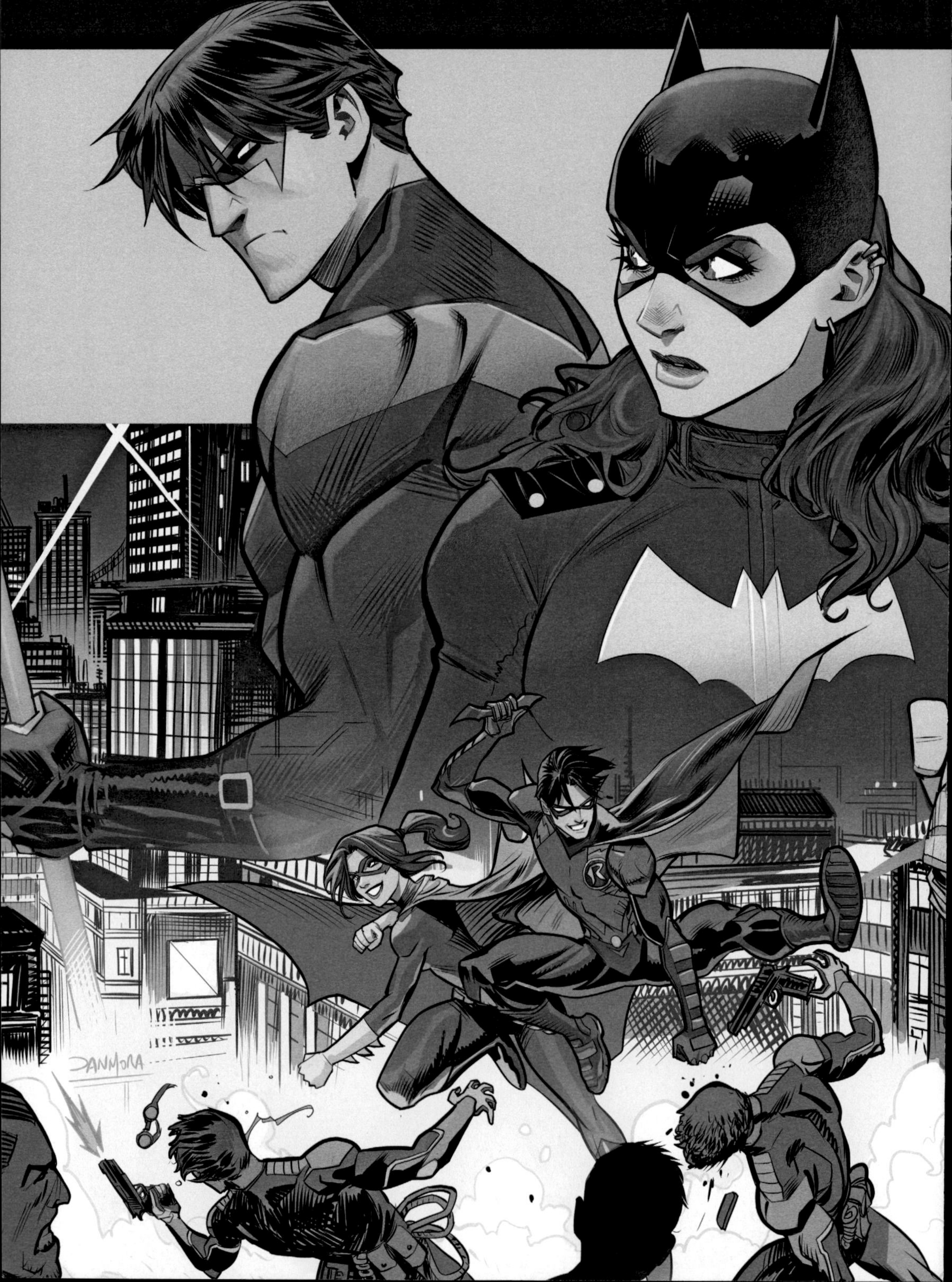
DANMORA

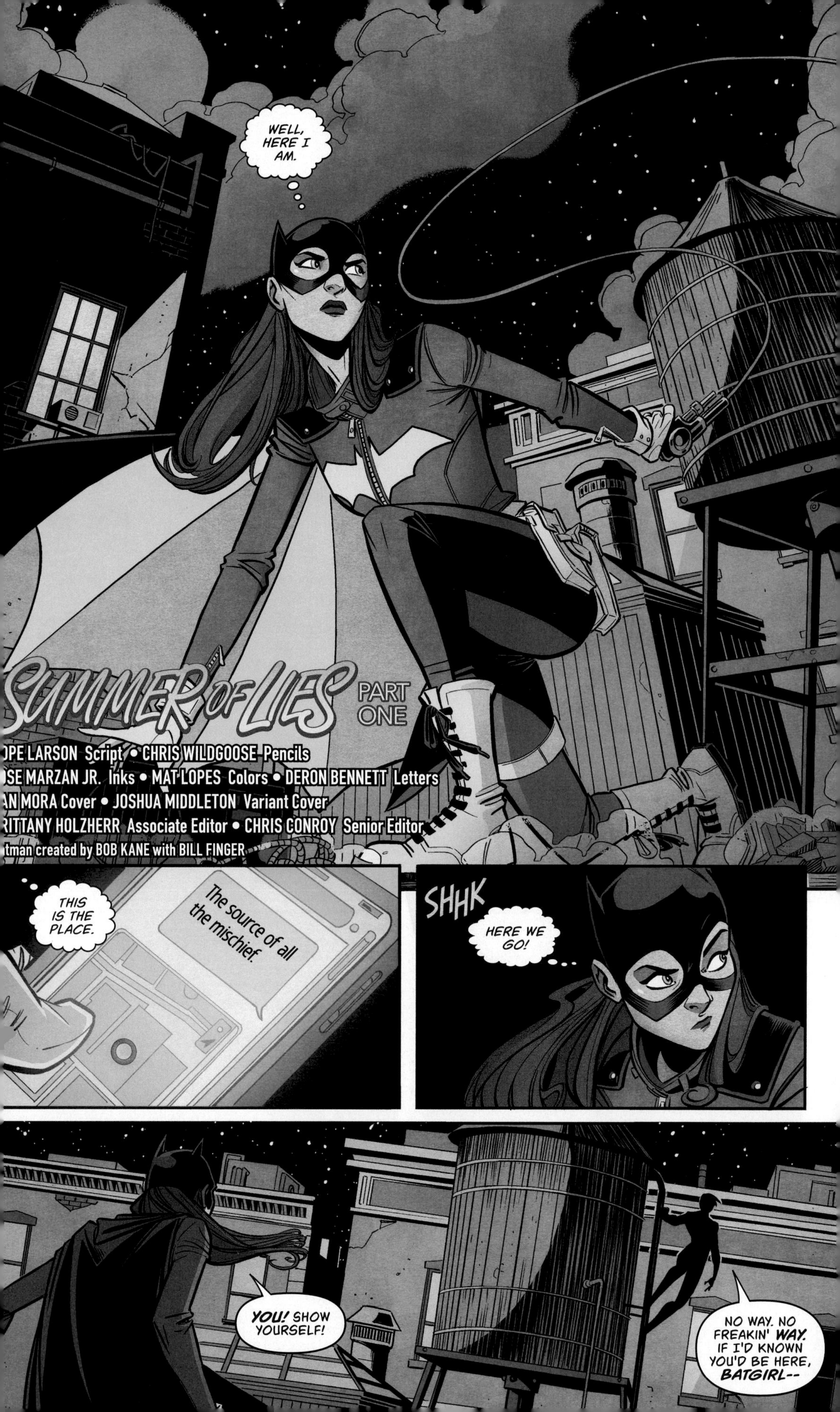
WELL, HERE I AM.
SUMMER OF LIES PART ONE
OPE LARSON Script • CHRIS WILDGOOSE Pencils
SE MARZAN JR. Inks • MAT LOPES Colors • DERON BENNETT Letters
AN MORA Cover • JOSHUA MIDDLETON Variant Cover
RITTANY HOLZHERR Associate Editor • CHRIS CONROY Senior Editor
tman created by BOB KANE with BILL FINGER
THIS IS THE PLACE.
The source of all the mischief.
SHHK
HERE WE GO!
YOU! SHOW YOURSELF!
NO WAY. NO FREAKIN' WAY. IF I'D KNOWN YOU'D BE HERE, BATGIRL--

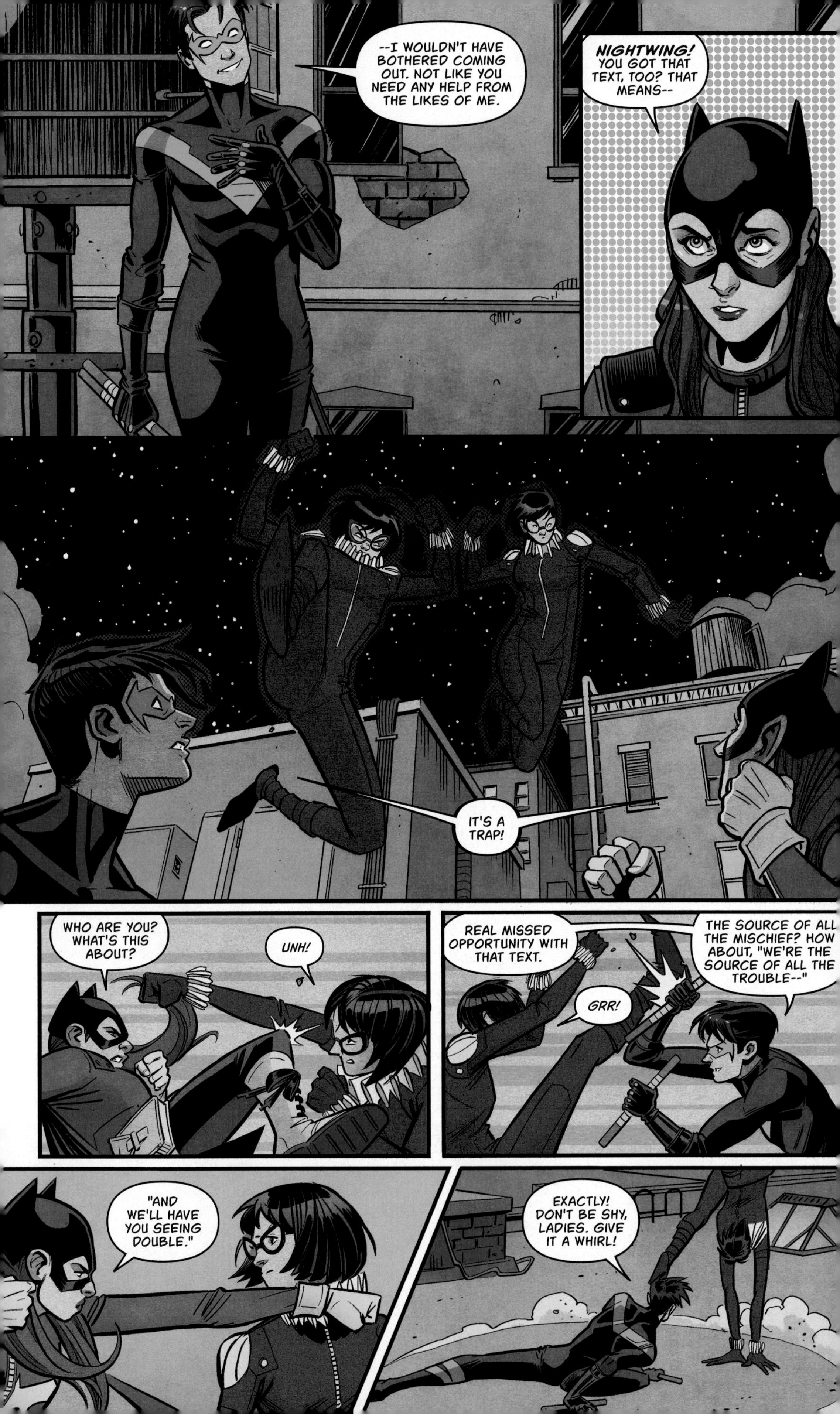
--I WOULDN'T HAVE BOTHERED COMING OUT. NOT LIKE YOU NEED ANY HELP FROM THE LIKES OF ME.
NIGHTWING! YOU GOT THAT TEXT, TOO? THAT MEANS--
IT'S A TRAP!
WHO ARE YOU? WHAT'S THIS ABOUT?
UNH!
REAL MISSED OPPORTUNITY WITH THAT TEXT.
THE SOURCE OF ALL THE MISCHIEF? HOW ABOUT, "WE'RE THE SOURCE OF ALL THE TROUBLE--"
GRR!
"AND WE'LL HAVE YOU SEEING DOUBLE."
EXACTLY! DON'T BE SHY, LADIES. GIVE IT A WHIRL!

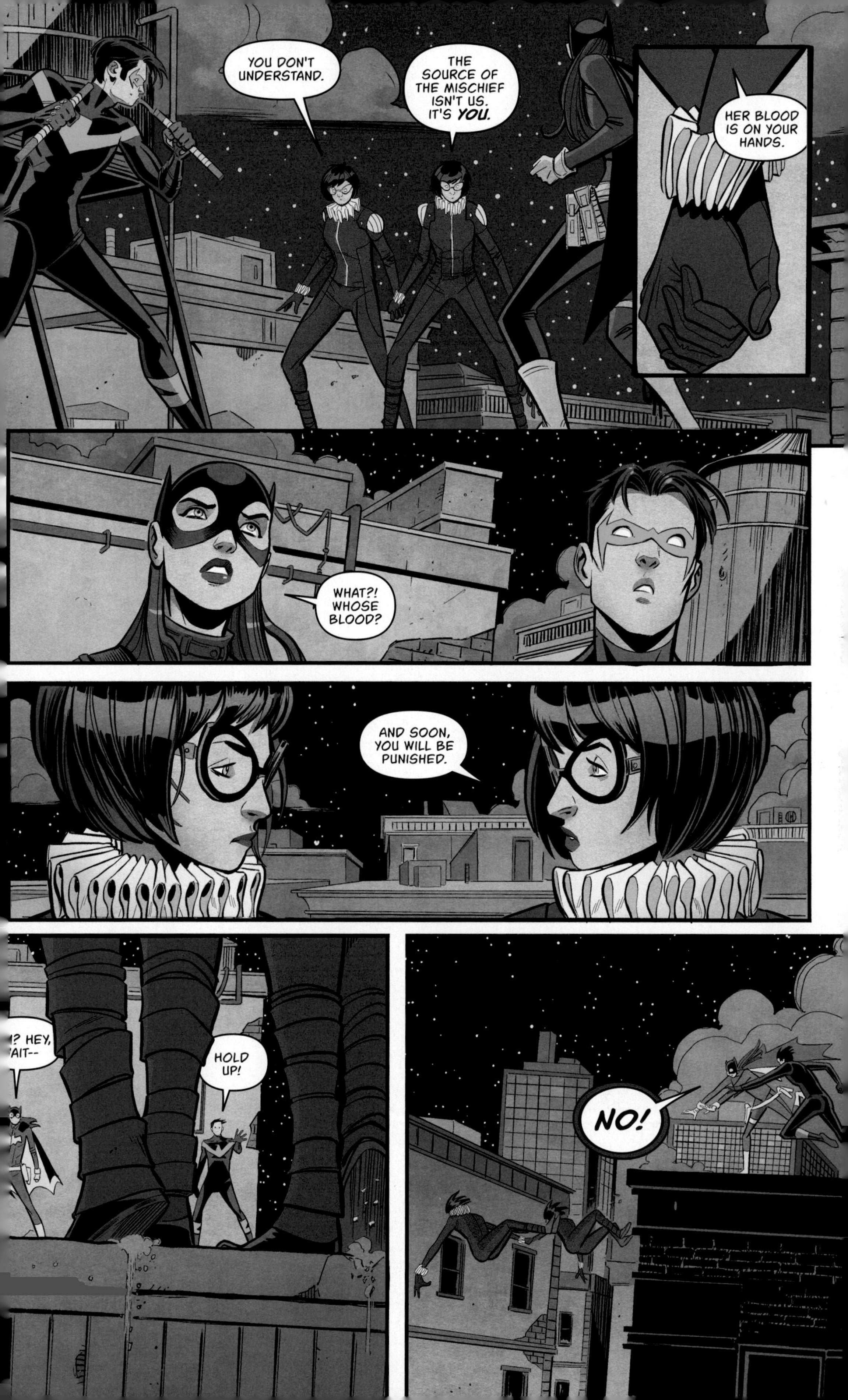
YOU DON'T UNDERSTAND.
THE SOURCE OF THE MISCHIEF ISN'T US. IT'S *YOU.*
HER BLOOD IS ON YOUR HANDS.
WHAT?! WHOSE BLOOD?
AND SOON, YOU WILL BE PUNISHED.
HOLD UP!
NO!

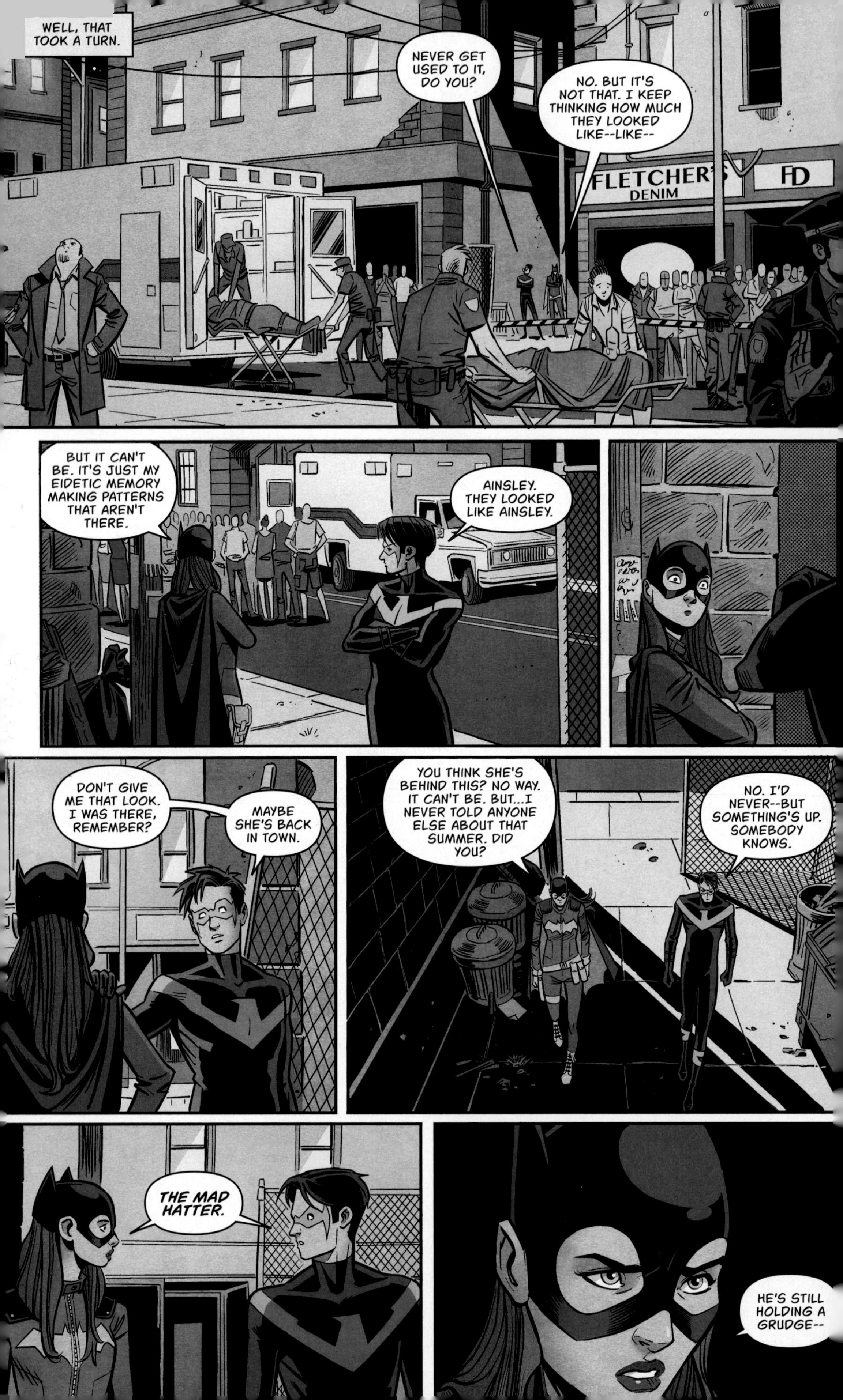

WELL, THAT TOOK A TURN.
NEVER GET USED TO IT, DO YOU?
NO. BUT IT'S NOT THAT. I KEEP THINKING HOW MUCH THEY LOOKED LIKE--LIKE--
FLETCHER'S DENIM
FD
BUT IT CAN'T BE. IT'S JUST MY EIDETIC MEMORY MAKING PATTERNS THAT AREN'T THERE.
AINSLEY. THEY LOOKED LIKE AINSLEY.
DON'T GIVE ME THAT LOOK. I WAS THERE, REMEMBER?
MAYBE SHE'S BACK IN TOWN.
YOU THINK SHE'S BEHIND THIS? NO WAY. IT CAN'T BE. BUT...I NEVER TOLD ANYONE ELSE ABOUT THAT SUMMER. DID YOU?
NO. I'D NEVER--BUT SOMETHING'S UP. SOMEBODY KNOWS.
THE MAD HATTER.
HE'S STILL HOLDING A GRUDGE--

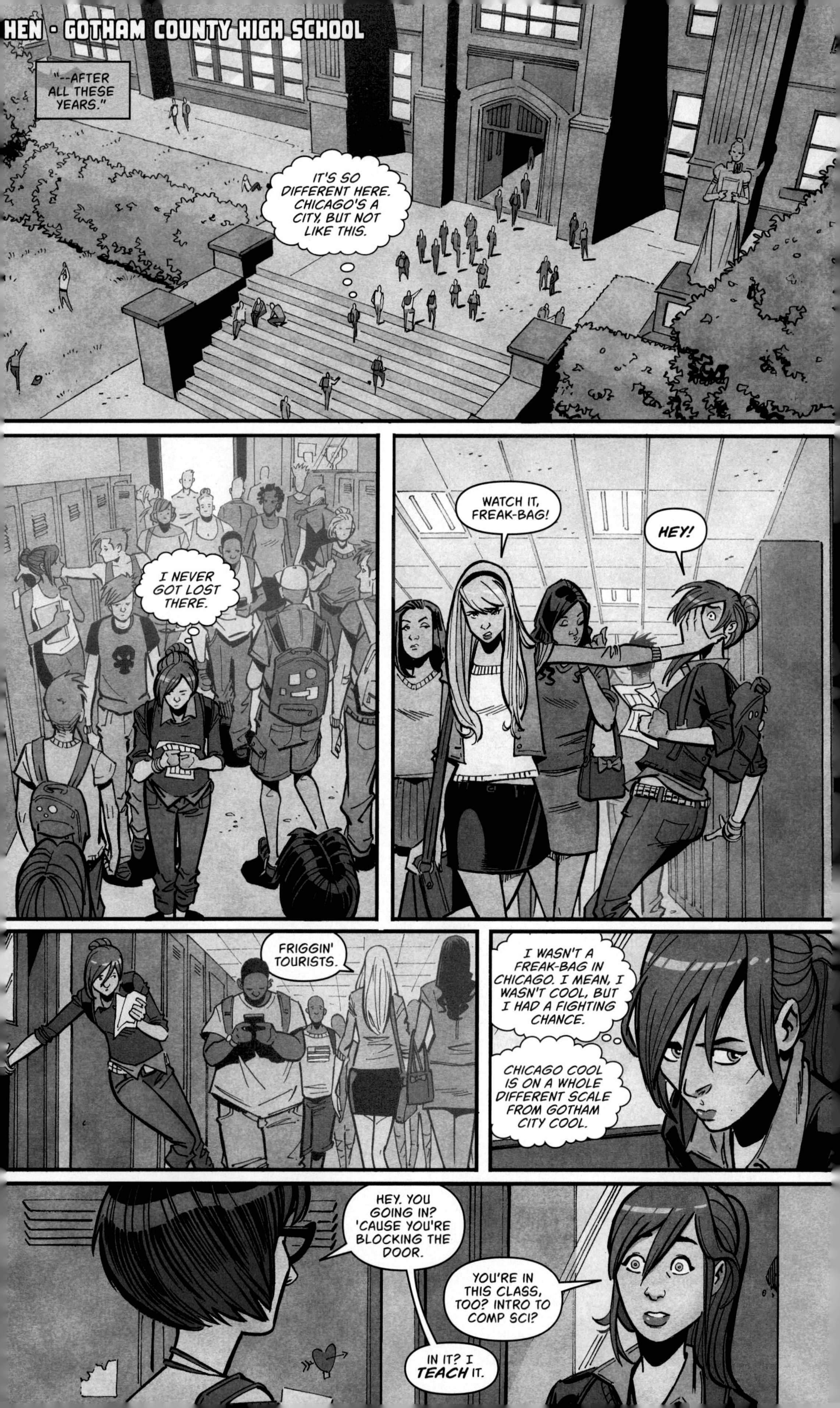
HEN - GOTHAM COUNTY HIGH SCHOOL
"--AFTER ALL THESE YEARS."
IT'S SO DIFFERENT HERE. CHICAGO'S A CITY, BUT NOT LIKE THIS.
I NEVER GOT LOST THERE.
WATCH IT, FREAK-BAG!
HEY!
FRIGGIN' TOURISTS.
I WASN'T A FREAK-BAG IN CHICAGO. I MEAN, I WASN'T COOL, BUT I HAD A FIGHTING CHANCE.
CHICAGO COOL IS ON A WHOLE DIFFERENT SCALE FROM GOTHAM CITY COOL.
HEY. YOU GOING IN? 'CAUSE YOU'RE BLOCKING THE DOOR.
YOU'RE IN THIS CLASS, TOO? INTRO TO COMP SCI?
IN IT? I TEACH IT.

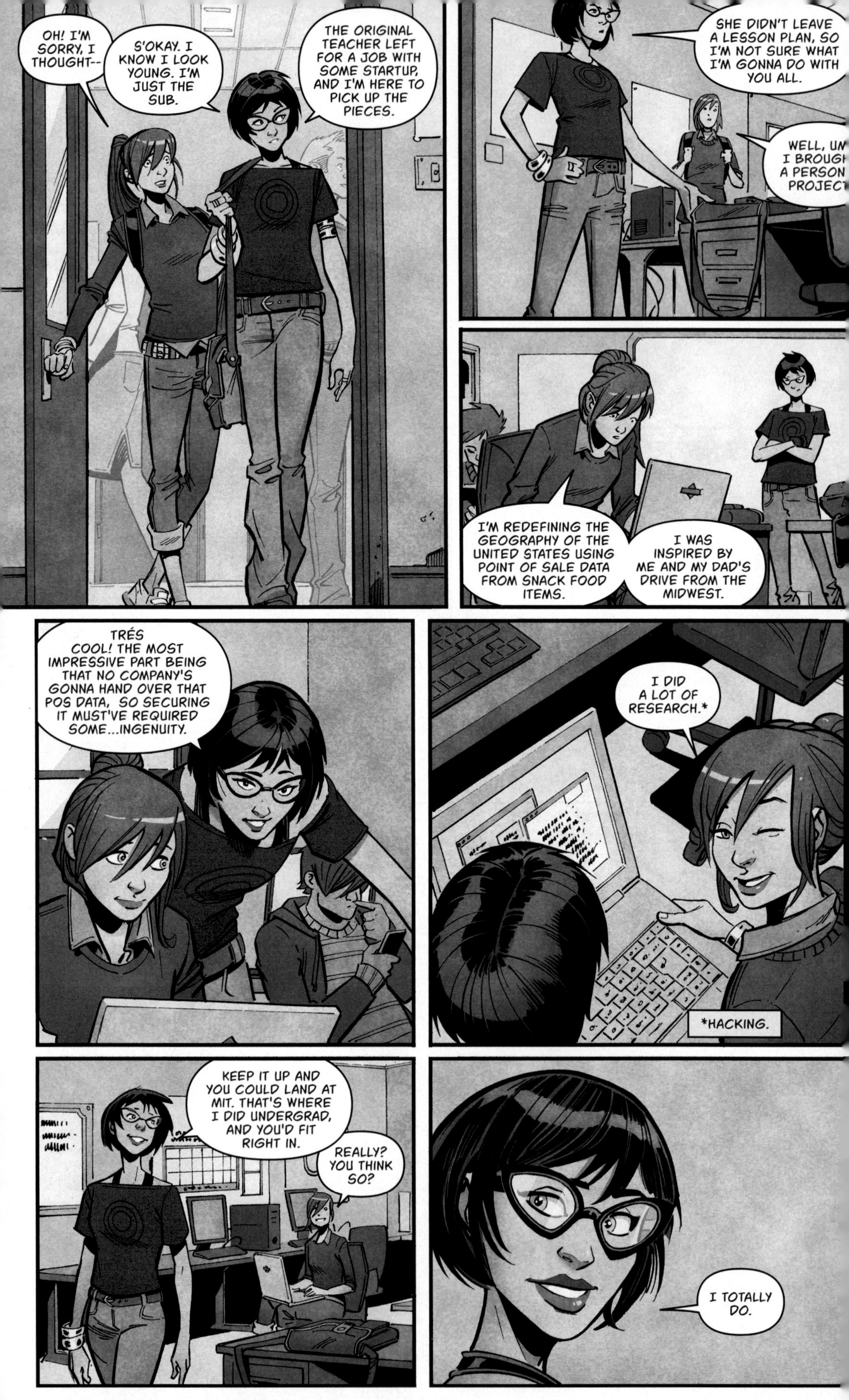
OH! I'M SORRY, I THOUGHT--
S'OKAY. I KNOW I LOOK YOUNG. I'M JUST THE SUB.
THE ORIGINAL TEACHER LEFT FOR A JOB WITH SOME STARTUP, AND I'M HERE TO PICK UP THE PIECES.
SHE DIDN'T LEAVE A LESSON PLAN, SO I'M NOT SURE WHAT I'M GONNA DO WITH YOU ALL.
WELL, UM I BROUGH A PERSON PROJECT
I'M REDEFINING THE GEOGRAPHY OF THE UNITED STATES USING POINT OF SALE DATA FROM SNACK FOOD ITEMS.
I WAS INSPIRED BY ME AND MY DAD'S DRIVE FROM THE MIDWEST.
TRÉS COOL! THE MOST IMPRESSIVE PART BEING THAT NO COMPANY'S GONNA HAND OVER THAT POS DATA, SO SECURING IT MUST'VE REQUIRED SOME...INGENUITY.
I DID A LOT OF RESEARCH.*
*HACKING.
KEEP IT UP AND YOU COULD LAND AT MIT. THAT'S WHERE I DID UNDERGRAD, AND YOU'D FIT RIGHT IN.
REALLY? YOU THINK SO?
I TOTALLY DO.

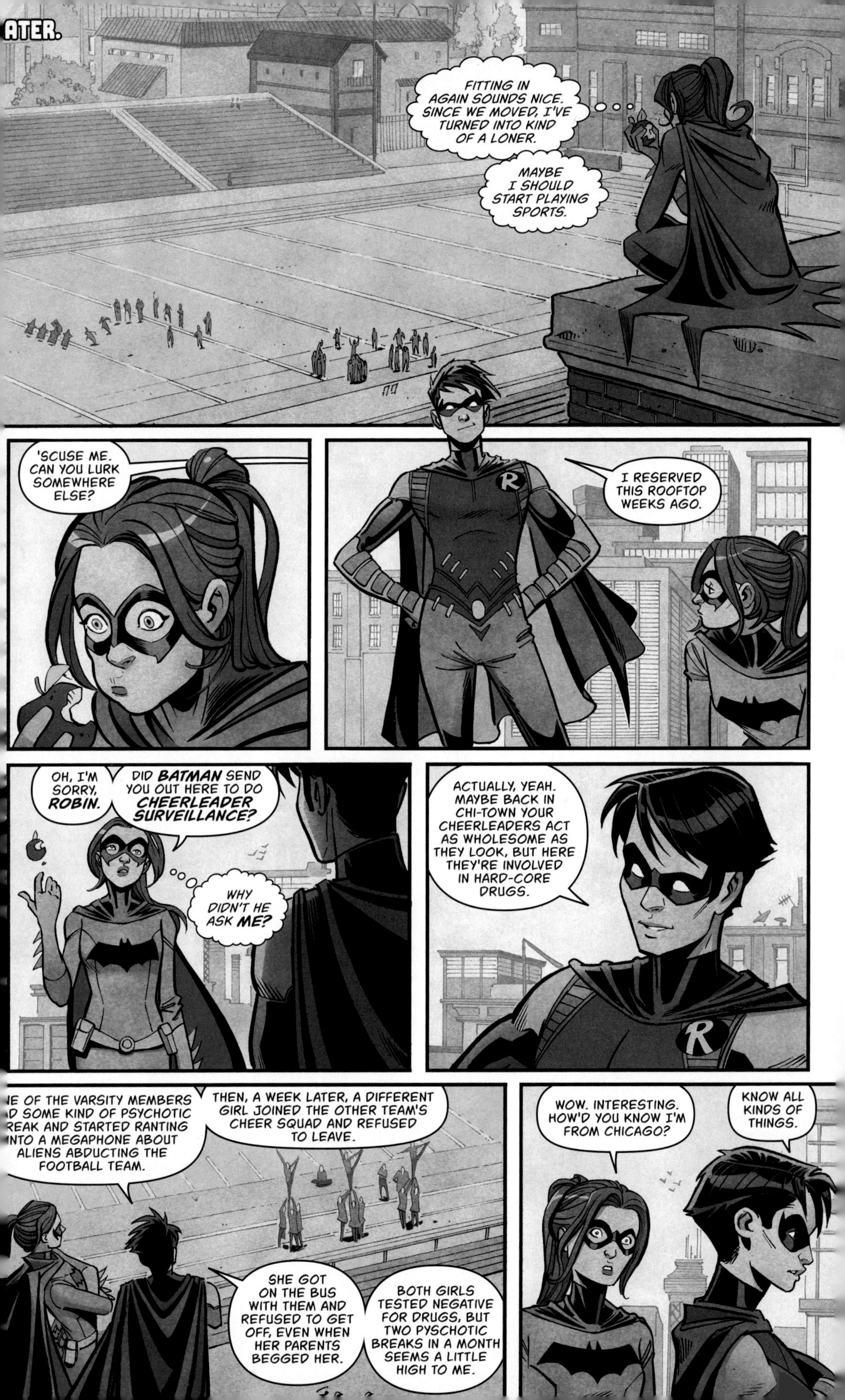
ATER.
FITTING IN AGAIN SOUNDS NICE. SINCE WE MOVED, I'VE TURNED INTO KIND OF A LONER.
MAYBE I SHOULD START PLAYING SPORTS.
'SCUSE ME. CAN YOU LURK SOMEWHERE ELSE?
I RESERVED THIS ROOFTOP WEEKS AGO.
OH, I'M SORRY, ROBIN.
DID BATMAN SEND YOU OUT HERE TO DO CHEERLEADER SURVEILLANCE?
WHY DIDN'T HE ASK ME?
ACTUALLY, YEAH. MAYBE BACK IN CHI-TOWN YOUR CHEERLEADERS ACT AS WHOLESOME AS THEY LOOK, BUT HERE THEY'RE INVOLVED IN HARD-CORE DRUGS.
IE OF THE VARSITY MEMBERS D SOME KIND OF PSYCHOTIC REAK AND STARTED RANTING INTO A MEGAPHONE ABOUT ALIENS ABDUCTING THE FOOTBALL TEAM.
THEN, A WEEK LATER, A DIFFERENT GIRL JOINED THE OTHER TEAM'S CHEER SQUAD AND REFUSED TO LEAVE.
SHE GOT ON THE BUS WITH THEM AND REFUSED TO GET OFF, EVEN WHEN HER PARENTS BEGGED HER.
BOTH GIRLS TESTED NEGATIVE FOR DRUGS, BUT TWO PYSCHOTIC BREAKS IN A MONTH SEEMS A LITTLE HIGH TO ME.
WOW. INTERESTING. HOW'D YOU KNOW I'M FROM CHICAGO?
KNOW ALL KINDS OF THINGS.

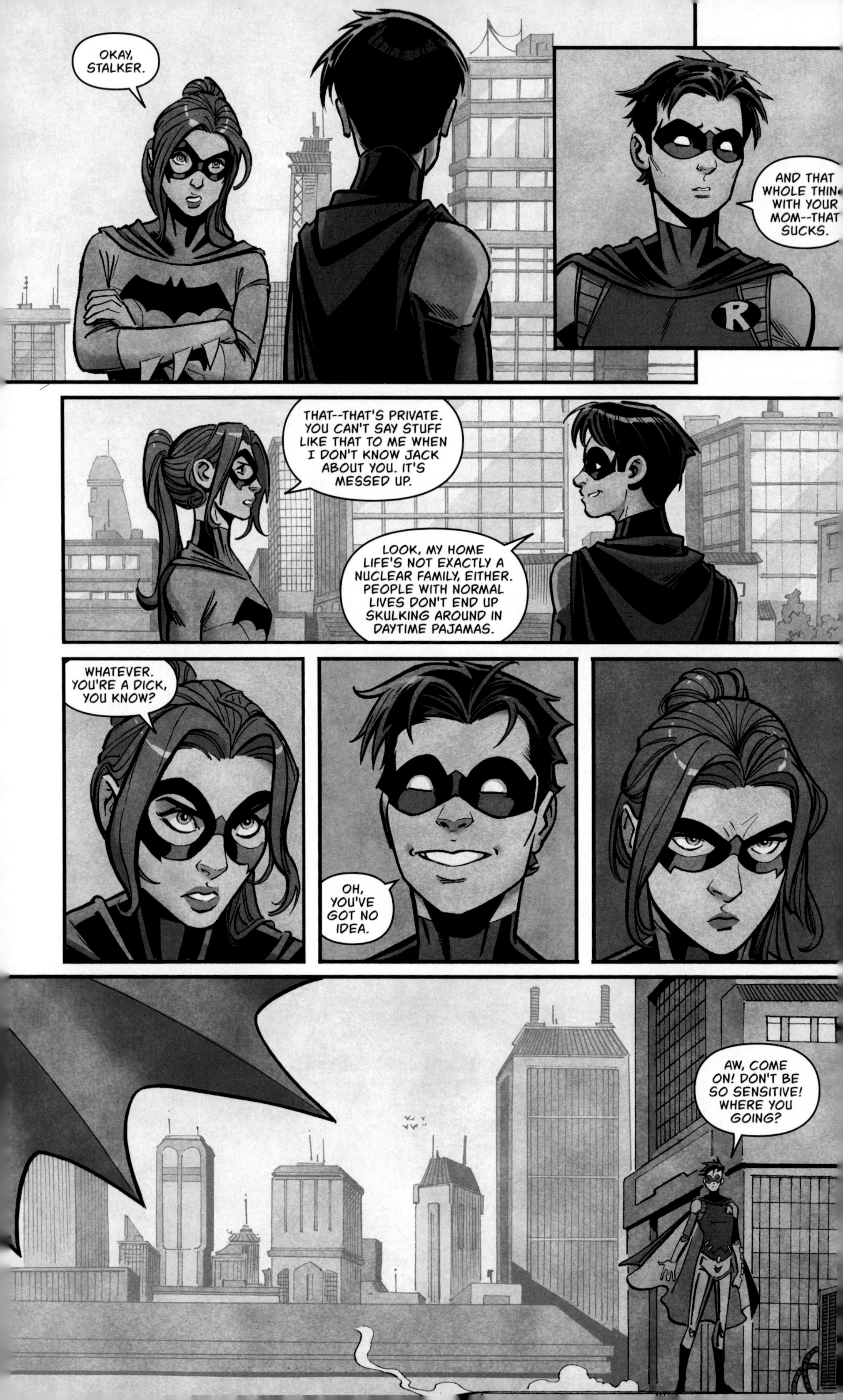
OKAY, STALKER.
AND THAT WHOLE THIN WITH YOUR MOM--THAT SUCKS.
THAT--THAT'S PRIVATE. YOU CAN'T SAY STUFF LIKE THAT TO ME WHEN I DON'T KNOW JACK ABOUT YOU. IT'S MESSED UP.
LOOK, MY HOME LIFE'S NOT EXACTLY A NUCLEAR FAMILY, EITHER. PEOPLE WITH NORMAL LIVES DON'T END UP SKULKING AROUND IN DAYTIME PAJAMAS.
WHATEVER. YOU'RE A DICK, YOU KNOW?
OH, YOU'VE GOT NO IDEA.
AW, COME ON! DON'T BE SO SENSITIVE! WHERE YOU GOING?

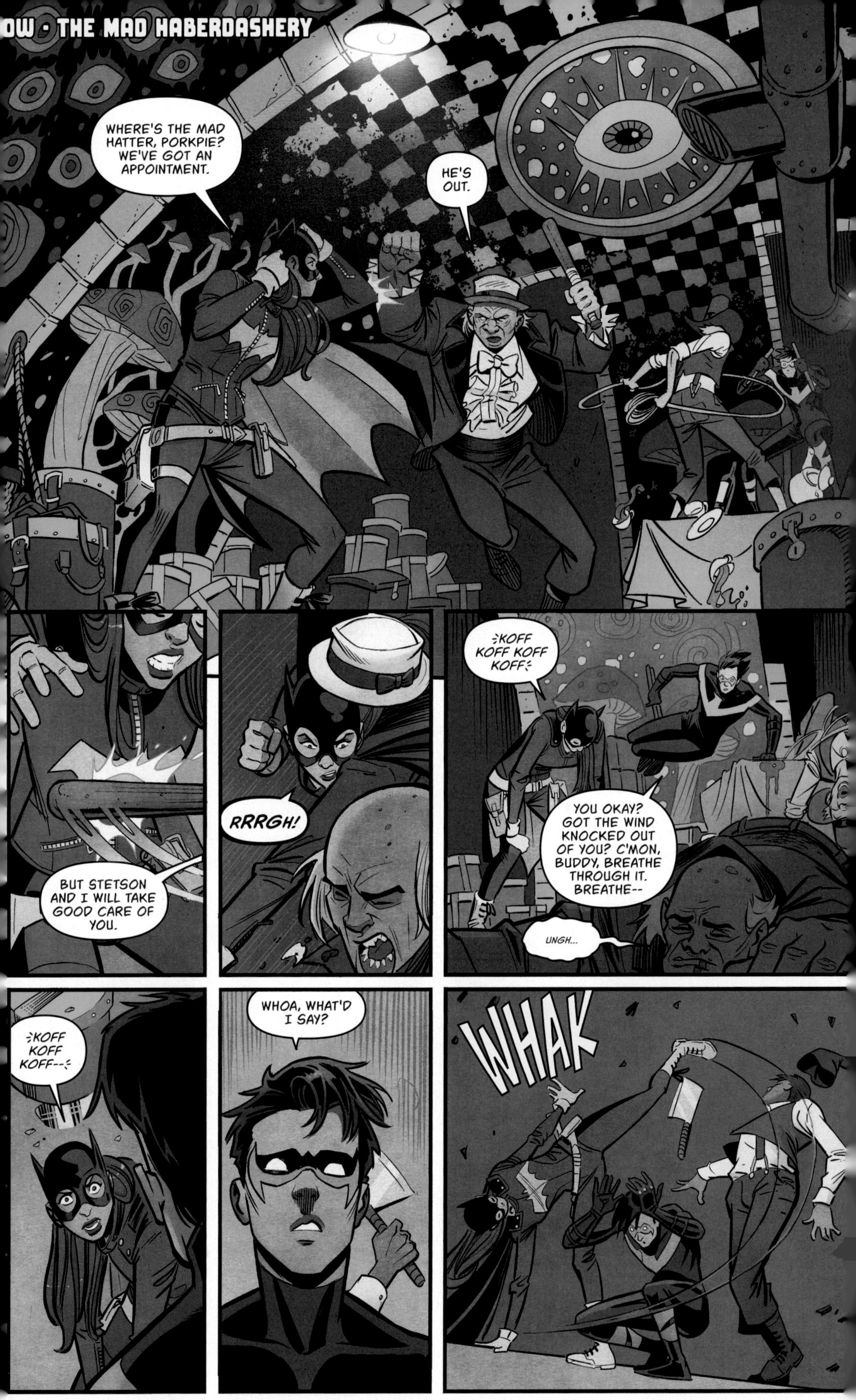
OW - THE MAD HABERDASHERY
WHERE'S THE MAD HATTER, PORKPIE? WE'VE GOT AN APPOINTMENT.
HE'S OUT.
BUT STETSON AND I WILL TAKE GOOD CARE OF YOU.
RRRGH!
KOFF KOFF KOFF KOFF
YOU OKAY? GOT THE WIND KNOCKED OUT OF YOU? C'MON, BUDDY, BREATHE THROUGH IT. BREATHE--
UNGH...
KOFF KOFF KOFF--
WHOA, WHAT'D I SAY?
WHAK

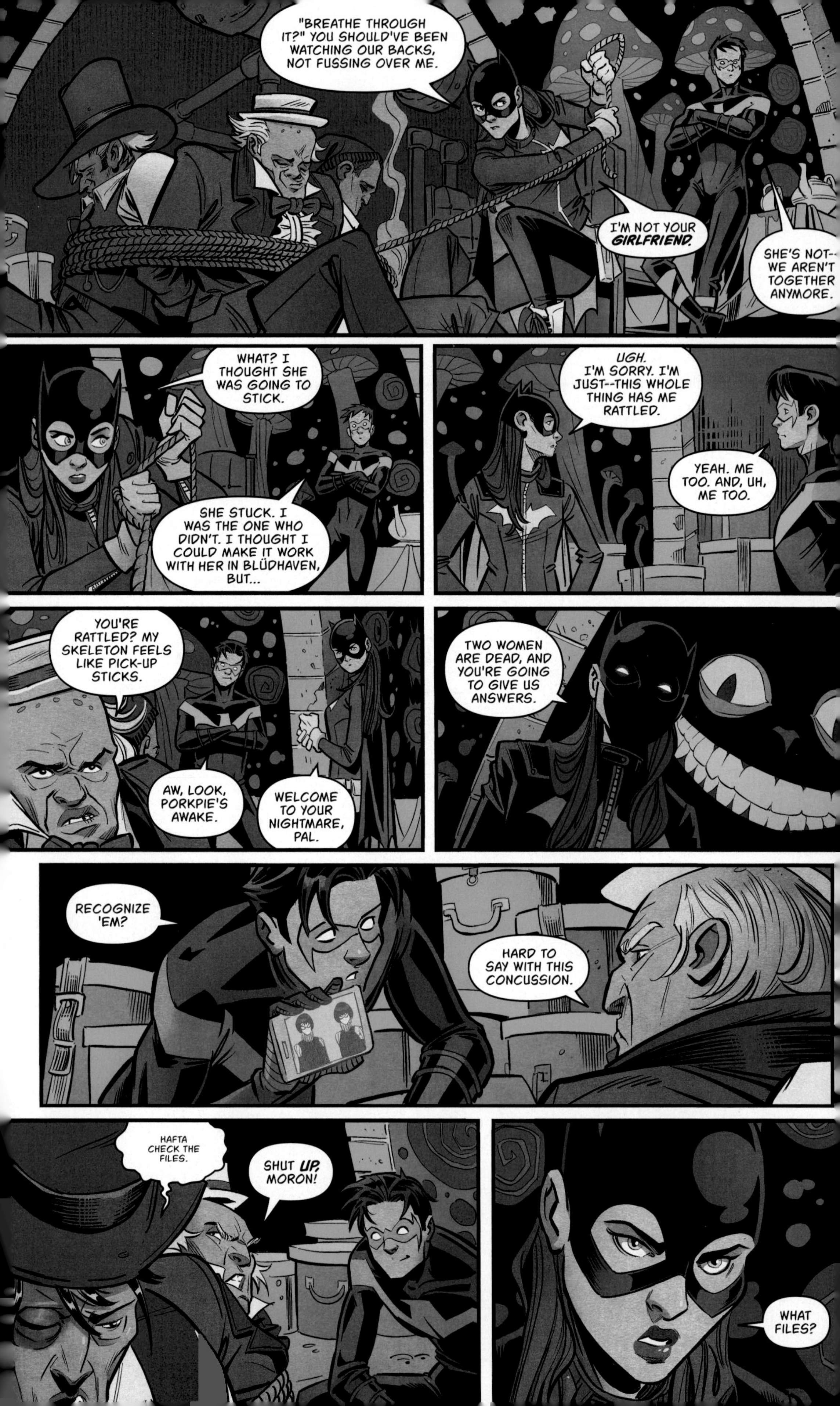
"BREATHE THROUGH IT?" YOU SHOULD'VE BEEN WATCHING OUR BACKS, NOT FUSSING OVER ME.
I'M NOT YOUR *GIRLFRIEND.*
SHE'S NOT-- WE AREN'T TOGETHER ANYMORE.
WHAT? I THOUGHT SHE WAS GOING TO STICK.
SHE STUCK. I WAS THE ONE WHO DIDN'T. I THOUGHT I COULD MAKE IT WORK WITH HER IN BLÜDHAVEN, BUT...
UGH. I'M SORRY. I'M JUST--THIS WHOLE THING HAS ME RATTLED.
YEAH. ME TOO. AND, UH, ME TOO.
YOU'RE RATTLED? MY SKELETON FEELS LIKE PICK-UP STICKS.
AW, LOOK, PORKPIE'S AWAKE.
WELCOME TO YOUR NIGHTMARE, PAL.
TWO WOMEN ARE DEAD, AND YOU'RE GOING TO GIVE US ANSWERS.
RECOGNIZE 'EM?
HARD TO SAY WITH THIS CONCUSSION.
HAFTA CHECK THE FILES.
SHUT *UP,* MORON!
WHAT FILES?

GOTTA LOVE A CRIMINAL WHO PUTS THE *ORGANIZED* IN ORGANIZED CRIME.

BOOM! HERE THEY ARE. "BEANIE" AND "BERET." THESE MUST BE THEIR INTAKE PHOTOS.

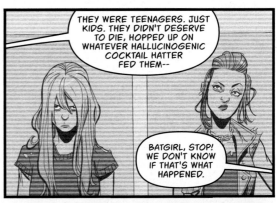

THEY WERE TEENAGERS. JUST KIDS. THEY DIDN'T DESERVE TO DIE, HOPPED UP ON WHATEVER HALLUCINOGENIC COCKTAIL HATTER FED THEM--

BATGIRL, STOP! WE DON'T KNOW IF THAT'S WHAT HAPPENED.

AND I KNOW THEY'RE YOUNG--

WERE YOUNG.

WERE YOUNG. *BUT* KIDS DO BAD THINGS, TOO. WE DID, BACK THEN.

I WAS TRYING TO DO THE RIGHT THING.

WE BOTH WERE.

OH, LOOK! IT--IT SAYS HERE THAT THE HATTER'S NOT JUST OUT--HE'S IN THE HOSPITAL.

WHAT ARE YOU WAITING FOR? LET'S GO.

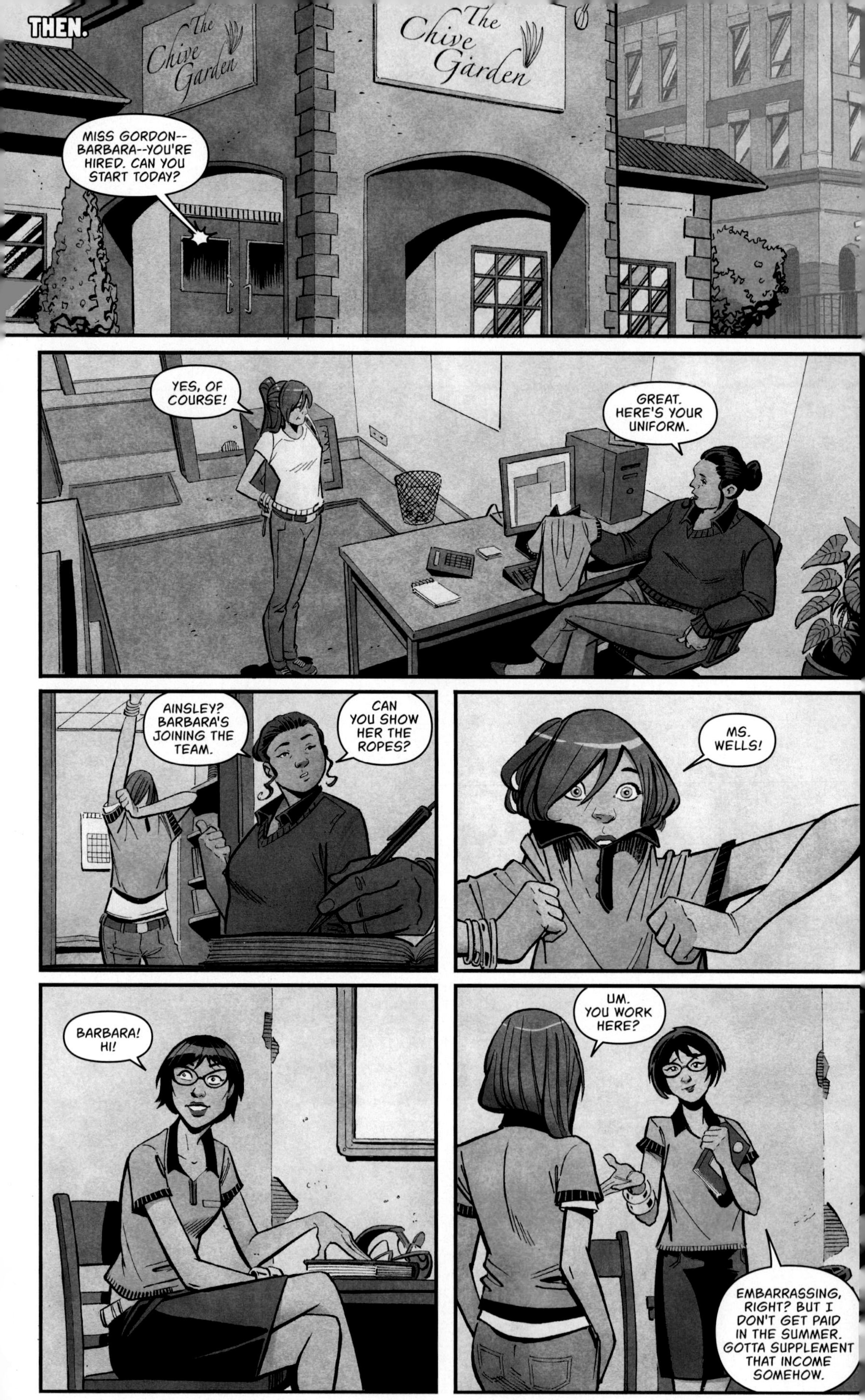
THEN.
The Chive Garden
The Chive Garden
MISS GORDON-- BARBARA--YOU'RE HIRED. CAN YOU START TODAY?
YES, OF COURSE!
GREAT. HERE'S YOUR UNIFORM.
AINSLEY? BARBARA'S JOINING THE TEAM.
CAN YOU SHOW HER THE ROPES?
MS. WELLS!
BARBARA! HI!
UM. YOU WORK HERE?
EMBARRASSING, RIGHT? BUT I DON'T GET PAID IN THE SUMMER. GOTTA SUPPLEMENT THAT INCOME SOMEHOW.

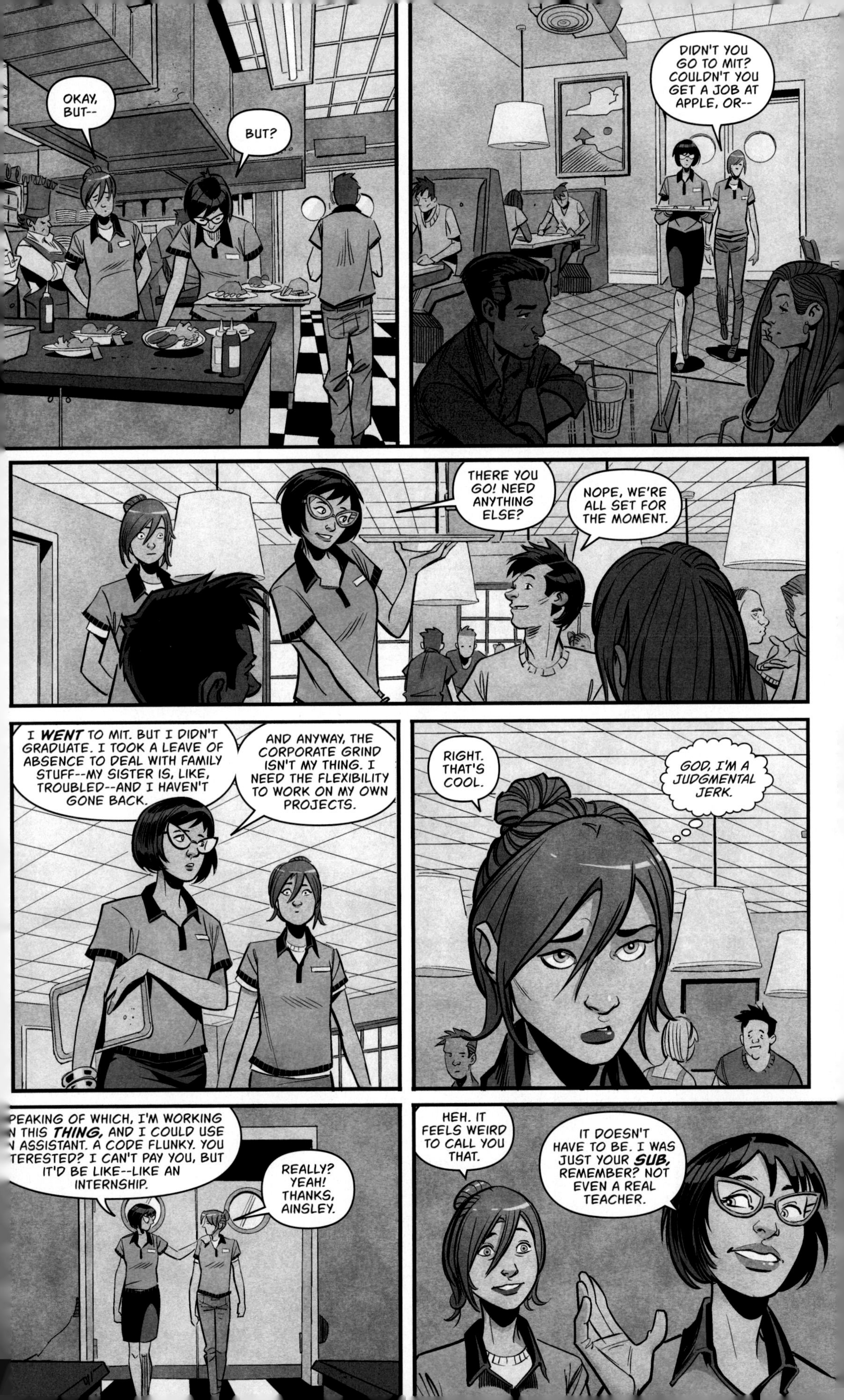
OKAY, BUT--
BUT?
DIDN'T YOU GO TO MIT? COULDN'T YOU GET A JOB AT APPLE, OR--
THERE YOU GO! NEED ANYTHING ELSE?
NOPE, WE'RE ALL SET FOR THE MOMENT.
I WENT TO MIT. BUT I DIDN'T GRADUATE. I TOOK A LEAVE OF ABSENCE TO DEAL WITH FAMILY STUFF--MY SISTER IS, LIKE, TROUBLED--AND I HAVEN'T GONE BACK.
AND ANYWAY, THE CORPORATE GRIND ISN'T MY THING. I NEED THE FLEXIBILITY TO WORK ON MY OWN PROJECTS.
RIGHT. THAT'S COOL.
GOD, I'M A JUDGMENTAL JERK.
PEAKING OF WHICH, I'M WORKING N THIS THING, AND I COULD USE N ASSISTANT. A CODE FLUNKY. YOU TERESTED? I CAN'T PAY YOU, BUT IT'D BE LIKE--LIKE AN INTERNSHIP.
REALLY? YEAH! THANKS, AINSLEY.
HEH. IT FEELS WEIRD TO CALL YOU THAT.
IT DOESN'T HAVE TO BE. I WAS JUST YOUR SUB, REMEMBER? NOT EVEN A REAL TEACHER.

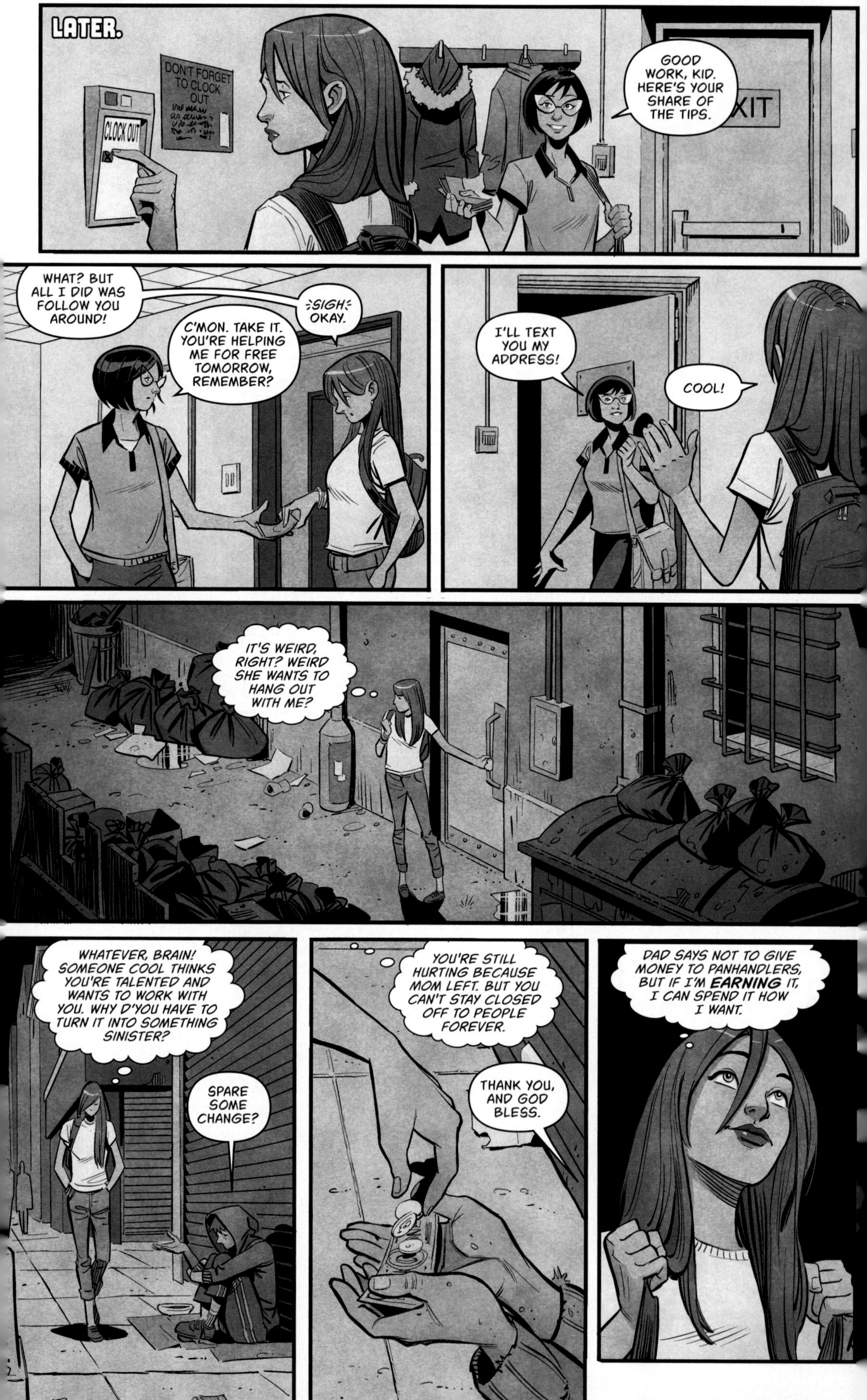

LATER.
DON'T FORGET TO CLOCK OUT
CLOCK OUT
GOOD WORK, KID. HERE'S YOUR SHARE OF THE TIPS.
EXIT
WHAT? BUT ALL I DID WAS FOLLOW YOU AROUND!
C'MON. TAKE IT. YOU'RE HELPING ME FOR FREE TOMORROW, REMEMBER?
SIGH OKAY.
I'LL TEXT YOU MY ADDRESS!
COOL!
IT'S WEIRD, RIGHT? WEIRD SHE WANTS TO HANG OUT WITH ME?
WHATEVER, BRAIN! SOMEONE COOL THINKS YOU'RE TALENTED AND WANTS TO WORK WITH YOU. WHY D'YOU HAVE TO TURN IT INTO SOMETHING SINISTER?
SPARE SOME CHANGE?
YOU'RE STILL HURTING BECAUSE MOM LEFT. BUT YOU CAN'T STAY CLOSED OFF TO PEOPLE FOREVER.
THANK YOU, AND GOD BLESS.
DAD SAYS NOT TO GIVE MONEY TO PANHANDLERS, BUT IF I'M **EARNING** IT, I CAN SPEND IT HOW I WANT.

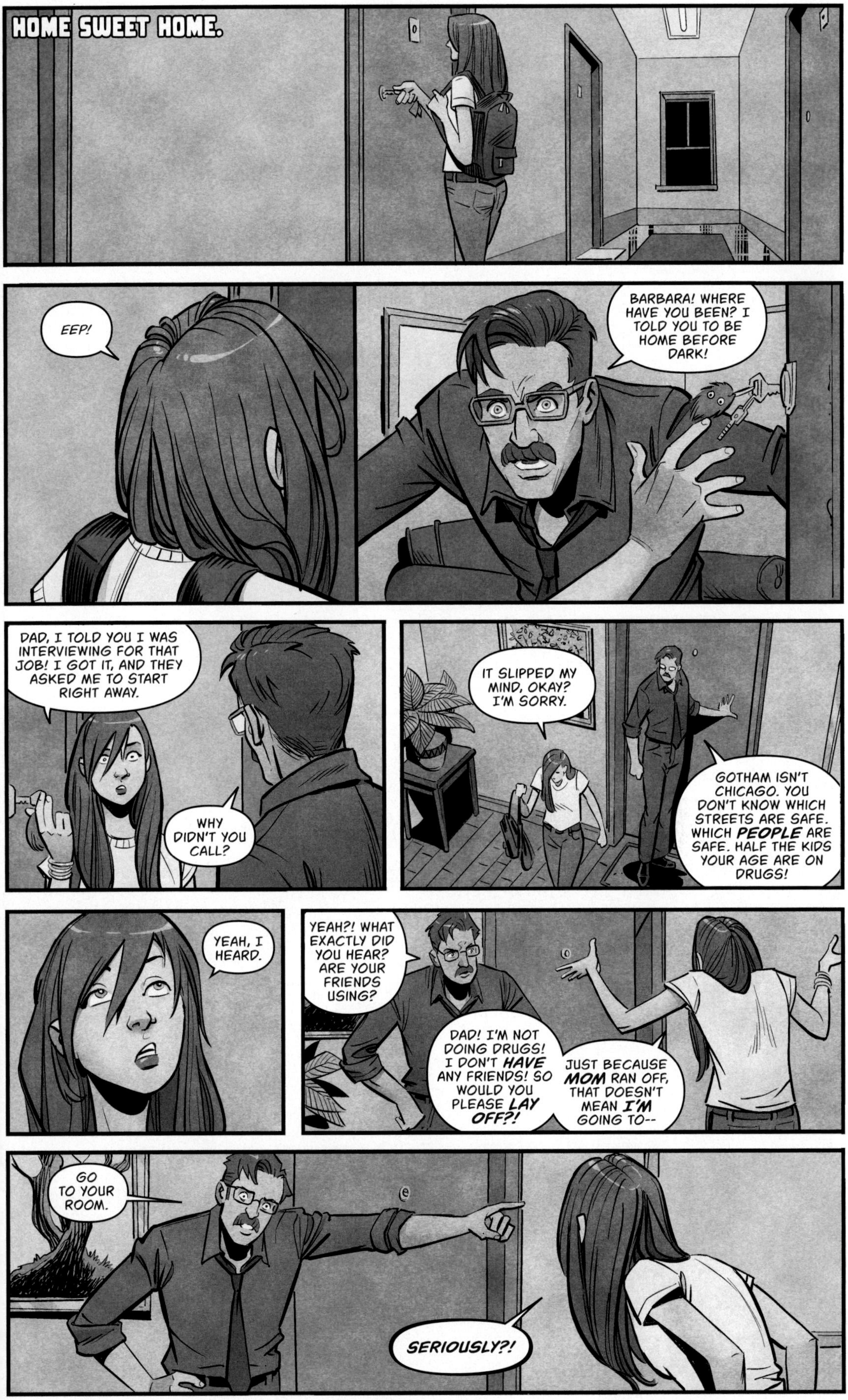
HOME SWEET HOME.
EEP!
BARBARA! WHERE HAVE YOU BEEN? I TOLD YOU TO BE HOME BEFORE DARK!
DAD, I TOLD YOU I WAS INTERVIEWING FOR THAT JOB! I GOT IT, AND THEY ASKED ME TO START RIGHT AWAY.
WHY DIDN'T YOU CALL?
IT SLIPPED MY MIND, OKAY? I'M SORRY.
GOTHAM ISN'T CHICAGO. YOU DON'T KNOW WHICH STREETS ARE SAFE. WHICH PEOPLE ARE SAFE. HALF THE KIDS YOUR AGE ARE ON DRUGS!
YEAH, I HEARD.
YEAH?! WHAT EXACTLY DID YOU HEAR? ARE YOUR FRIENDS USING?
DAD! I'M NOT DOING DRUGS! I DON'T HAVE ANY FRIENDS! SO WOULD YOU PLEASE LAY OFF?!
JUST BECAUSE MOM RAN OFF, THAT DOESN'T MEAN I'M GOING TO--
GO TO YOUR ROOM.
SERIOUSLY?!

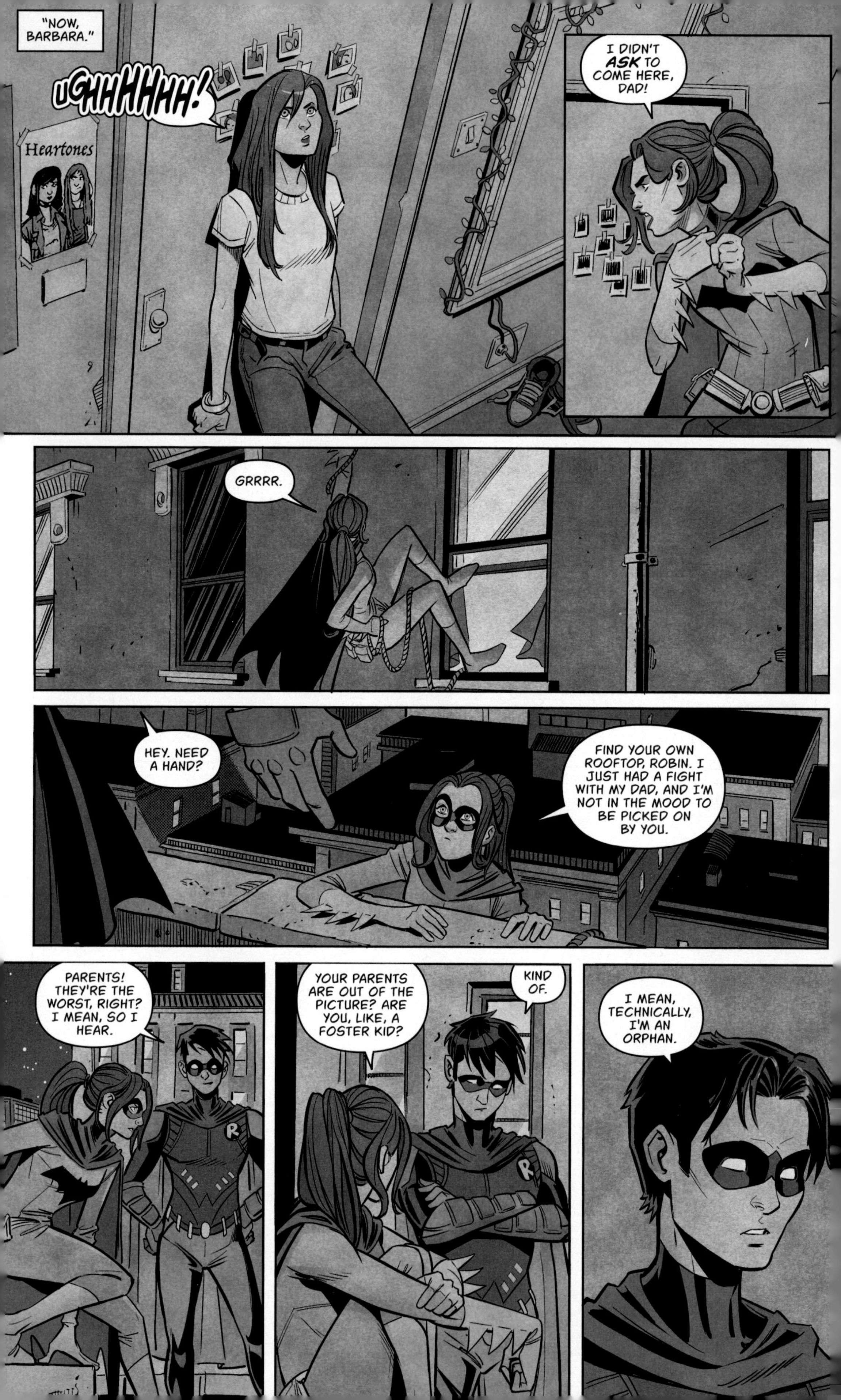
"NOW, BARBARA."
UGHHHHHH!
Heartones
I DIDN'T ASK TO COME HERE, DAD!
GRRRR.
HEY. NEED A HAND?
FIND YOUR OWN ROOFTOP, ROBIN. I JUST HAD A FIGHT WITH MY DAD, AND I'M NOT IN THE MOOD TO BE PICKED ON BY YOU.
PARENTS! THEY'RE THE WORST, RIGHT? I MEAN, SO I HEAR.
YOUR PARENTS ARE OUT OF THE PICTURE? ARE YOU, LIKE, A FOSTER KID?
KIND OF.
I MEAN, TECHNICALLY, I'M AN ORPHAN.

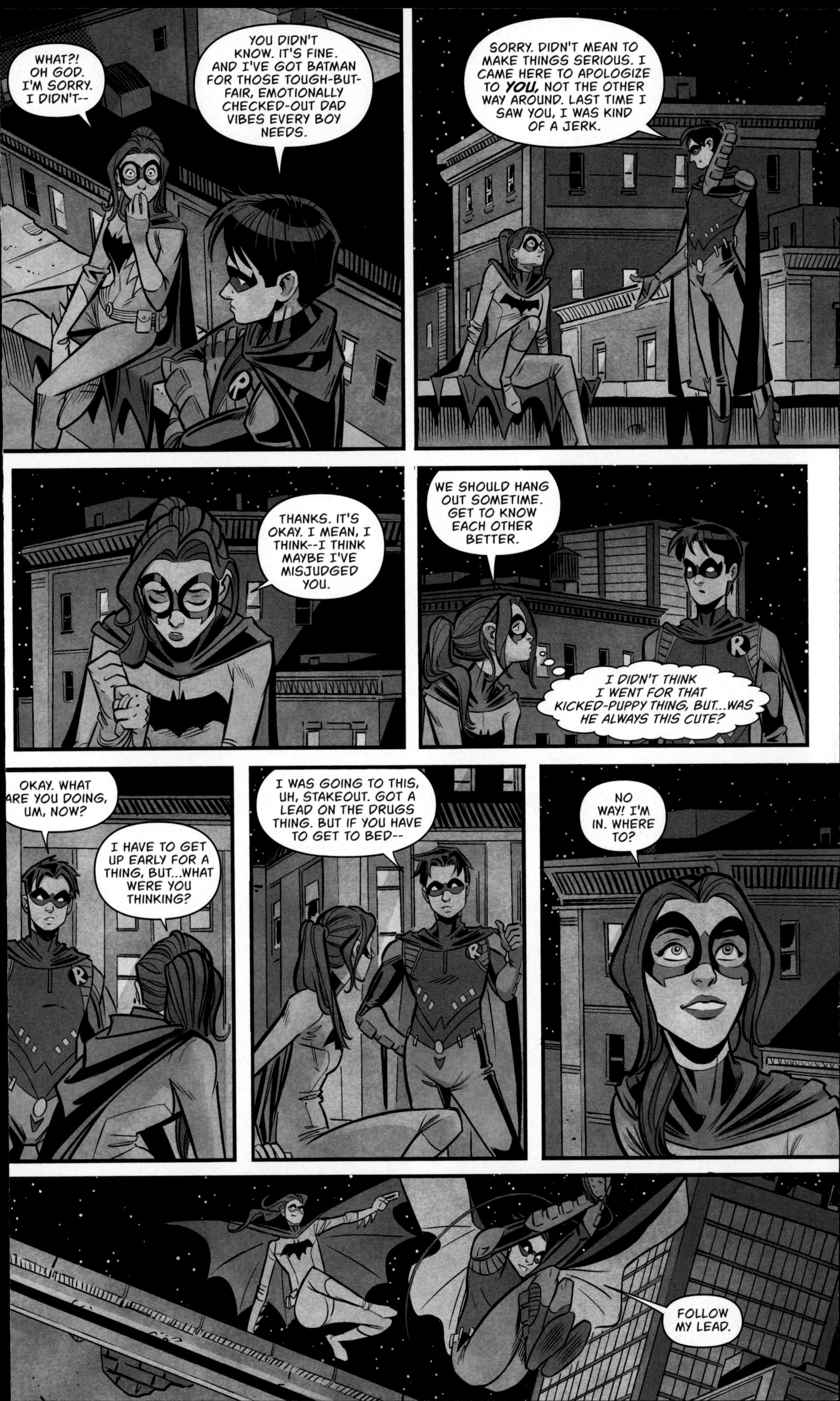
WHAT?! OH GOD. I'M SORRY. I DIDN'T--
YOU DIDN'T KNOW. IT'S FINE. AND I'VE GOT BATMAN FOR THOSE TOUGH-BUT-FAIR, EMOTIONALLY CHECKED-OUT DAD VIBES EVERY BOY NEEDS.
SORRY. DIDN'T MEAN TO MAKE THINGS SERIOUS. I CAME HERE TO APOLOGIZE TO YOU, NOT THE OTHER WAY AROUND. LAST TIME I SAW YOU, I WAS KIND OF A JERK.
THANKS. IT'S OKAY. I MEAN, I THINK--I THINK MAYBE I'VE MISJUDGED YOU.
WE SHOULD HANG OUT SOMETIME. GET TO KNOW EACH OTHER BETTER.
I DIDN'T THINK I WENT FOR THAT KICKED-PUPPY THING, BUT...WAS HE ALWAYS THIS CUTE?
OKAY. WHAT ARE YOU DOING, UM, NOW?
I HAVE TO GET UP EARLY FOR A THING, BUT...WHAT WERE YOU THINKING?
I WAS GOING TO THIS, UH, STAKEOUT. GOT A LEAD ON THE DRUGS THING. BUT IF YOU HAVE TO GET TO BED--
NO WAY! I'M IN. WHERE TO?
FOLLOW MY LEAD.

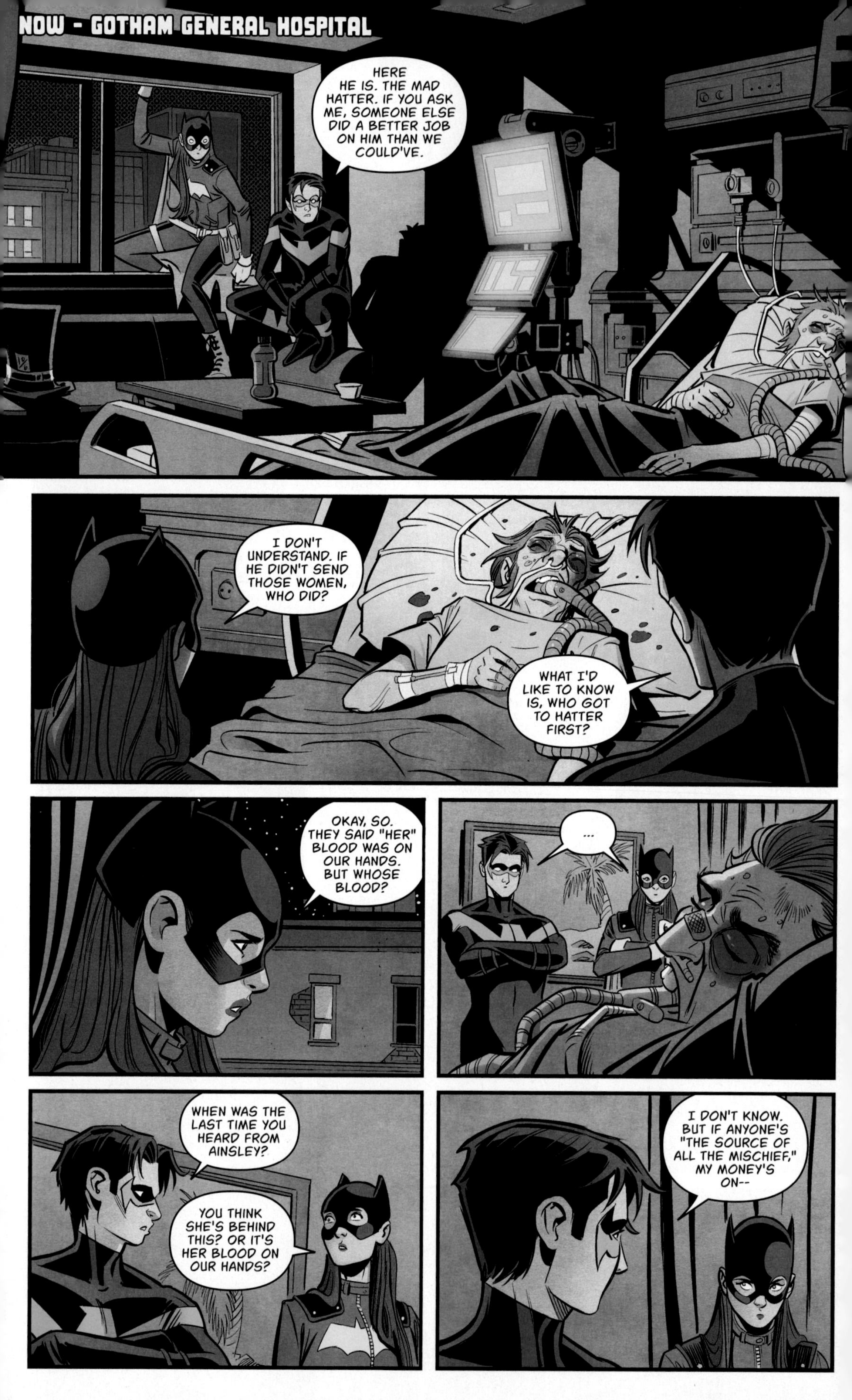
NOW - GOTHAM GENERAL HOSPITAL
HERE HE IS. THE MAD HATTER. IF YOU ASK ME, SOMEONE ELSE DID A BETTER JOB ON HIM THAN WE COULD'VE.
I DON'T UNDERSTAND. IF HE DIDN'T SEND THOSE WOMEN, WHO DID?
WHAT I'D LIKE TO KNOW IS, WHO GOT TO HATTER FIRST?
OKAY, SO. THEY SAID "HER" BLOOD WAS ON OUR HANDS. BUT WHOSE BLOOD?
...
WHEN WAS THE LAST TIME YOU HEARD FROM AINSLEY?
YOU THINK SHE'S BEHIND THIS? OR IT'S HER BLOOD ON OUR HANDS?
I DON'T KNOW. BUT IF ANYONE'S "THE SOURCE OF ALL THE MISCHIEF," MY MONEY'S ON--

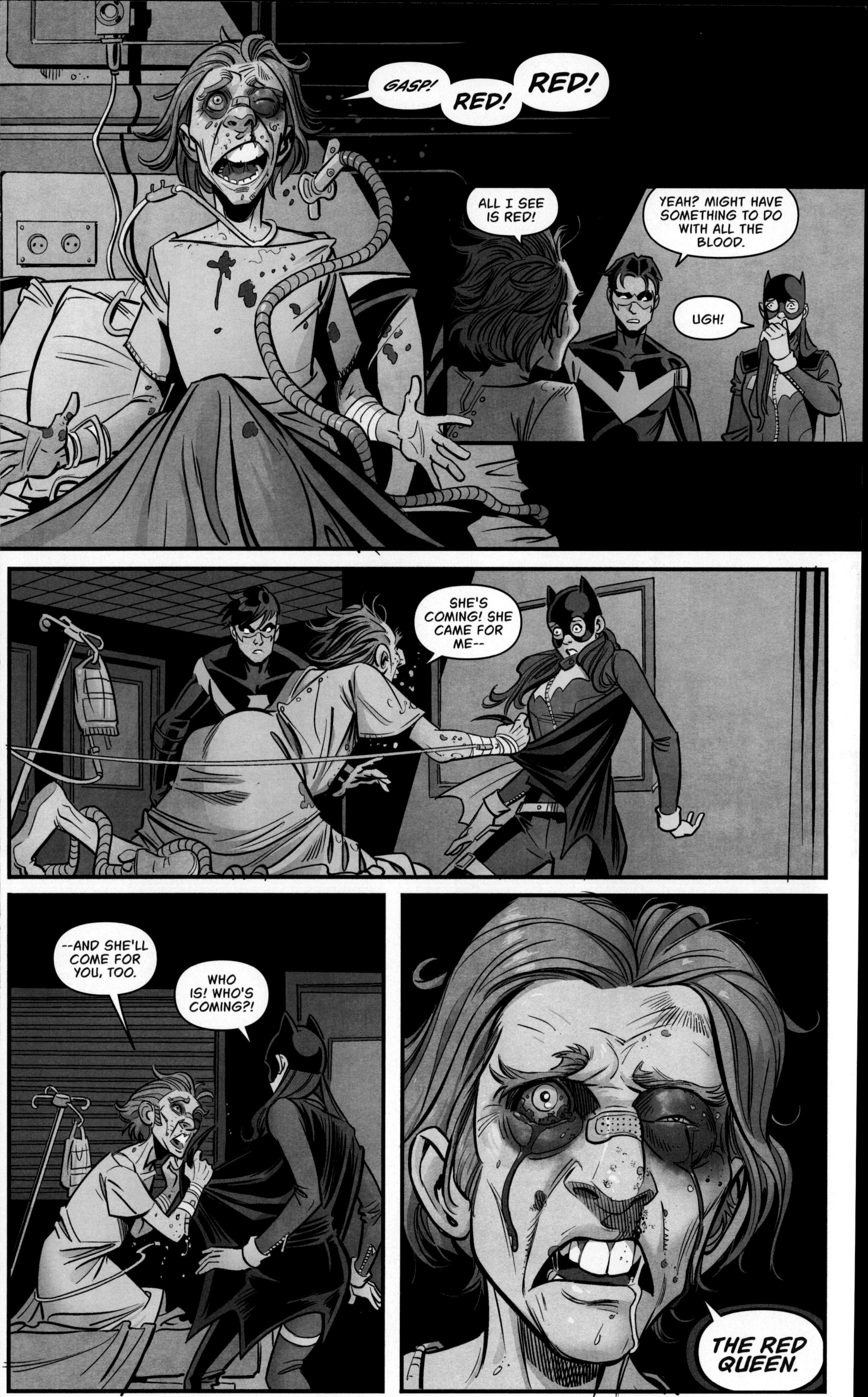
GASP!
RED!
RED!
ALL I SEE IS RED!
YEAH? MIGHT HAVE SOMETHING TO DO WITH ALL THE BLOOD.
UGH!
SHE'S COMING! SHE CAME FOR ME--
--AND SHE'LL COME FOR YOU, TOO.
WHO IS! WHO'S COMING?!
THE RED QUEEN.

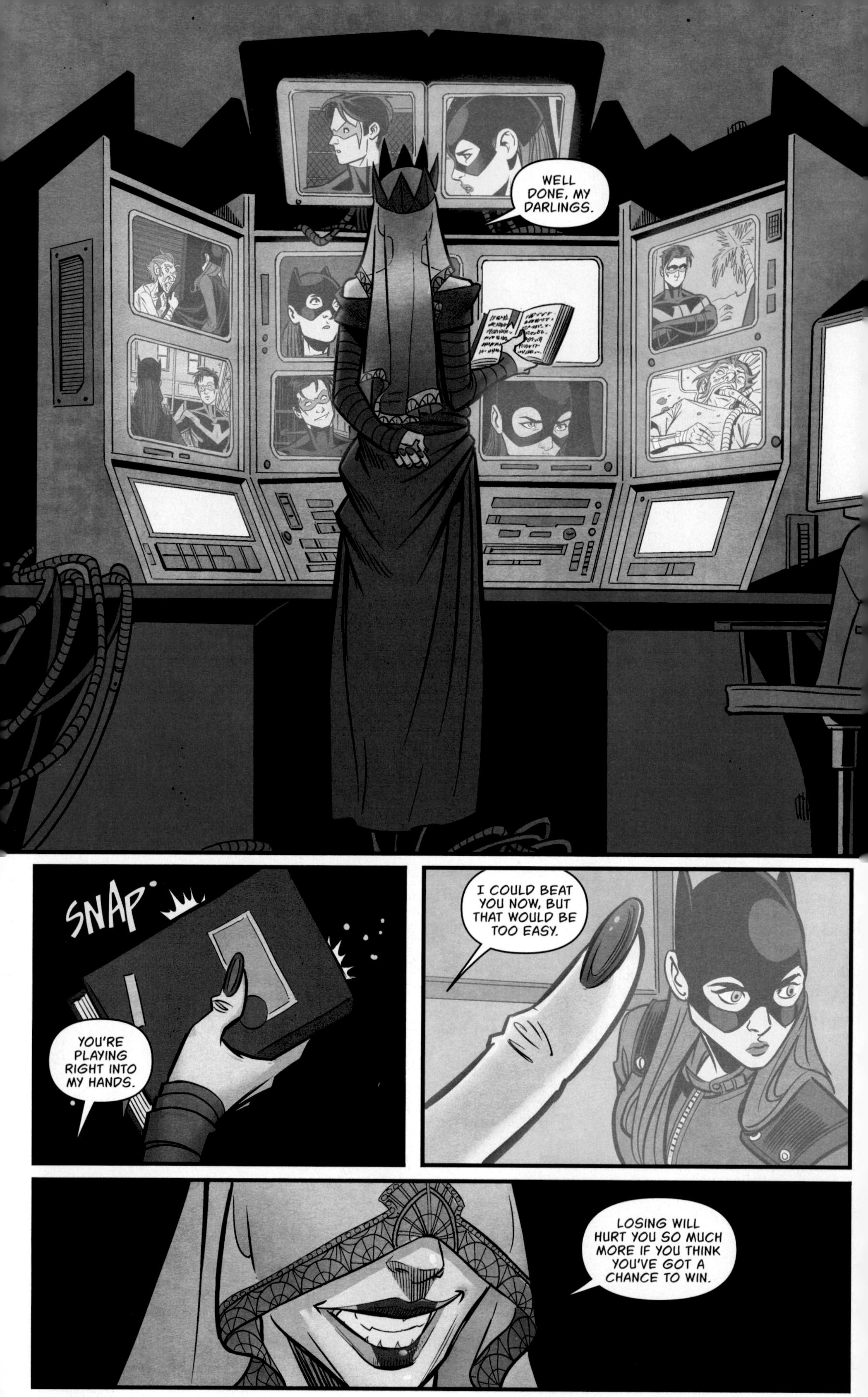

WELL DONE, MY DARLINGS.
SNAP
YOU'RE PLAYING RIGHT INTO MY HANDS.
I COULD BEAT YOU NOW, BUT THAT WOULD BE TOO EASY.
LOSING WILL HURT YOU SO MUCH MORE IF YOU THINK YOU'VE GOT A CHANCE TO WIN.

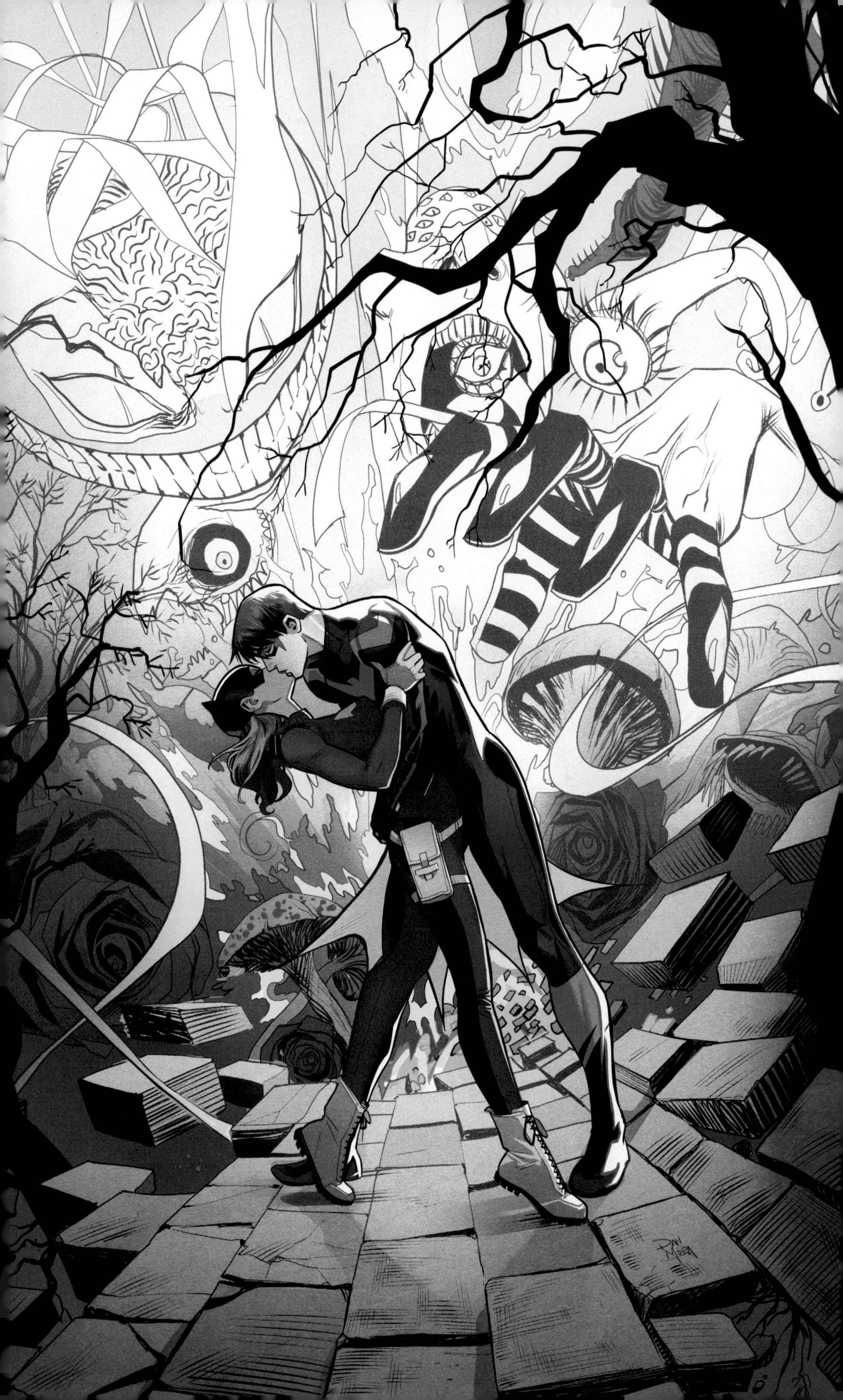
DAN MORA

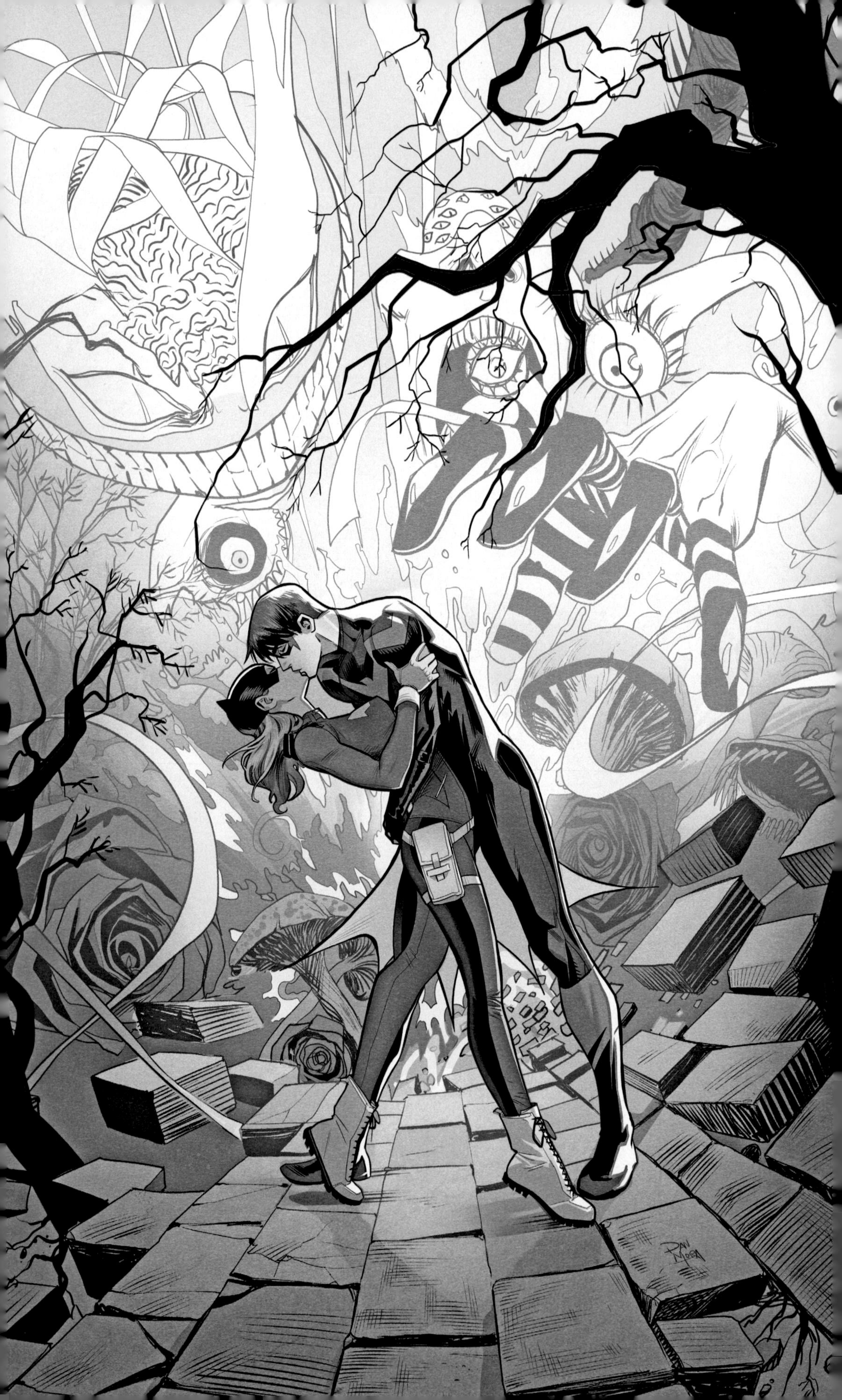
DAN MORA

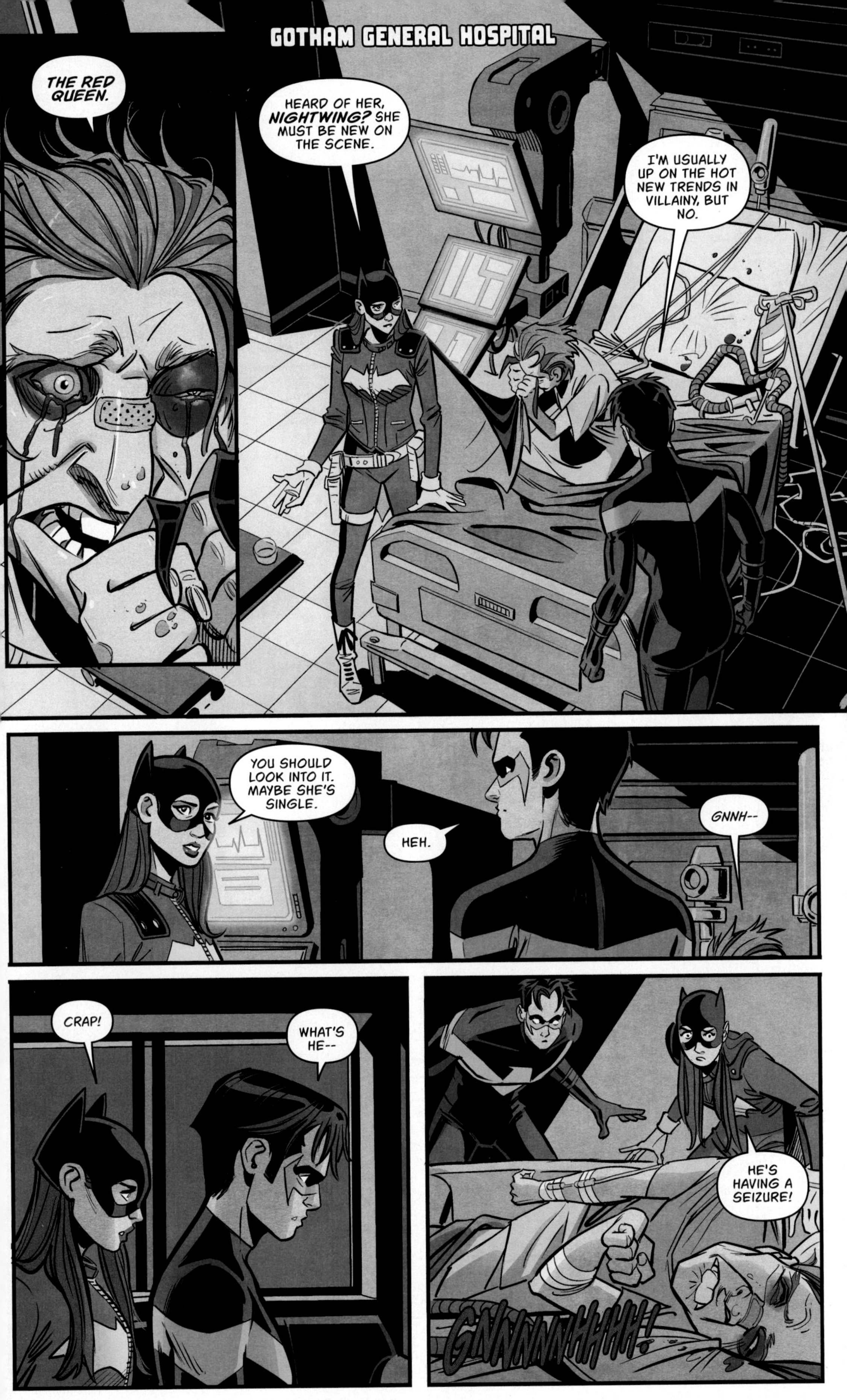
GOTHAM GENERAL HOSPITAL
THE RED QUEEN.
HEARD OF HER, NIGHTWING? SHE MUST BE NEW ON THE SCENE.
I'M USUALLY UP ON THE HOT NEW TRENDS IN VILLAINY, BUT NO.
YOU SHOULD LOOK INTO IT. MAYBE SHE'S SINGLE.
HEH.
GNNH--
CRAP!
WHAT'S HE--
HE'S HAVING A SEIZURE!
GNNNNHHHH!

BREEEEEEEET BREEEEEEEET

HIS HEART JUST STOPPED!

WE SHOULD GET OUT OF HERE BEFORE THE NURSE SHOWS UP AND STARTS ASKING QUESTIONS WE CAN'T--

CR...

PLEASE USE HANDWASH
Hygiene protect patients & visitors

DID YOU KNOW!?

HELP! HELP!

THE STAFF SOUNDS PREOCCUPIED.

GIVE HATTER'S HEART A *REBOOT* WHILE I GO SEE WHAT'S UP.

GKK--

YOU GOT IT, BATS!

BEEP BEEP BEEP BEEP BREEEEEE--

WHOOM

HELP! SOMEBODY!

LEVEL 4

NURSE STATION →

I'M ON MY WAY!

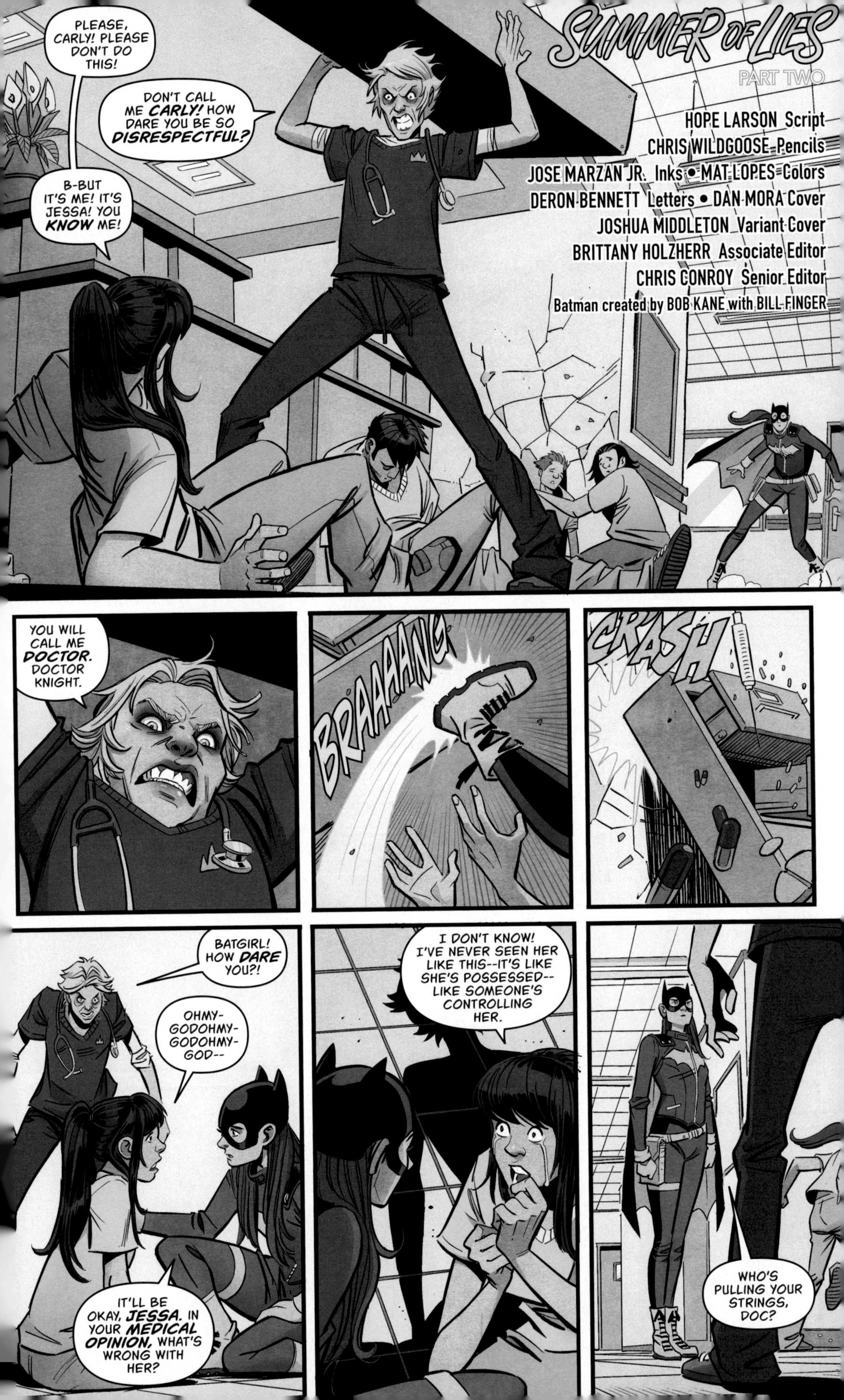
SUMMER OF LIES
PART TWO
HOPE LARSON Script
CHRIS WILDGOOSE Pencils
JOSE MARZAN JR. Inks • MAT LOPES Colors
DERON BENNETT Letters • DAN MORA Cover
JOSHUA MIDDLETON Variant Cover
BRITTANY HOLZHERR Associate Editor
CHRIS CONROY Senior Editor
Batman created by BOB KANE with BILL FINGER
PLEASE, CARLY! PLEASE DON'T DO THIS!
DON'T CALL ME CARLY! HOW DARE YOU BE SO DISRESPECTFUL?
B-BUT IT'S ME! IT'S JESSA! YOU KNOW ME!
YOU WILL CALL ME DOCTOR. DOCTOR KNIGHT.
BRAAAANG
CRASH
BATGIRL! HOW DARE YOU?!
OHMY-GODOHMY-GODOHMY-GOD--
IT'LL BE OKAY, JESSA. IN YOUR MEDICAL OPINION, WHAT'S WRONG WITH HER?
I DON'T KNOW! I'VE NEVER SEEN HER LIKE THIS--IT'S LIKE SHE'S POSSESSED--LIKE SOMEONE'S CONTROLLING HER.
WHO'S PULLING YOUR STRINGS, DOC?

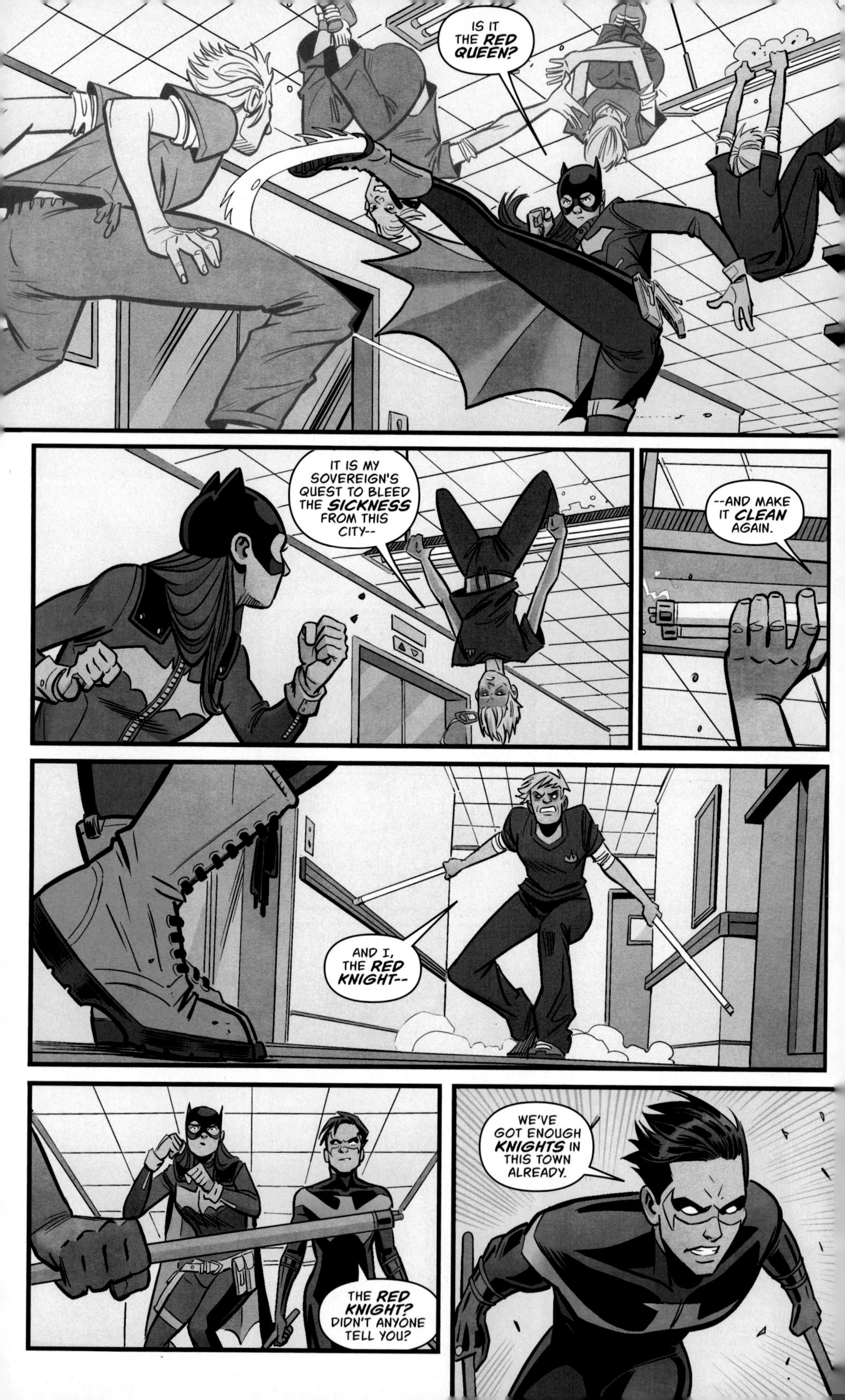
IS IT THE RED QUEEN?
IT IS MY SOVEREIGN'S QUEST TO BLEED THE SICKNESS FROM THIS CITY--
--AND MAKE IT CLEAN AGAIN.
AND I, THE RED KNIGHT--
THE RED KNIGHT? DIDN'T ANYONE TELL YOU?
WE'VE GOT ENOUGH KNIGHTS IN THIS TOWN ALREADY.

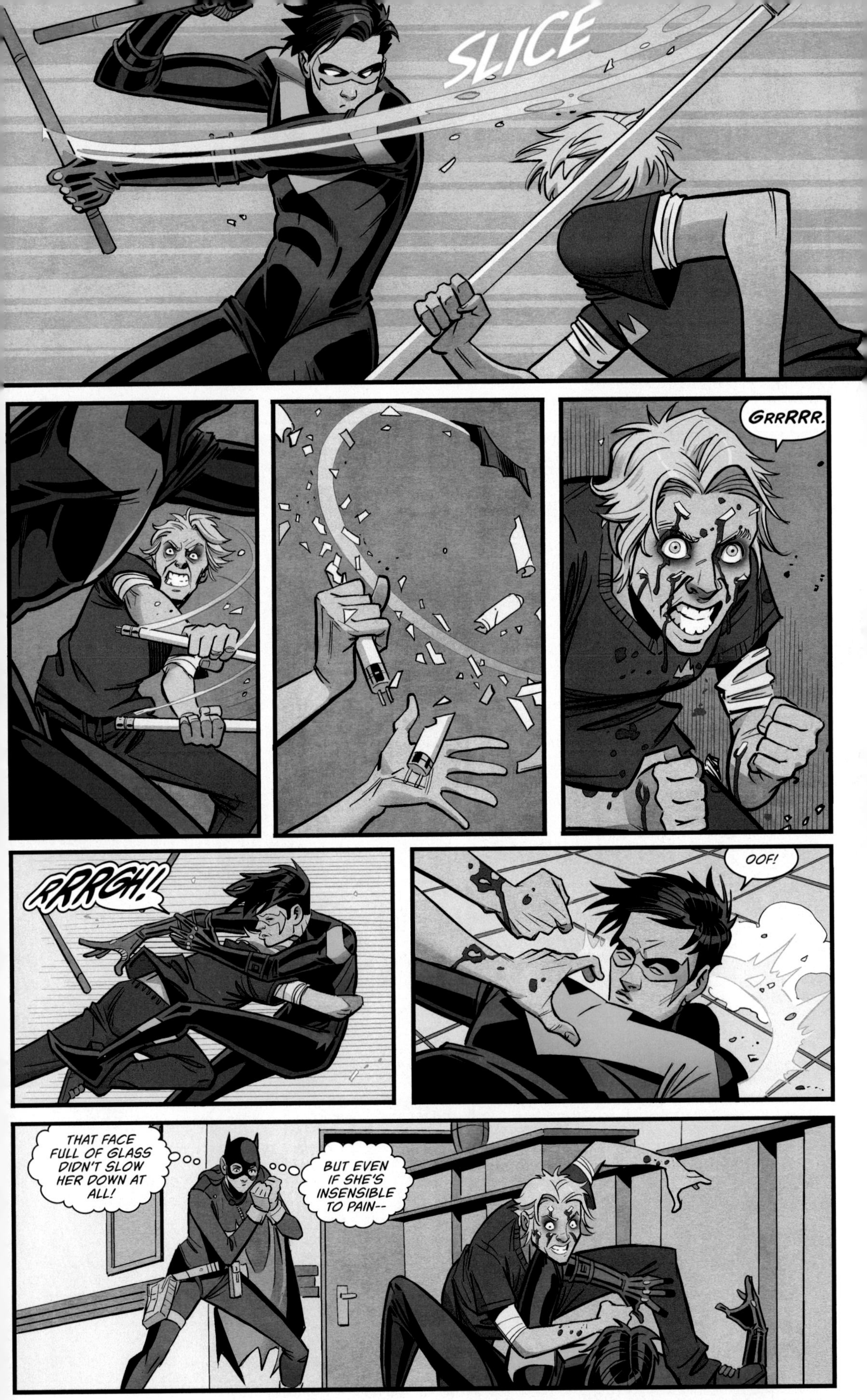
SLICE
GrrRRR.
RRRGH!
OOF!
THAT FACE FULL OF GLASS DIDN'T SLOW HER DOWN AT ALL!
BUT EVEN IF SHE'S INSENSIBLE TO PAIN--

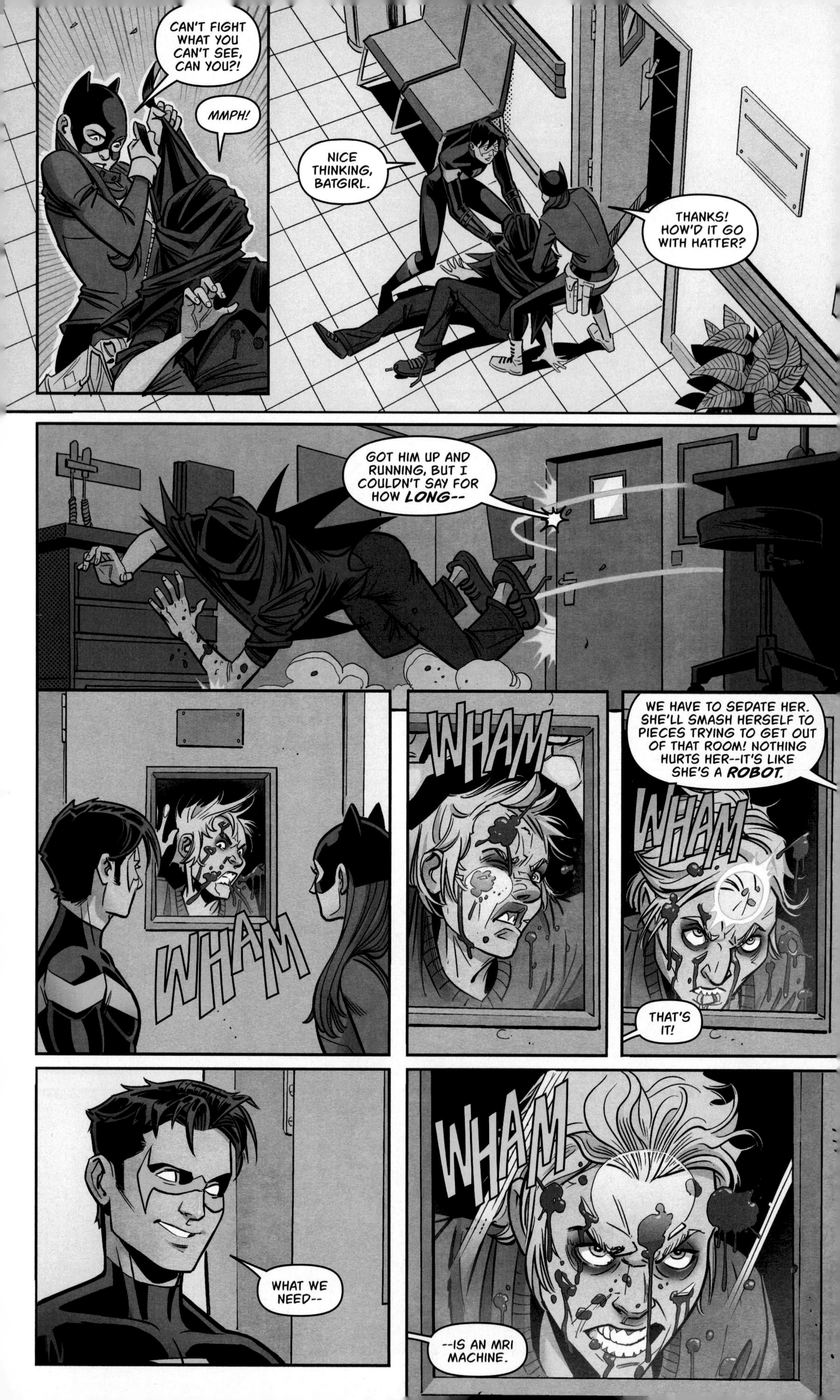
CAN'T FIGHT WHAT YOU CAN'T SEE, CAN YOU?!
MMPH!
NICE THINKING, BATGIRL.
THANKS! HOW'D IT GO WITH HATTER?
GOT HIM UP AND RUNNING, BUT I COULDN'T SAY FOR HOW LONG--
WHAM
WHAM
WE HAVE TO SEDATE HER. SHE'LL SMASH HERSELF TO PIECES TRYING TO GET OUT OF THAT ROOM! NOTHING HURTS HER--IT'S LIKE SHE'S A ROBOT.
WHAM
THAT'S IT!
WHAT WE NEED--
WHAM
--IS AN MRI MACHINE.

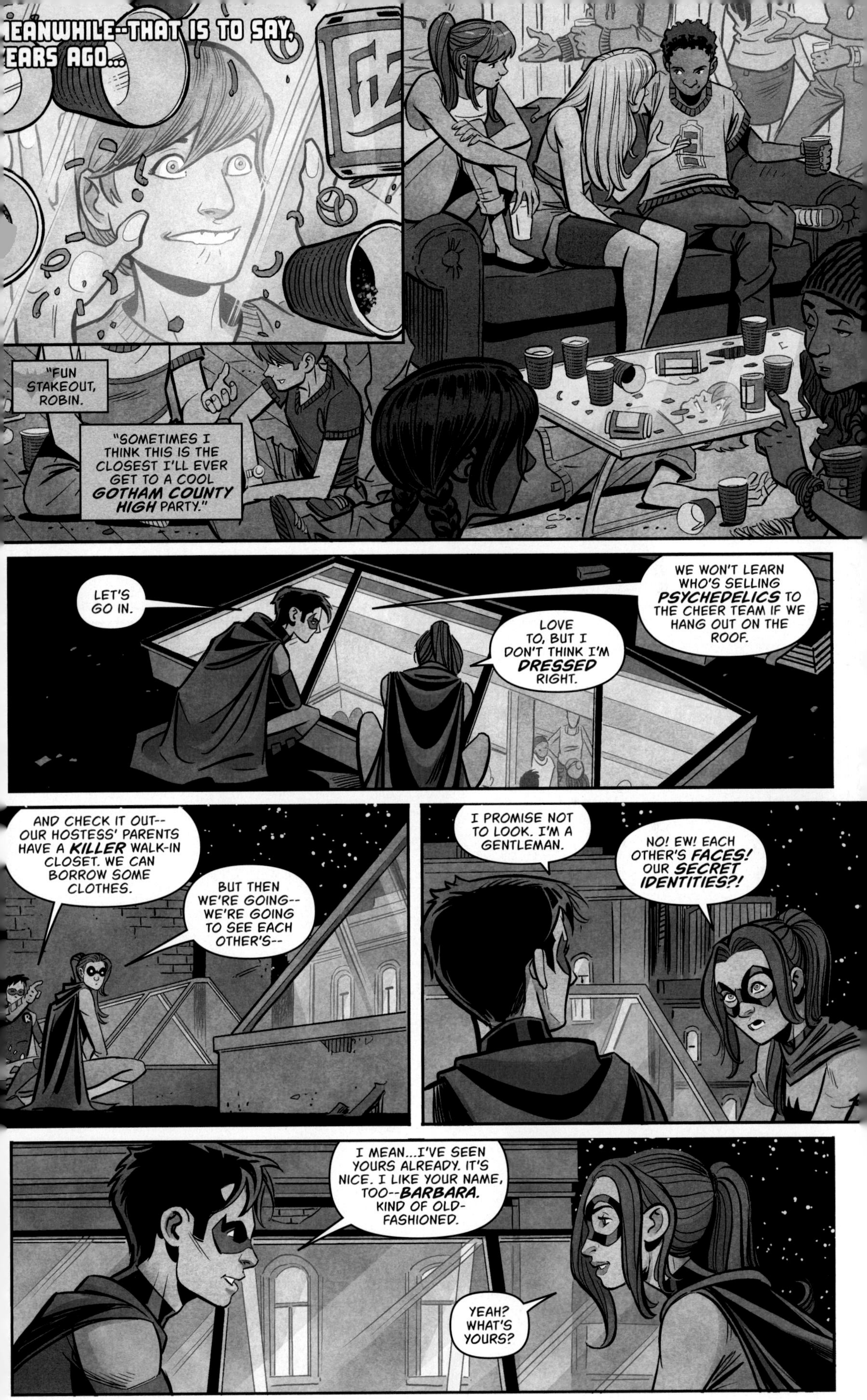

IEANWHILE--THAT IS TO SAY, EARS AGO...
"FUN STAKEOUT, ROBIN.
"SOMETIMES I THINK THIS IS THE CLOSEST I'LL EVER GET TO A COOL GOTHAM COUNTY HIGH PARTY."
LET'S GO IN.
WE WON'T LEARN WHO'S SELLING PSYCHEDELICS TO THE CHEER TEAM IF WE HANG OUT ON THE ROOF.
LOVE TO, BUT I DON'T THINK I'M DRESSED RIGHT.
AND CHECK IT OUT-- OUR HOSTESS' PARENTS HAVE A KILLER WALK-IN CLOSET. WE CAN BORROW SOME CLOTHES.
BUT THEN WE'RE GOING-- WE'RE GOING TO SEE EACH OTHER'S--
I PROMISE NOT TO LOOK. I'M A GENTLEMAN.
NO! EW! EACH OTHER'S FACES! OUR SECRET IDENTITIES?!
I MEAN...I'VE SEEN YOURS ALREADY. IT'S NICE. I LIKE YOUR NAME, TOO--BARBARA. KIND OF OLD-FASHIONED.
YEAH? WHAT'S YOURS?

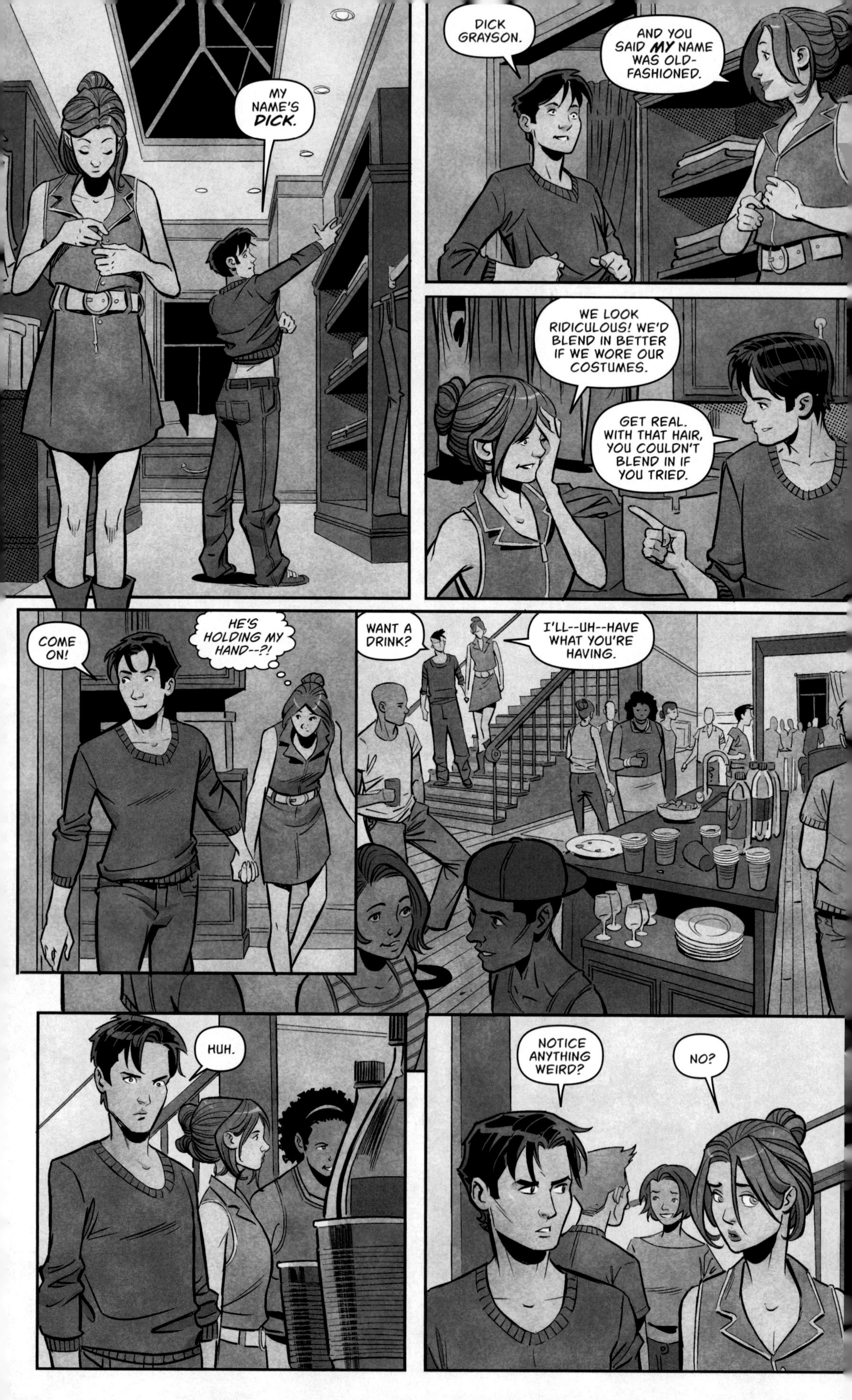
MY NAME'S *DICK.*
DICK GRAYSON.
AND YOU SAID *MY* NAME WAS OLD-FASHIONED.
WE LOOK RIDICULOUS! WE'D BLEND IN BETTER IF WE WORE OUR COSTUMES.
GET REAL. WITH THAT HAIR, YOU COULDN'T BLEND IN IF YOU TRIED.
COME ON!
HE'S HOLDING MY HAND--?!
WANT A DRINK?
I'LL--UH--HAVE WHAT YOU'RE HAVING.
HUH.
NOTICE ANYTHING WEIRD?
NO?

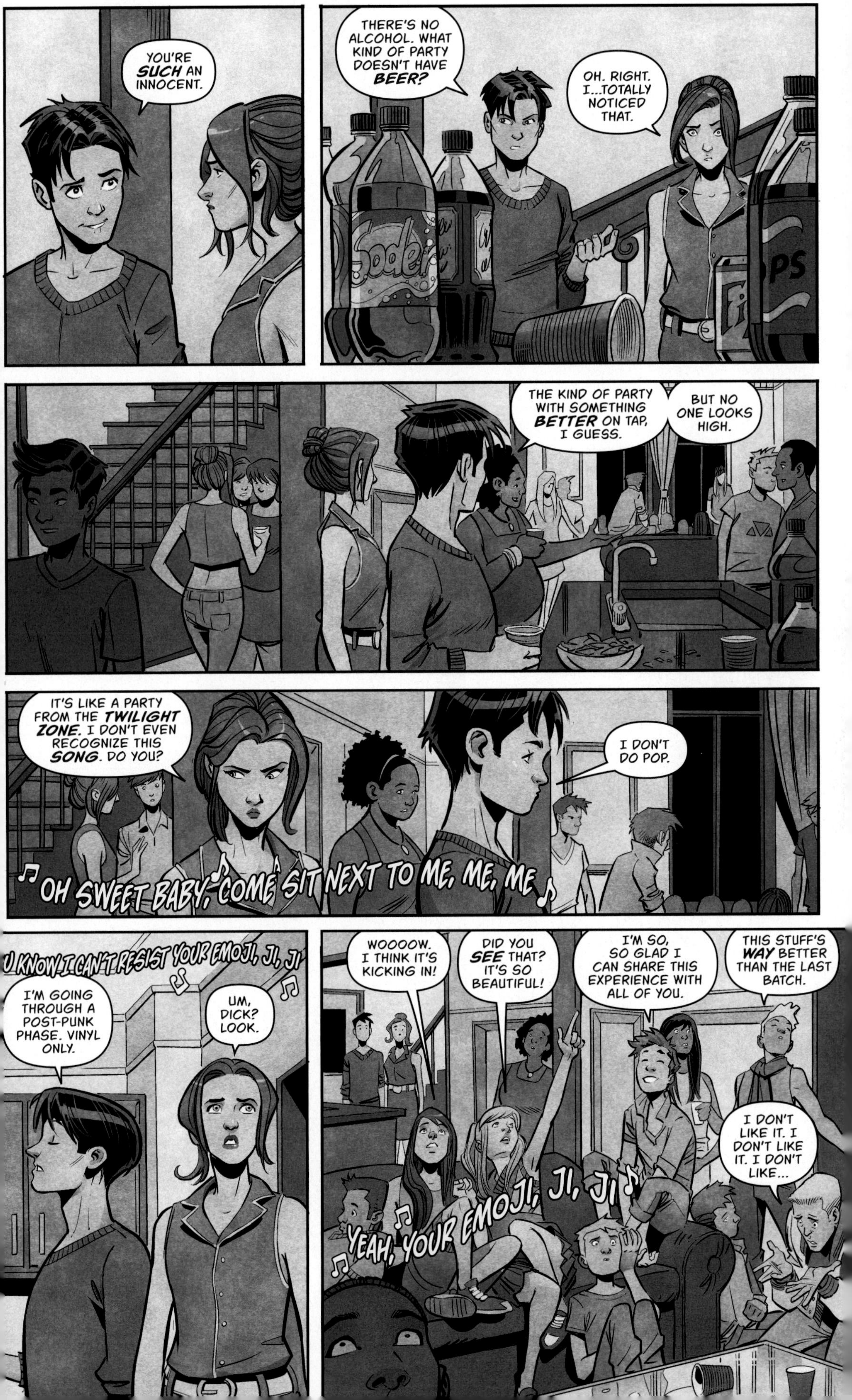
YOU'RE **SUCH** AN INNOCENT.
THERE'S NO ALCOHOL. WHAT KIND OF PARTY DOESN'T HAVE **BEER?**
OH. RIGHT. I...TOTALLY NOTICED THAT.
THE KIND OF PARTY WITH SOMETHING **BETTER** ON TAP, I GUESS.
BUT NO ONE LOOKS HIGH.
IT'S LIKE A PARTY FROM THE **TWILIGHT ZONE**. I DON'T EVEN RECOGNIZE THIS **SONG**. DO YOU?
I DON'T DO POP.
♪ OH SWEET BABY, COME SIT NEXT TO ME, ME, ME ♪
U KNOW I CAN'T RESIST YOUR EMOJI, JI, JI ♪
I'M GOING THROUGH A POST-PUNK PHASE. VINYL ONLY.
UM, DICK? LOOK.
WOOOOW. I THINK IT'S KICKING IN!
DID YOU **SEE** THAT? IT'S SO BEAUTIFUL!
I'M SO, SO GLAD I CAN SHARE THIS EXPERIENCE WITH ALL OF YOU.
THIS STUFF'S **WAY** BETTER THAN THE LAST BATCH.
I DON'T LIKE IT. I DON'T LIKE IT. I DON'T LIKE...
♪ YEAH, YOUR EMOJI, JI, JI ♪

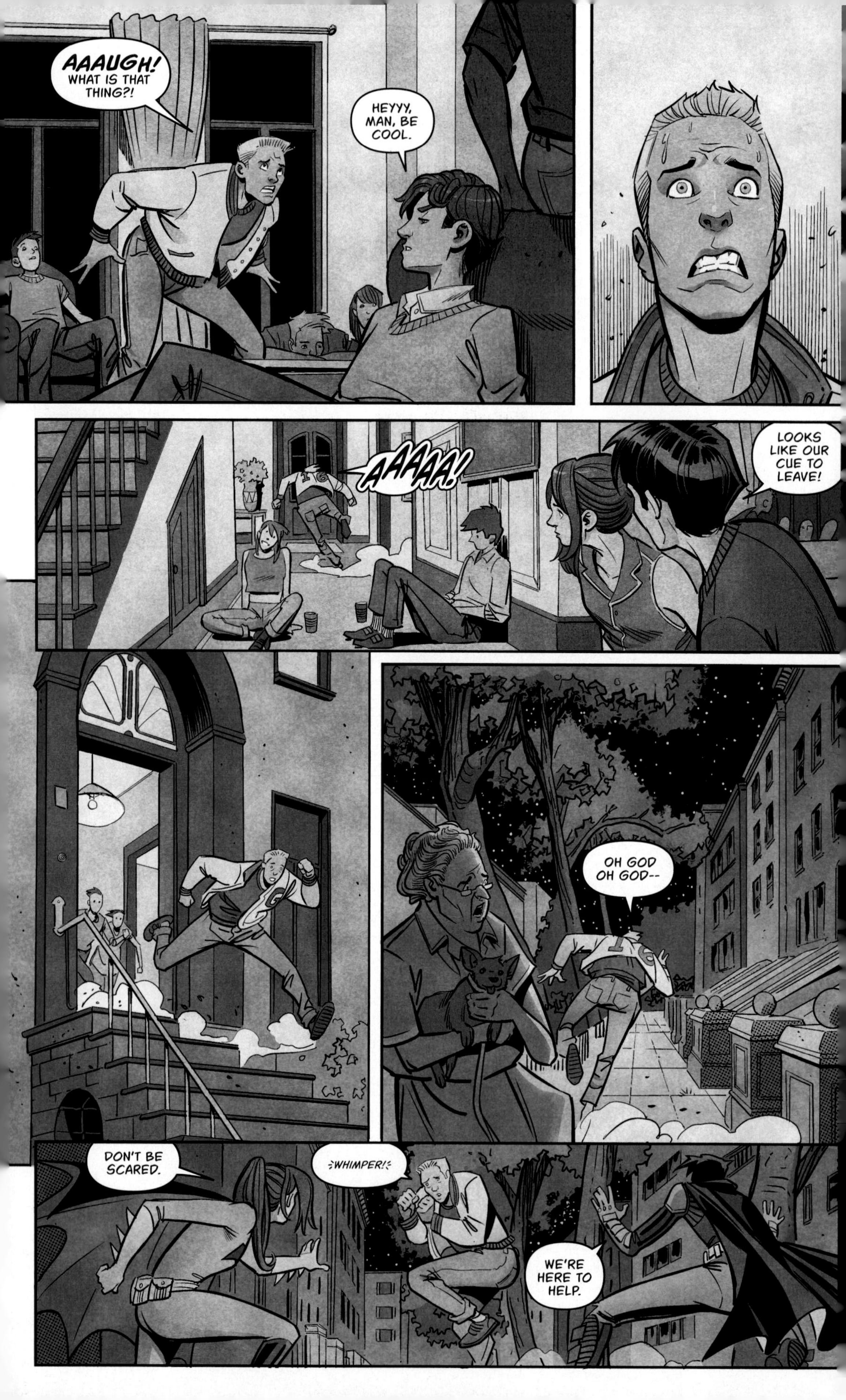
AAAUGH! WHAT IS THAT THING?!
HEYYY, MAN, BE COOL.
AAAAA!
LOOKS LIKE OUR CUE TO LEAVE!
OH GOD OH GOD--
DON'T BE SCARED.
WHIMPER!
WE'RE HERE TO HELP.

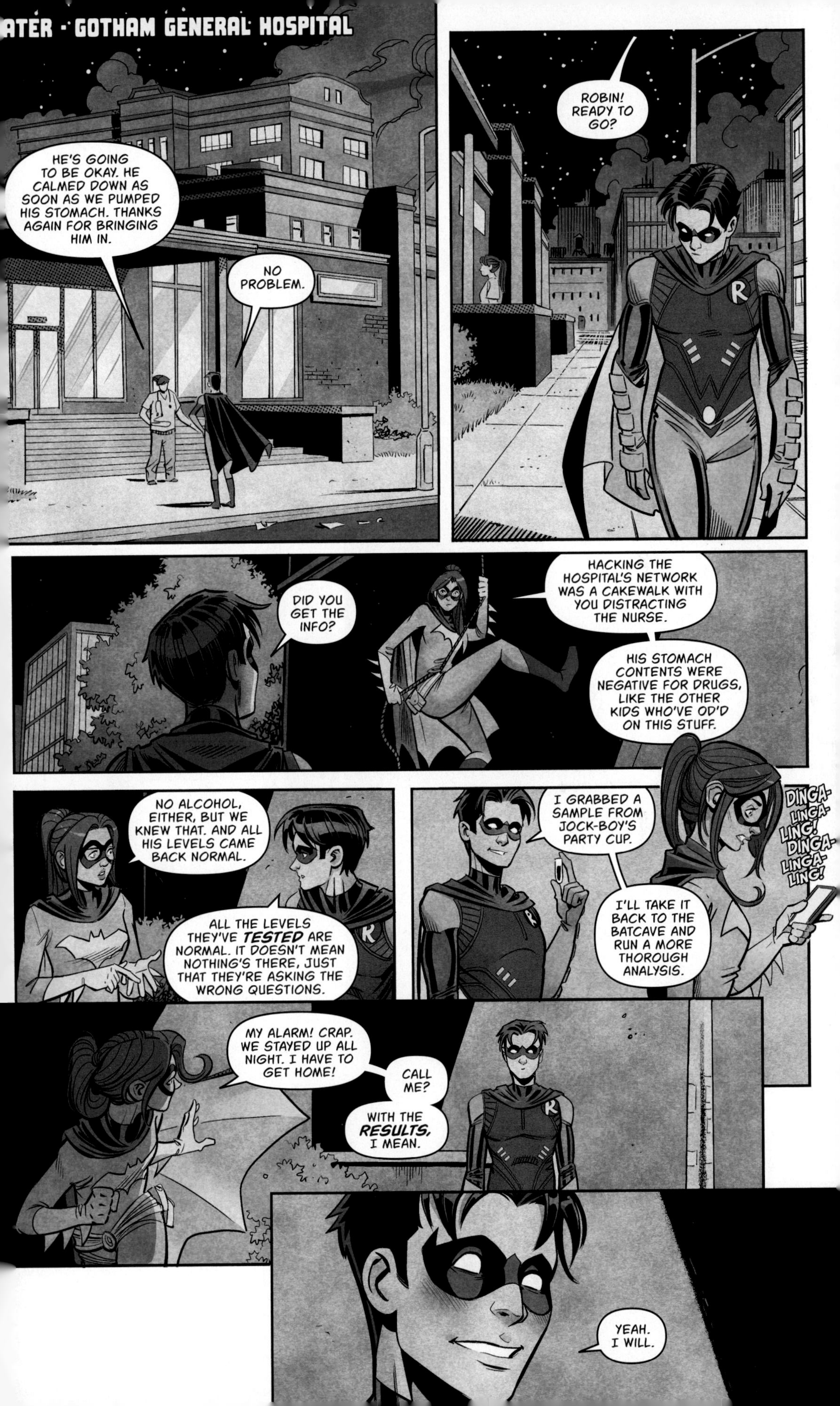

ATER · GOTHAM GENERAL HOSPITAL
HE'S GOING TO BE OKAY. HE CALMED DOWN AS SOON AS WE PUMPED HIS STOMACH. THANKS AGAIN FOR BRINGING HIM IN.
NO PROBLEM.
ROBIN! READY TO GO?
DID YOU GET THE INFO?
HACKING THE HOSPITAL'S NETWORK WAS A CAKEWALK WITH YOU DISTRACTING THE NURSE.
HIS STOMACH CONTENTS WERE NEGATIVE FOR DRUGS, LIKE THE OTHER KIDS WHO'VE OD'D ON THIS STUFF.
NO ALCOHOL, EITHER, BUT WE KNEW THAT. AND ALL HIS LEVELS CAME BACK NORMAL.
ALL THE LEVELS THEY'VE *TESTED* ARE NORMAL. IT DOESN'T MEAN NOTHING'S THERE, JUST THAT THEY'RE ASKING THE WRONG QUESTIONS.
I GRABBED A SAMPLE FROM JOCK-BOY'S PARTY CUP.
I'LL TAKE IT BACK TO THE BATCAVE AND RUN A MORE THOROUGH ANALYSIS.
DINGA-LINGA-LING! DINGA-LINGA-LING!
MY ALARM! CRAP. WE STAYED UP ALL NIGHT. I HAVE TO GET HOME!
CALL ME?
WITH THE ***RESULTS,*** I MEAN.
YEAH. I WILL.

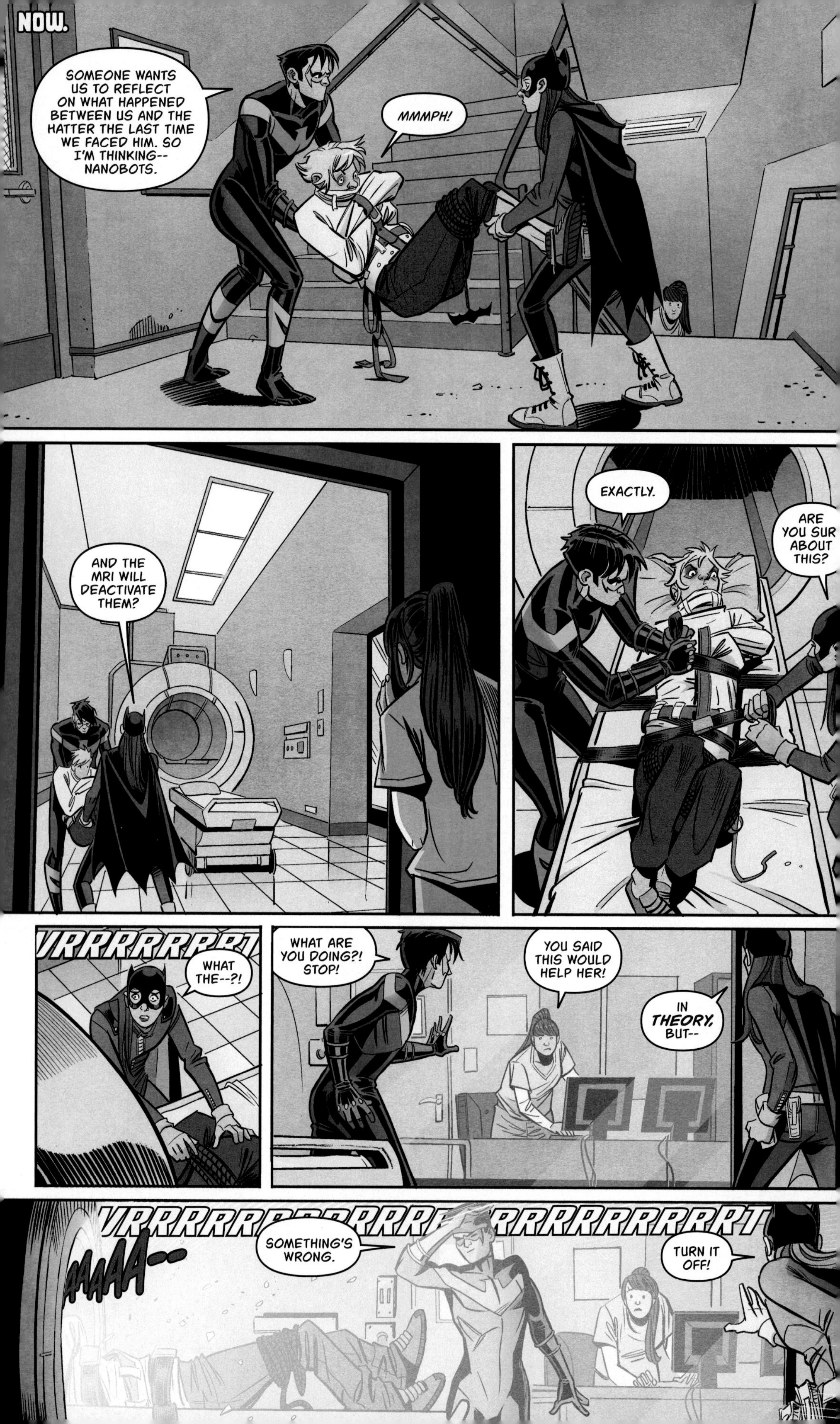
NOW.
SOMEONE WANTS US TO REFLECT ON WHAT HAPPENED BETWEEN US AND THE HATTER THE LAST TIME WE FACED HIM. SO I'M THINKING-- NANOBOTS.
MMMPH!
AND THE MRI WILL DEACTIVATE THEM?
EXACTLY.
ARE YOU SUR ABOUT THIS?
VRRRRRRRRT
WHAT THE--?!
WHAT ARE YOU DOING?! STOP!
YOU SAID THIS WOULD HELP HER!
IN THEORY, BUT--
VRRRRRRRRRRRRRRRRRRRRRRRRRRT
AAAAA--
SOMETHING'S WRONG.
TURN IT OFF!

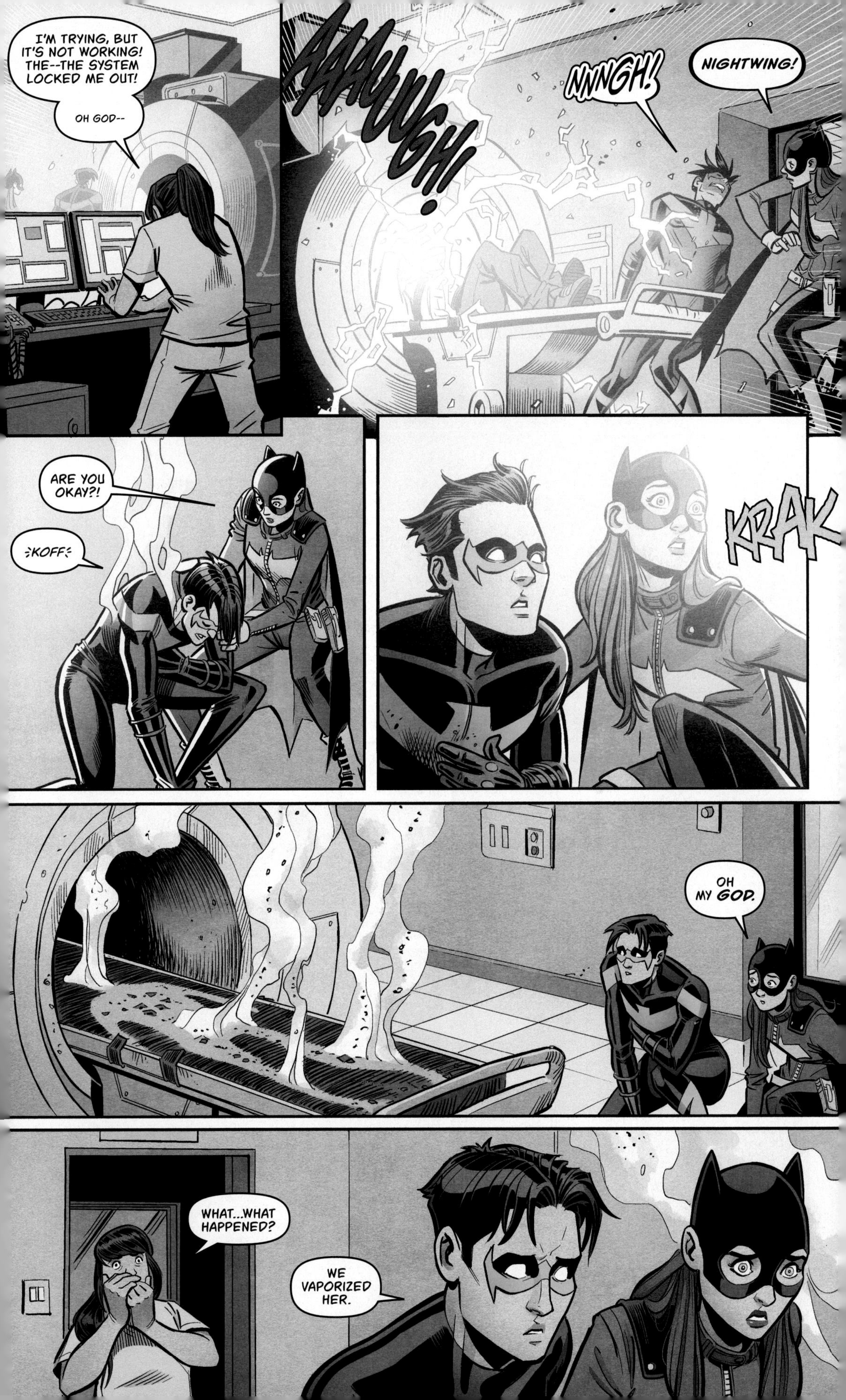
I'M TRYING, BUT IT'S NOT WORKING! THE--THE SYSTEM LOCKED ME OUT!
OH GOD--
AAAUUUGH!!
NNNGH!
NIGHTWING!
ARE YOU OKAY?!
KOFF
KRAK
OH MY GOD.
WHAT...WHAT HAPPENED?
WE VAPORIZED HER.

I'VE ANALYZED THE RESIDUE LEFT BEHIND IN THE MRI MACHINE...

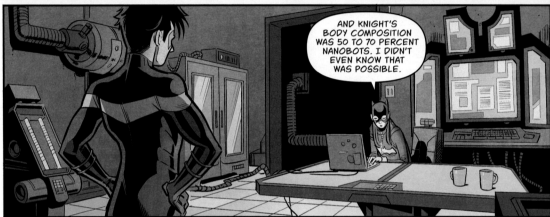

AND KNIGHT'S BODY COMPOSITION WAS 50 TO 70 PERCENT NANOBOTS. I DIDN'T EVEN KNOW THAT WAS POSSIBLE.

Z@#&!

I MEANT TO SHORT HER OUT, NOT *SNUFF* HER OUT.

HEY, DICK--IT WAS AN ACCIDENT.

RED KNIGHT WASN'T IN CONTROL OF HERSELF ANY MORE THAN THOSE *OTHER* TWO GIRLS WERE.

SHE WAS A VICTIM. SHE NEEDED OUR HELP.

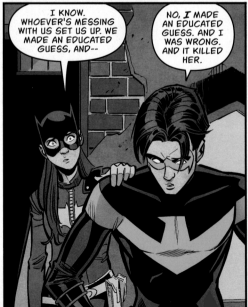

I KNOW. WHOEVER'S MESSING WITH US SET US UP. WE MADE AN EDUCATED GUESS, AND--

NO, *I* MADE AN EDUCATED GUESS. AND I WAS WRONG. AND IT KILLED HER.

DICK, *STOP.* IT'S NOT OKAY, BUT IT'S NOT YOUR FAULT. YOU WEREN'T THE ONE AT THE CONTROLS.

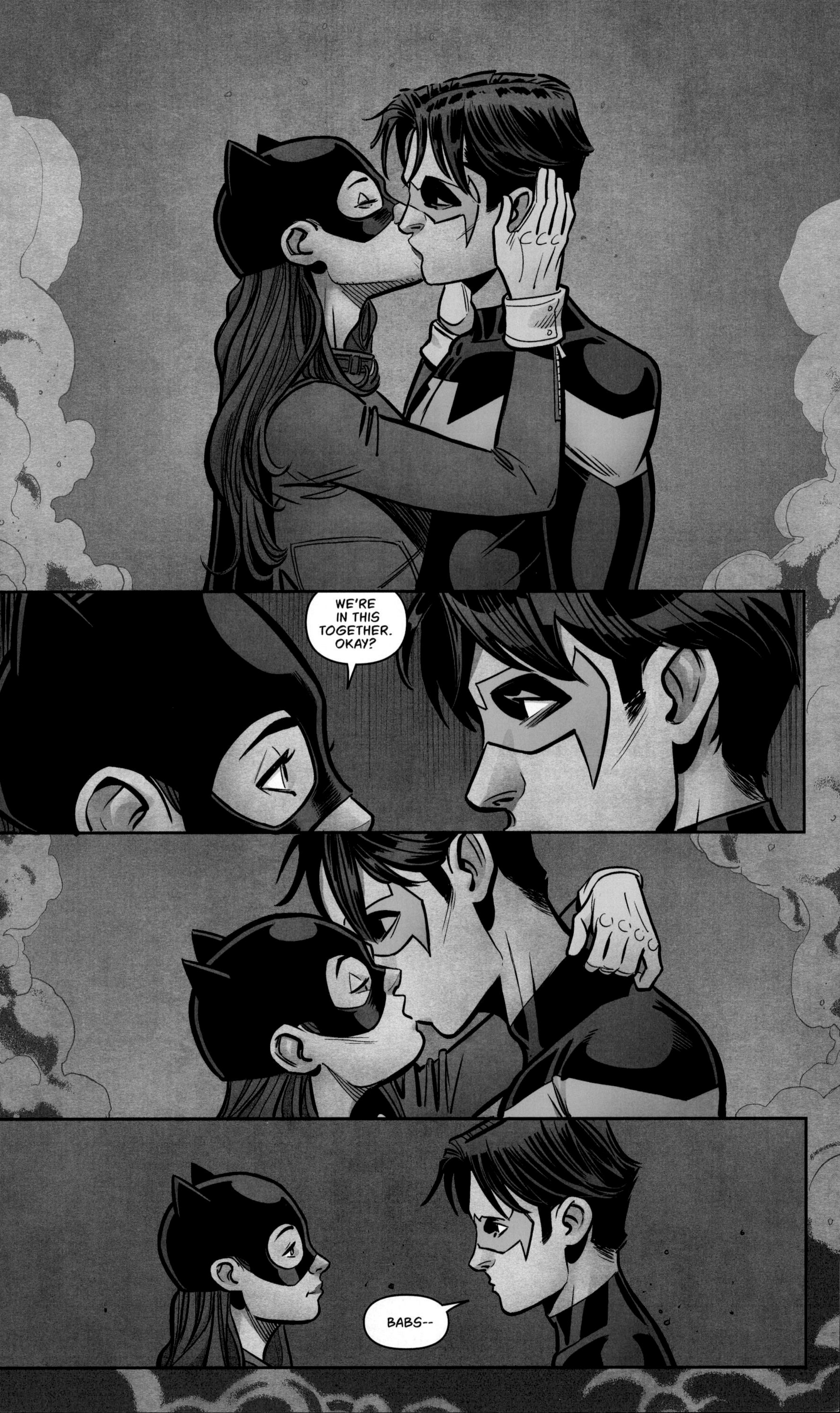
WE'RE IN THIS TOGETHER. OKAY?
BABS--

I CAN'T DO THIS RIGHT NOW.

I'M SORRY. I--I WASN'T THINKING.

IT'S OKAY. WE WERE BOTH NOT-THINKING IT. BUT WE SHOULDN'T--

DEFINITELY NOT. SO--

SO, UH--

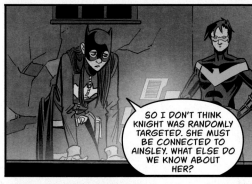

SO I DON'T THINK KNIGHT WAS RANDOMLY TARGETED. SHE MUST BE CONNECTED TO AINSLEY. WHAT ELSE DO WE KNOW ABOUT HER?

SHE WAS A PSYCHIATRIST. NO KIDS.

MARRIED?

DIVORCED. MAIDEN NAME PHILBERT.

PHILBERT? WITH A P.H.?

YEAH.

I KNOW THAT NAME.

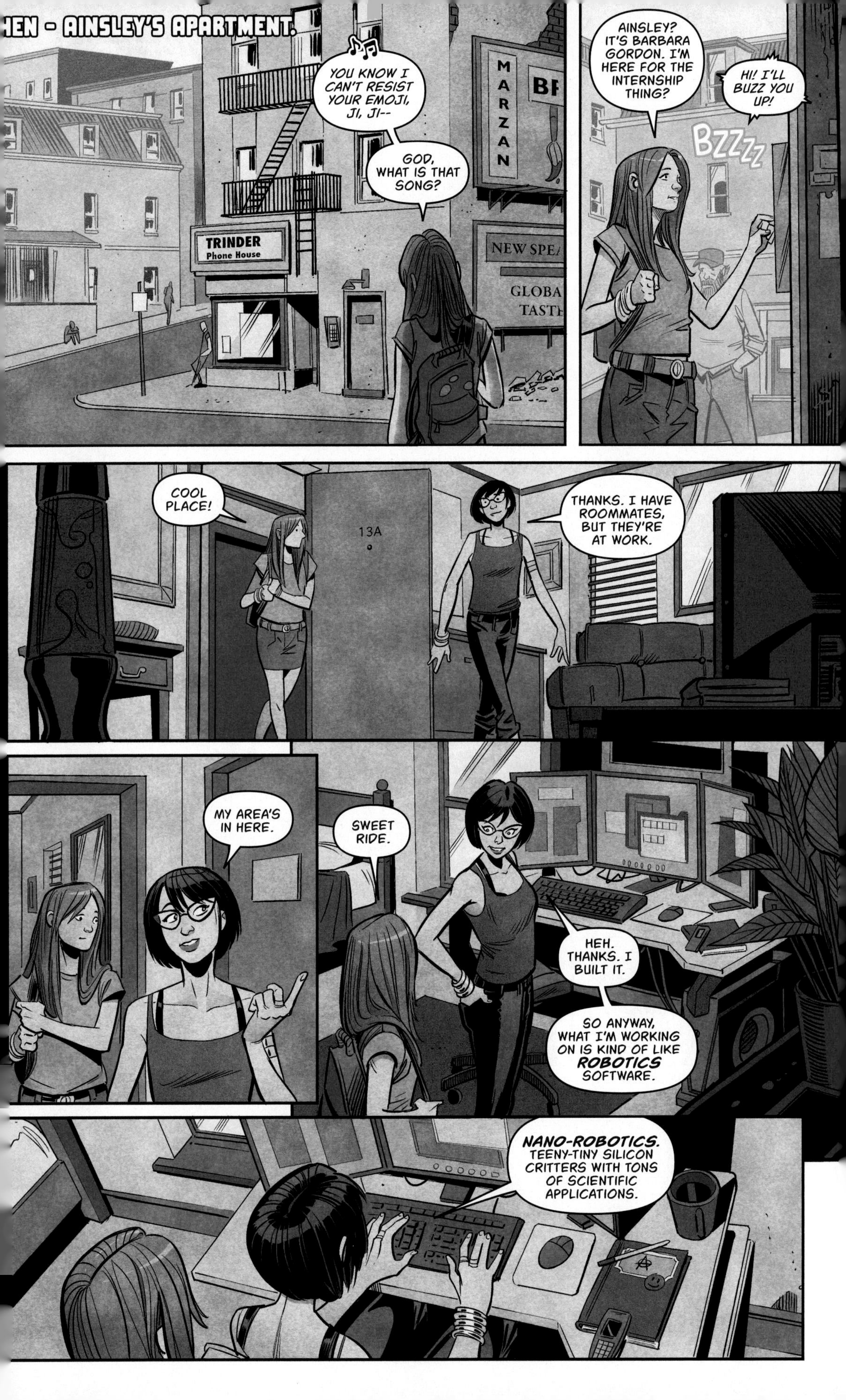

HEN - AINSLEY'S APARTMENT.
YOU KNOW I CAN'T RESIST YOUR EMOJI, JI, JI--
GOD, WHAT IS THAT SONG?
TRINDER
Phone House
MARZAN
NEW SPEA
GLOBA
TASTE
AINSLEY? IT'S BARBARA GORDON. I'M HERE FOR THE INTERNSHIP THING?
HI! I'LL BUZZ YOU UP!
BZZZZ
COOL PLACE!
13A
THANKS. I HAVE ROOMMATES, BUT THEY'RE AT WORK.
MY AREA'S IN HERE.
SWEET RIDE.
HEH. THANKS. I BUILT IT.
SO ANYWAY, WHAT I'M WORKING ON IS KIND OF LIKE ROBOTICS SOFTWARE.
NANO-ROBOTICS. TEENY-TINY SILICON CRITTERS WITH TONS OF SCIENTIFIC APPLICATIONS.

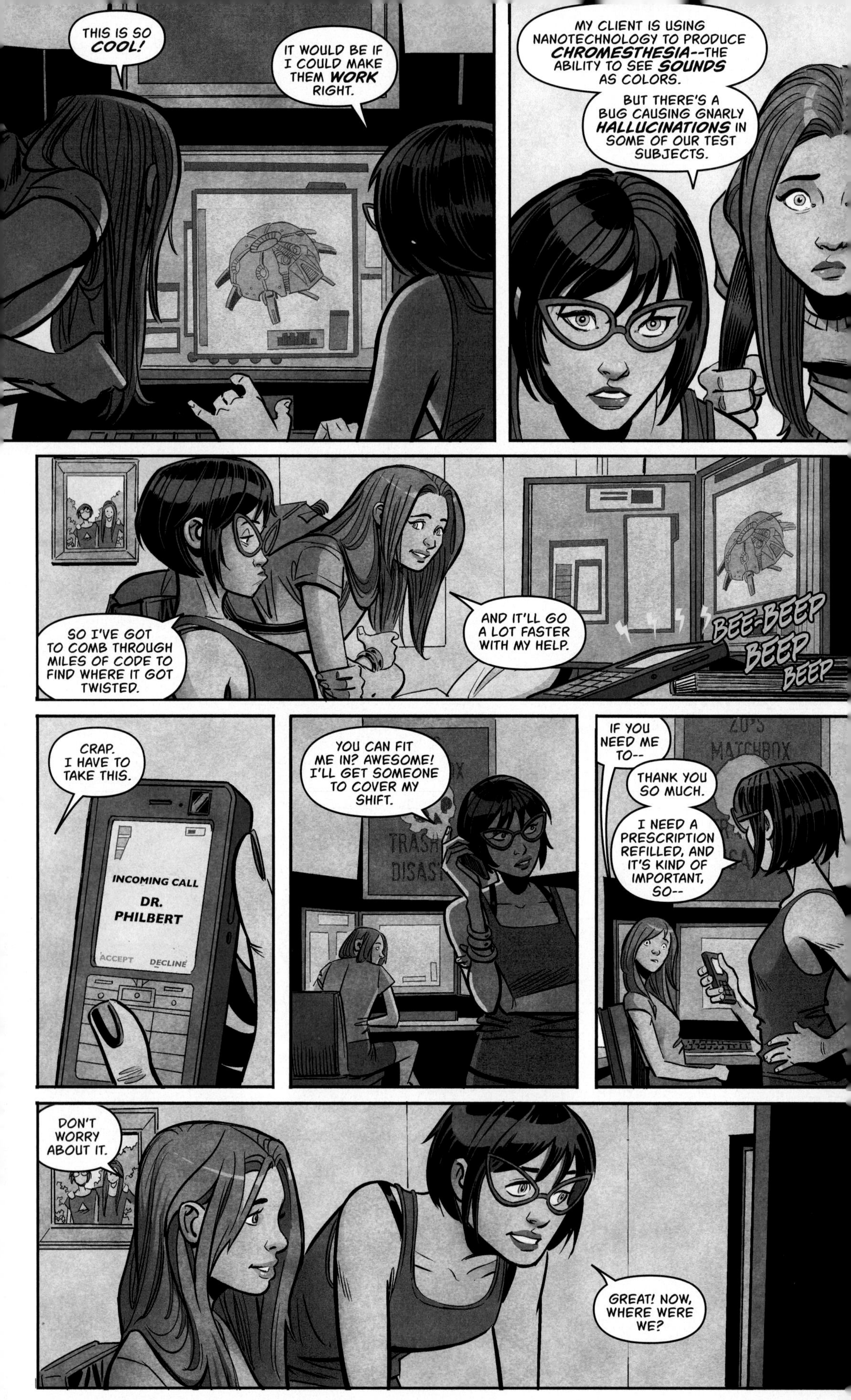
THIS IS SO COOL!
IT WOULD BE IF I COULD MAKE THEM WORK RIGHT.
MY CLIENT IS USING NANOTECHNOLOGY TO PRODUCE CHROMESTHESIA--THE ABILITY TO SEE SOUNDS AS COLORS.
BUT THERE'S A BUG CAUSING GNARLY HALLUCINATIONS IN SOME OF OUR TEST SUBJECTS.
SO I'VE GOT TO COMB THROUGH MILES OF CODE TO FIND WHERE IT GOT TWISTED.
AND IT'LL GO A LOT FASTER WITH MY HELP.
BEE-BEEP BEEP BEEP
CRAP. I HAVE TO TAKE THIS.
INCOMING CALL
DR. PHILBERT
ACCEPT
DECLINE
YOU CAN FIT ME IN? AWESOME! I'LL GET SOMEONE TO COVER MY SHIFT.
IF YOU NEED ME TO--
THANK YOU SO MUCH.
I NEED A PRESCRIPTION REFILLED, AND IT'S KIND OF IMPORTANT, SO--
DON'T WORRY ABOUT IT.
GREAT! NOW, WHERE WERE WE?

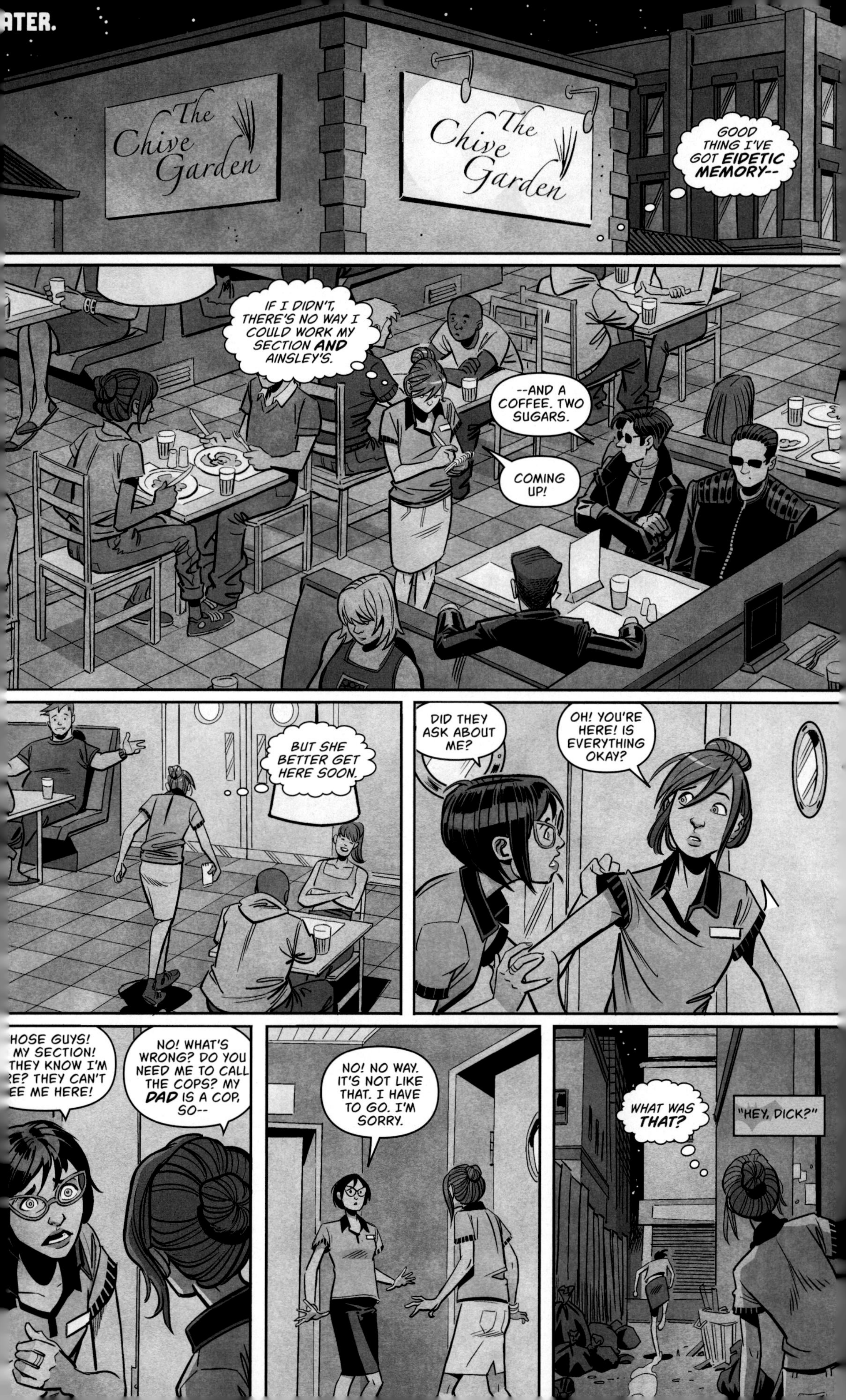

ATER.
The Chive Garden
The Chive Garden
GOOD THING I'VE GOT EIDETIC MEMORY--
IF I DIDN'T, THERE'S NO WAY I COULD WORK MY SECTION AND AINSLEY'S.
--AND A COFFEE. TWO SUGARS.
COMING UP!
BUT SHE BETTER GET HERE SOON.
DID THEY ASK ABOUT ME?
OH! YOU'RE HERE! IS EVERYTHING OKAY?
HOSE GUYS! MY SECTION! THEY KNOW I'M RE? THEY CAN'T EE ME HERE!
NO! WHAT'S WRONG? DO YOU NEED ME TO CALL THE COPS? MY DAD IS A COP, SO--
NO! NO WAY. IT'S NOT LIKE THAT. I HAVE TO GO. I'M SORRY.
WHAT WAS THAT?
"HEY, DICK?"

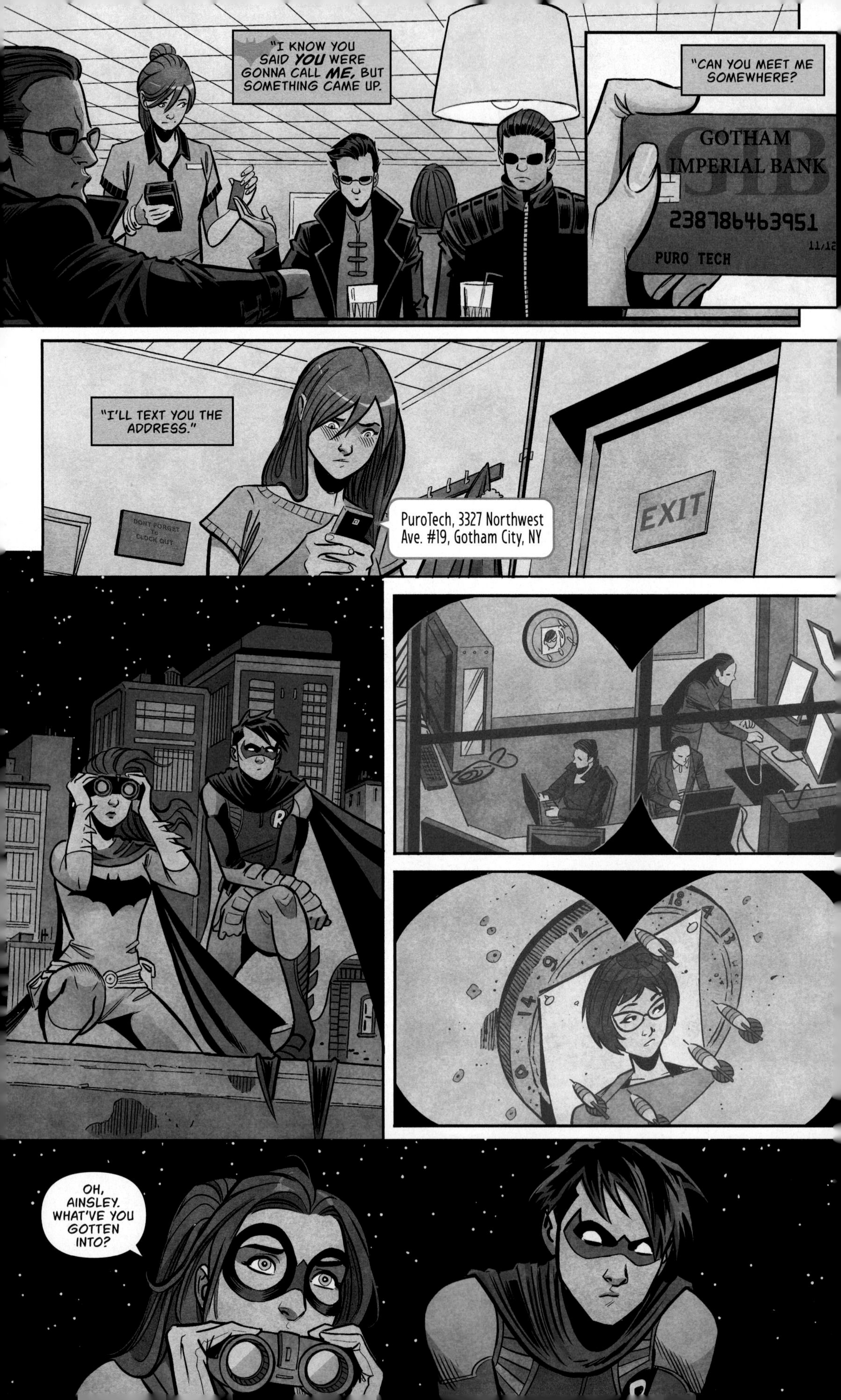
"I KNOW YOU SAID YOU WERE GONNA CALL ME, BUT SOMETHING CAME UP.
"CAN YOU MEET ME SOMEWHERE?
GOTHAM IMPERIAL BANK
238786463951
11/12
PURO TECH
"I'LL TEXT YOU THE ADDRESS."
DONT FORGET TO CLOCK OUT
PuroTech, 3327 Northwest Ave. #19, Gotham City, NY
EXIT
OH, AINSLEY. WHAT'VE YOU GOTTEN INTO?

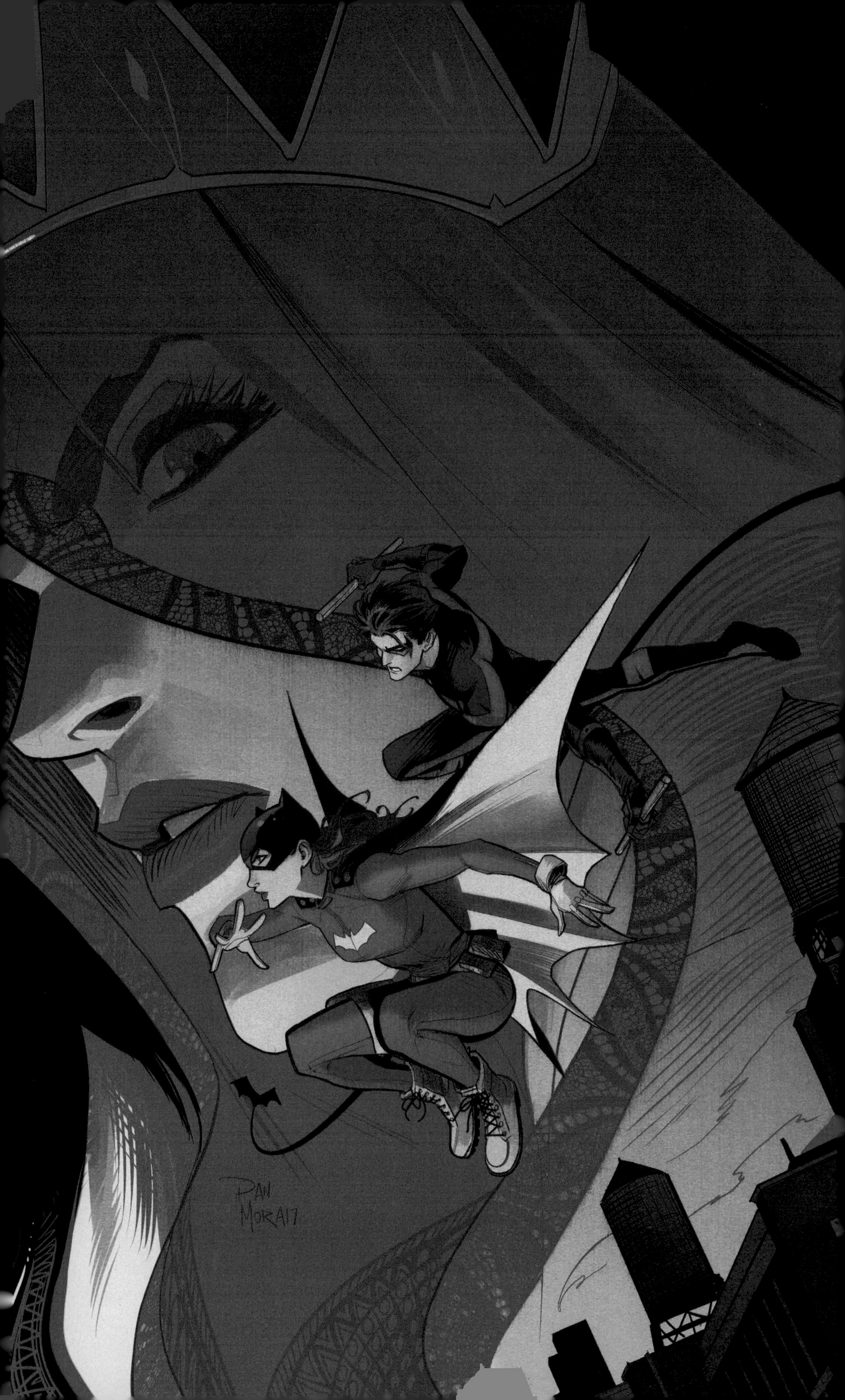
DAN
MORA17

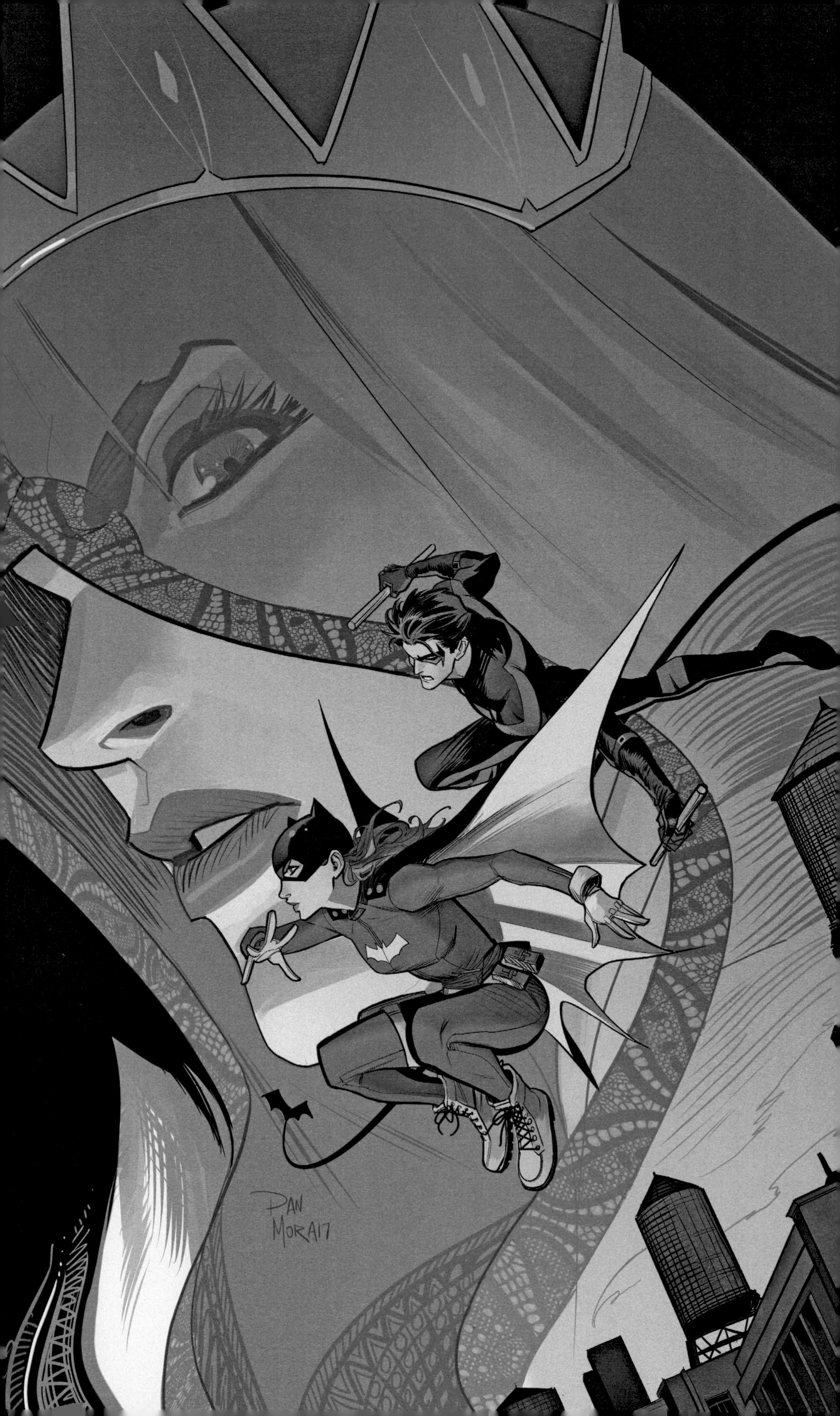
DAN
MORA17

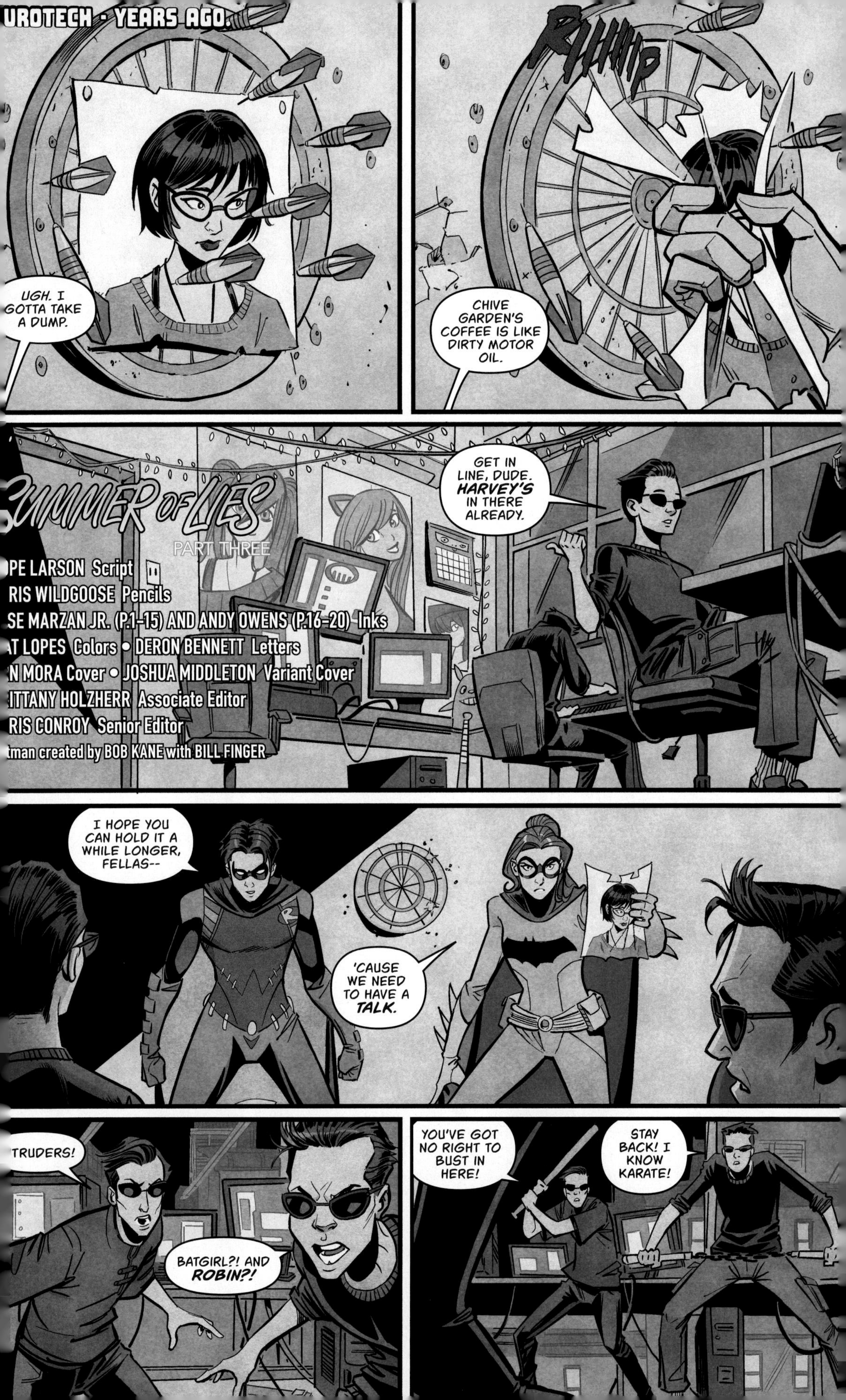

UROTECH - YEARS AGO.
UGH. I GOTTA TAKE A DUMP.
RIIIIP
CHIVE GARDEN'S COFFEE IS LIKE DIRTY MOTOR OIL.
SUMMER OF LIES
PART THREE
PE LARSON Script
RIS WILDGOOSE Pencils
SE MARZAN JR. (P.1-15) AND ANDY OWENS (P.16-20) Inks
AT LOPES Colors • DERON BENNETT Letters
N MORA Cover • JOSHUA MIDDLETON Variant Cover
ITTANY HOLZHERR Associate Editor
RIS CONROY Senior Editor
tman created by BOB KANE with BILL FINGER
GET IN LINE, DUDE. **HARVEY'S** IN THERE ALREADY.
I HOPE YOU CAN HOLD IT A WHILE LONGER, FELLAS--
'CAUSE WE NEED TO HAVE A **TALK.**
TRUDERS!
BATGIRL?! AND **ROBIN?!**
YOU'VE GOT NO RIGHT TO BUST IN HERE!
STAY BACK! I KNOW KARATE!

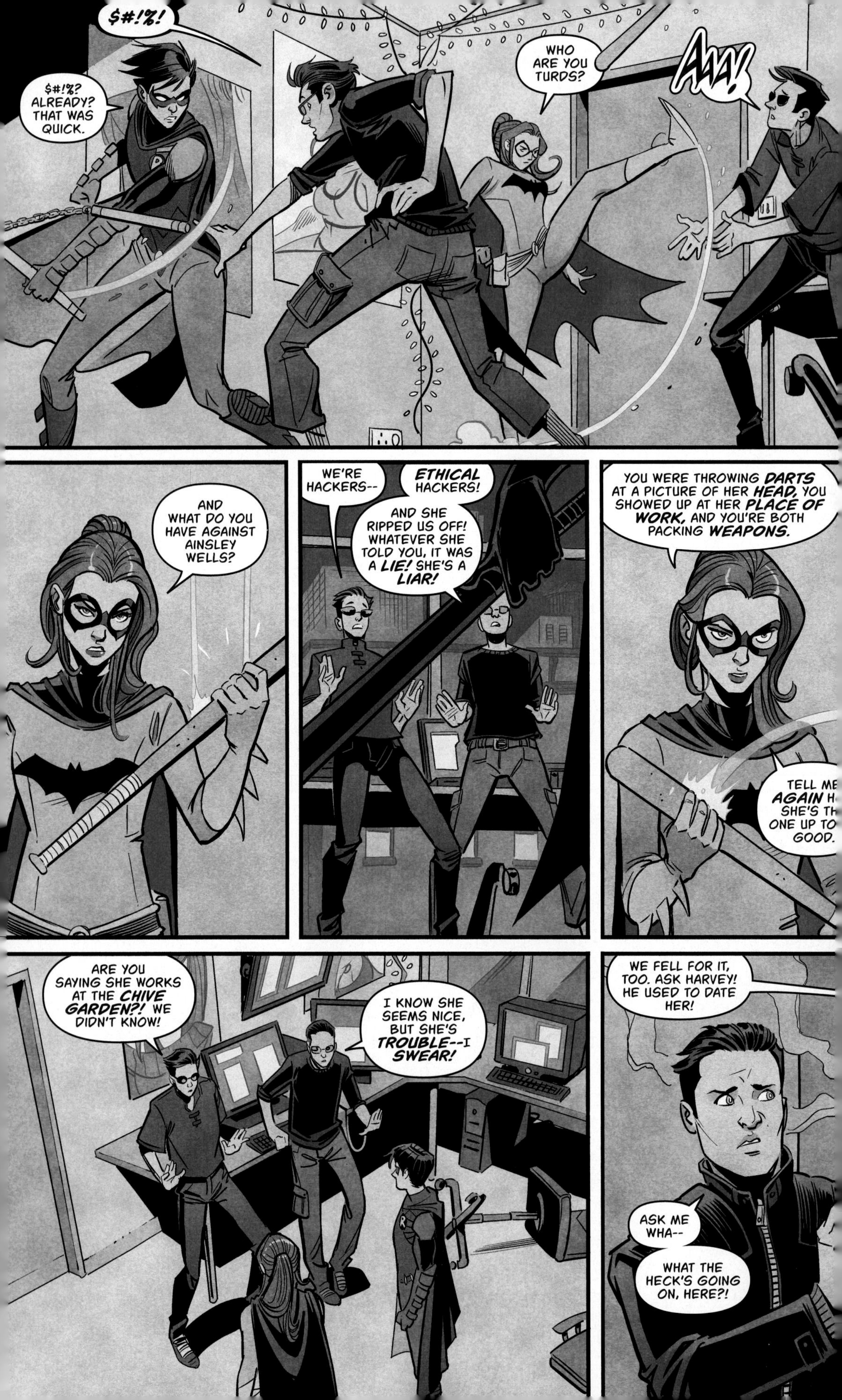
$#!%!
$#!%? ALREADY? THAT WAS QUICK.
WHO ARE YOU TURDS?
AAA!
AND WHAT DO YOU HAVE AGAINST AINSLEY WELLS?
WE'RE HACKERS--
ETHICAL HACKERS!
AND SHE RIPPED US OFF! WHATEVER SHE TOLD YOU, IT WAS A LIE! SHE'S A LIAR!
YOU WERE THROWING DARTS AT A PICTURE OF HER HEAD, YOU SHOWED UP AT HER PLACE OF WORK, AND YOU'RE BOTH PACKING WEAPONS.
TELL ME AGAIN H SHE'S TH ONE UP TO GOOD.
ARE YOU SAYING SHE WORKS AT THE CHIVE GARDEN?! WE DIDN'T KNOW!
I KNOW SHE SEEMS NICE, BUT SHE'S TROUBLE--I SWEAR!
WE FELL FOR IT, TOO. ASK HARVEY! HE USED TO DATE HER!
ASK ME WHA--
WHAT THE HECK'S GOING ON, HERE?!

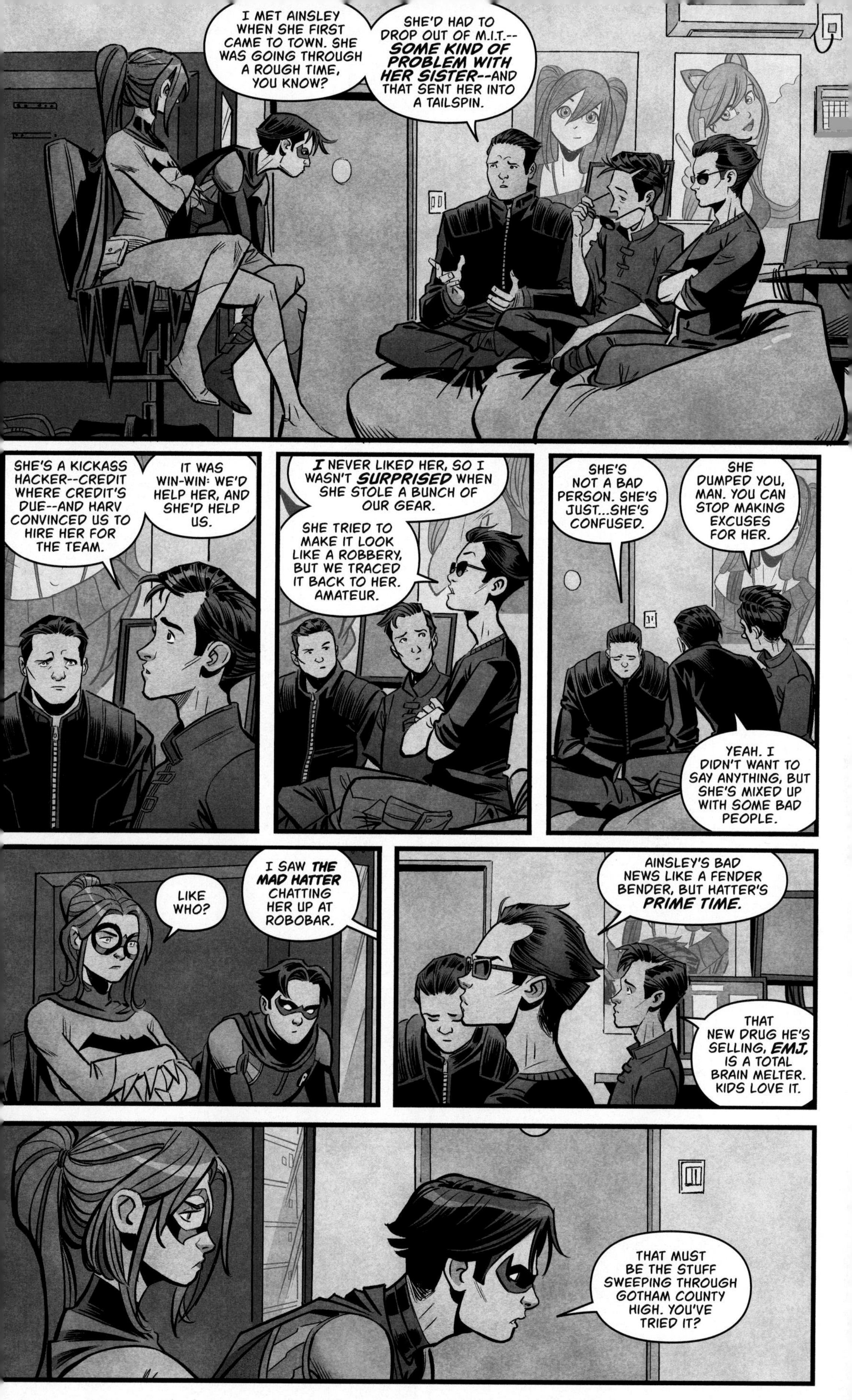

I MET AINSLEY WHEN SHE FIRST CAME TO TOWN. SHE WAS GOING THROUGH A ROUGH TIME, YOU KNOW?
SHE'D HAD TO DROP OUT OF M.I.T.-- SOME KIND OF PROBLEM WITH HER SISTER--AND THAT SENT HER INTO A TAILSPIN.
SHE'S A KICKASS HACKER--CREDIT WHERE CREDIT'S DUE--AND HARV CONVINCED US TO HIRE HER FOR THE TEAM.
IT WAS WIN-WIN: WE'D HELP HER, AND SHE'D HELP US.
I NEVER LIKED HER, SO I WASN'T SURPRISED WHEN SHE STOLE A BUNCH OF OUR GEAR.
SHE TRIED TO MAKE IT LOOK LIKE A ROBBERY, BUT WE TRACED IT BACK TO HER. AMATEUR.
SHE'S NOT A BAD PERSON. SHE'S JUST...SHE'S CONFUSED.
SHE DUMPED YOU, MAN. YOU CAN STOP MAKING EXCUSES FOR HER.
YEAH. I DIDN'T WANT TO SAY ANYTHING, BUT SHE'S MIXED UP WITH SOME BAD PEOPLE.
LIKE WHO?
I SAW THE MAD HATTER CHATTING HER UP AT ROBOBAR.
AINSLEY'S BAD NEWS LIKE A FENDER BENDER, BUT HATTER'S PRIME TIME.
THAT NEW DRUG HE'S SELLING, EMJ, IS A TOTAL BRAIN MELTER. KIDS LOVE IT.
THAT MUST BE THE STUFF SWEEPING THROUGH GOTHAM COUNTY HIGH. YOU'VE TRIED IT?

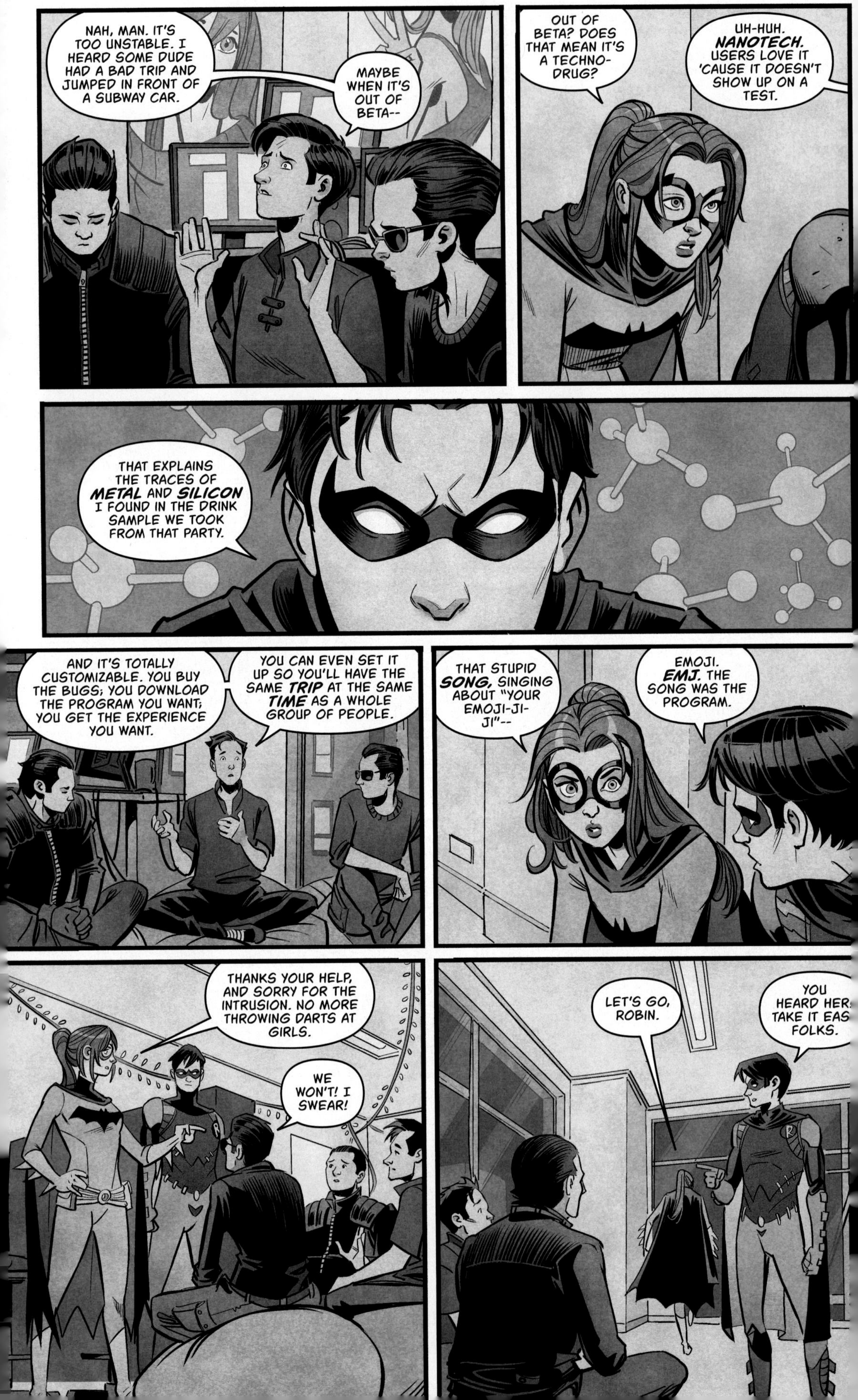

NAH, MAN. IT'S TOO UNSTABLE. I HEARD SOME DUDE HAD A BAD TRIP AND JUMPED IN FRONT OF A SUBWAY CAR.
MAYBE WHEN IT'S OUT OF BETA--
OUT OF BETA? DOES THAT MEAN IT'S A TECHNO-DRUG?
UH-HUH. NANOTECH. USERS LOVE IT 'CAUSE IT DOESN'T SHOW UP ON A TEST.
THAT EXPLAINS THE TRACES OF METAL AND SILICON I FOUND IN THE DRINK SAMPLE WE TOOK FROM THAT PARTY.
AND IT'S TOTALLY CUSTOMIZABLE. YOU BUY THE BUGS; YOU DOWNLOAD THE PROGRAM YOU WANT; YOU GET THE EXPERIENCE YOU WANT.
YOU CAN EVEN SET IT UP SO YOU'LL HAVE THE SAME TRIP AT THE SAME TIME AS A WHOLE GROUP OF PEOPLE.
THAT STUPID SONG, SINGING ABOUT "YOUR EMOJI-JI-JI"--
EMOJI. EMJ. THE SONG WAS THE PROGRAM.
THANKS YOUR HELP, AND SORRY FOR THE INTRUSION. NO MORE THROWING DARTS AT GIRLS.
WE WON'T! I SWEAR!
LET'S GO, ROBIN.
YOU HEARD HER
TAKE IT EAS
FOLKS.

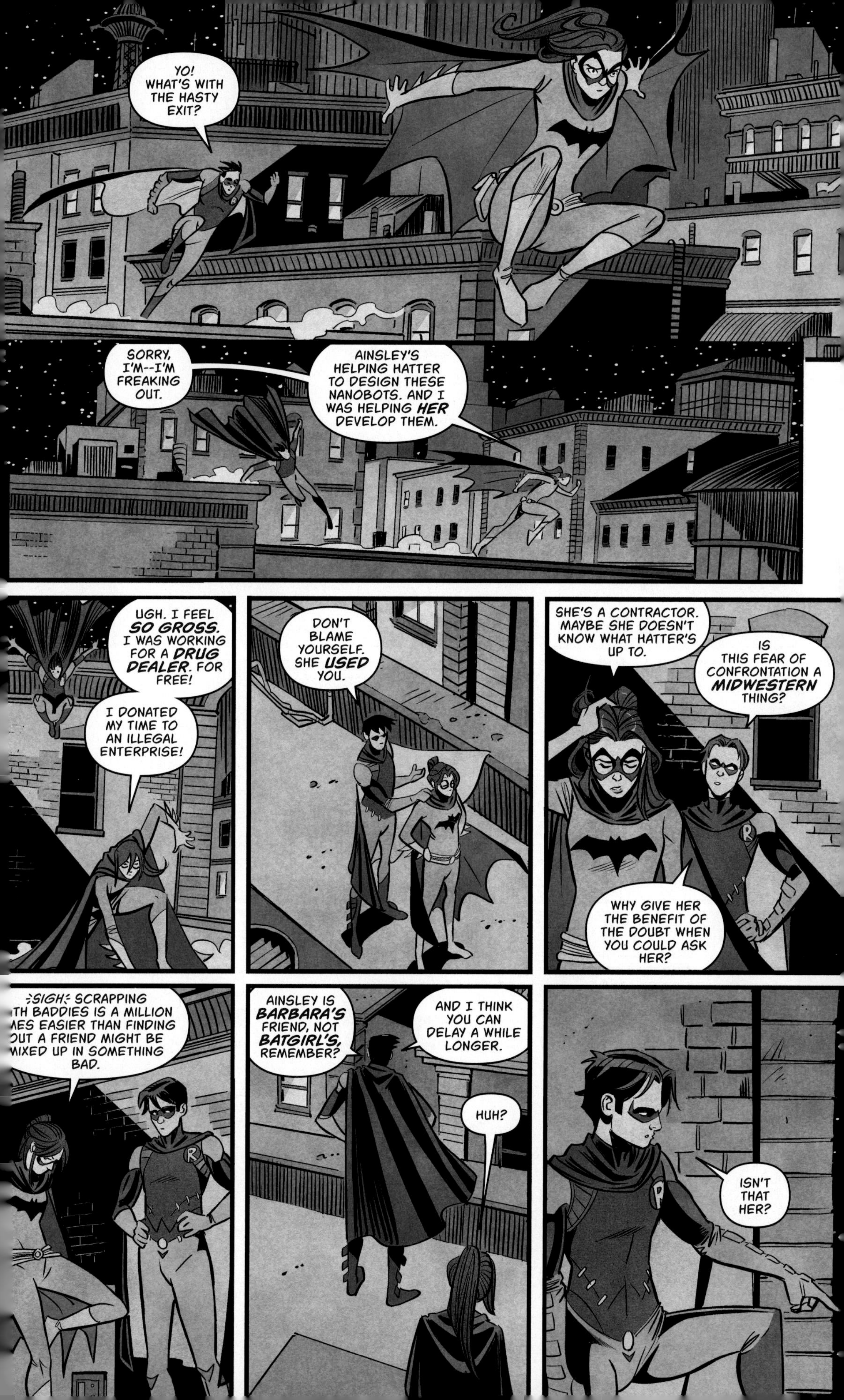

YO! WHAT'S WITH THE HASTY EXIT?
SORRY, I'M--I'M FREAKING OUT.
AINSLEY'S HELPING HATTER TO DESIGN THESE NANOBOTS. AND I WAS HELPING HER DEVELOP THEM.
UGH. I FEEL SO GROSS. I WAS WORKING FOR A DRUG DEALER. FOR FREE!
I DONATED MY TIME TO AN ILLEGAL ENTERPRISE!
DON'T BLAME YOURSELF. SHE USED YOU.
SHE'S A CONTRACTOR. MAYBE SHE DOESN'T KNOW WHAT HATTER'S UP TO.
IS THIS FEAR OF CONFRONTATION A MIDWESTERN THING?
WHY GIVE HER THE BENEFIT OF THE DOUBT WHEN YOU COULD ASK HER?
SIGH SCRAPPING ITH BADDIES IS A MILLION MES EASIER THAN FINDING OUT A FRIEND MIGHT BE MIXED UP IN SOMETHING BAD.
AINSLEY IS BARBARA'S FRIEND, NOT BATGIRL'S, REMEMBER?
AND I THINK YOU CAN DELAY A WHILE LONGER.
HUH?
ISN'T THAT HER?

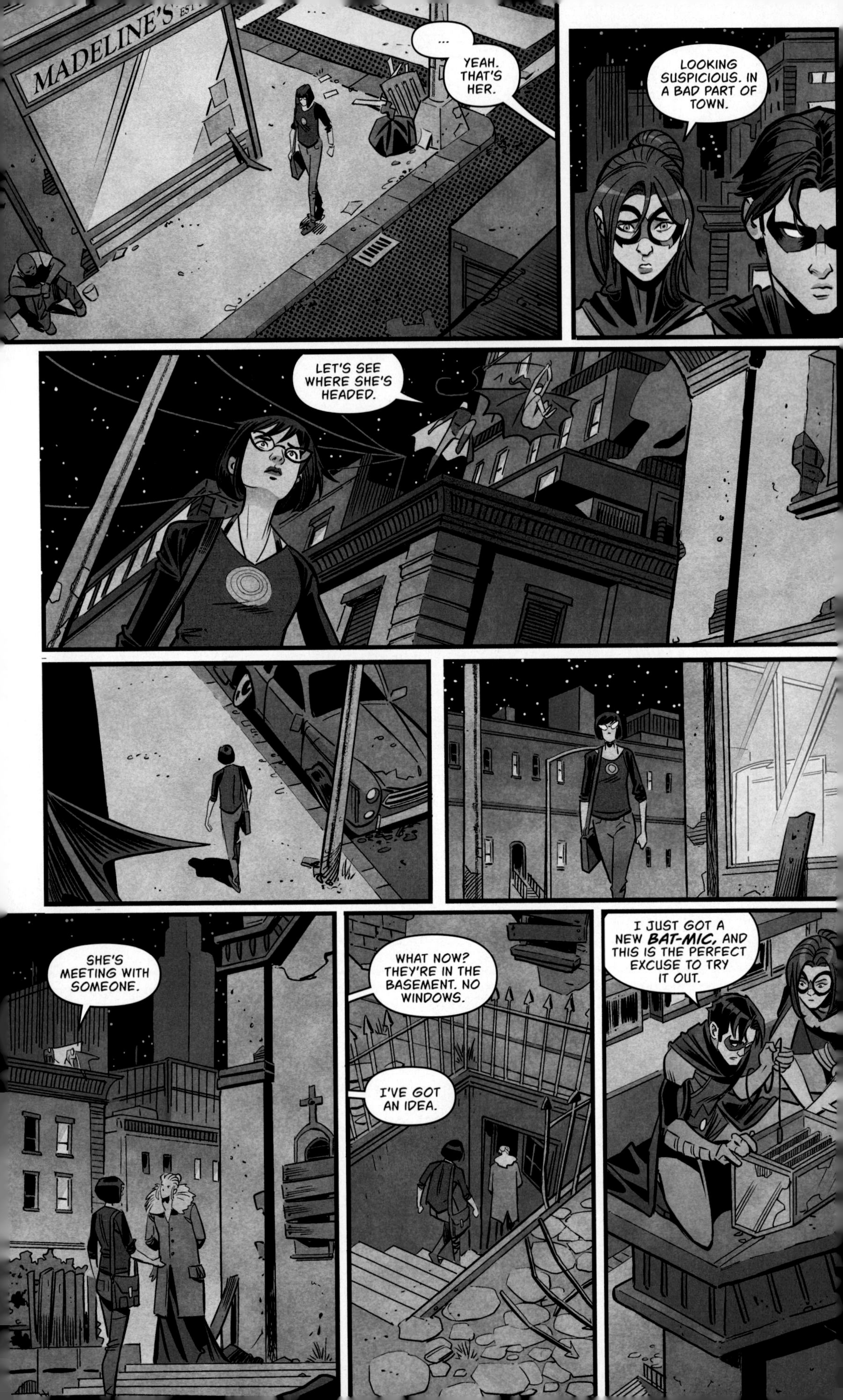
MADELINE'S
...
YEAH. THAT'S HER.
LOOKING SUSPICIOUS. IN A BAD PART OF TOWN.
LET'S SEE WHERE SHE'S HEADED.
SHE'S MEETING WITH SOMEONE.
WHAT NOW? THEY'RE IN THE BASEMENT. NO WINDOWS.
I'VE GOT AN IDEA.
I JUST GOT A NEW **BAT-MIC,** AND THIS IS THE PERFECT EXCUSE TO TRY IT OUT.

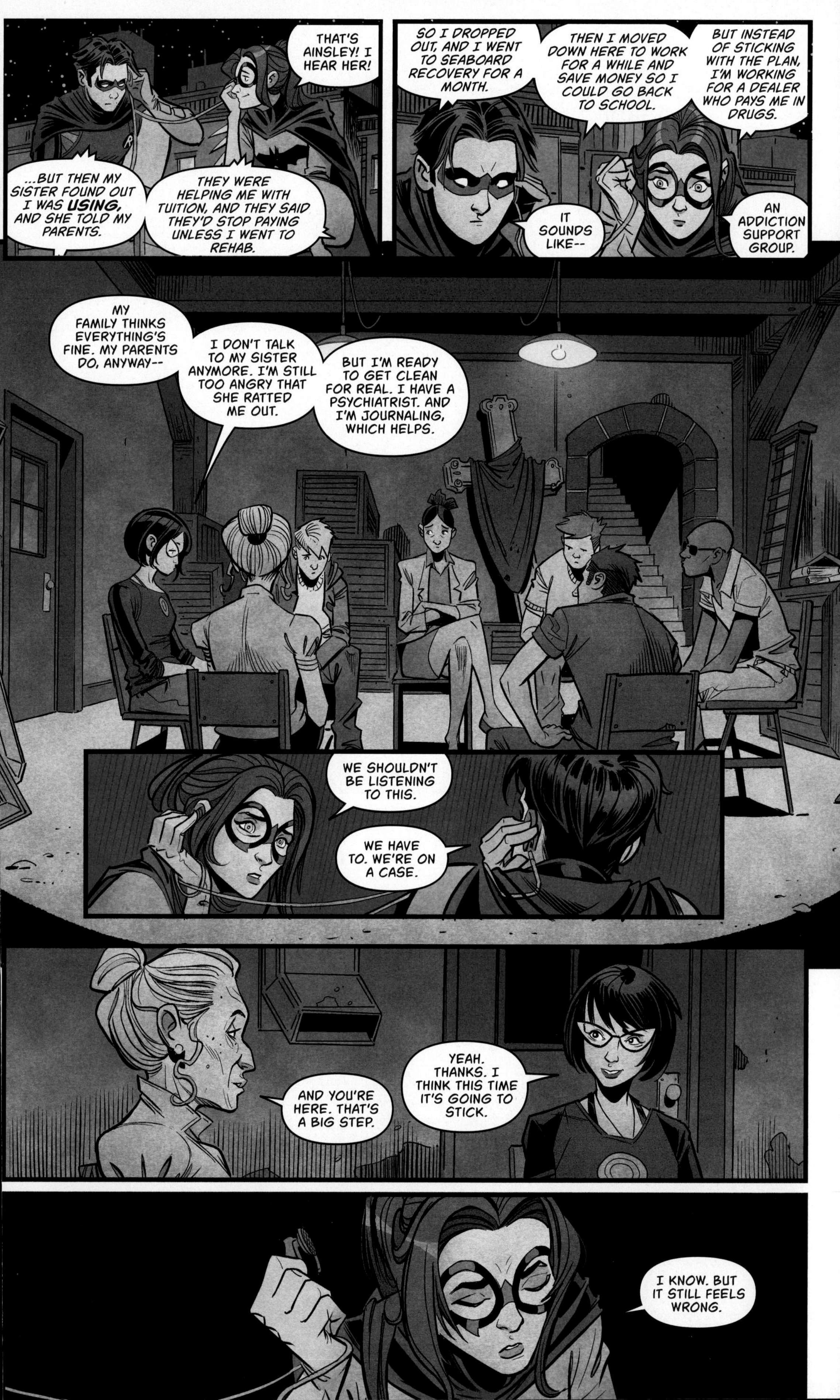
THAT'S AINSLEY! I HEAR HER!
...BUT THEN MY SISTER FOUND OUT I WAS **USING,** AND SHE TOLD MY PARENTS.
THEY WERE HELPING ME WITH TUITION, AND THEY SAID THEY'D STOP PAYING UNLESS I WENT TO REHAB.
SO I DROPPED OUT, AND I WENT TO SEABOARD RECOVERY FOR A MONTH.
THEN I MOVED DOWN HERE TO WORK FOR A WHILE AND SAVE MONEY SO I COULD GO BACK TO SCHOOL.
BUT INSTEAD OF STICKING WITH THE PLAN, I'M WORKING FOR A DEALER WHO PAYS ME IN DRUGS.
IT SOUNDS LIKE--
AN ADDICTION SUPPORT GROUP.
MY FAMILY THINKS EVERYTHING'S FINE. MY PARENTS DO, ANYWAY--
I DON'T TALK TO MY SISTER ANYMORE. I'M STILL TOO ANGRY THAT SHE RATTED ME OUT.
BUT I'M READY TO GET CLEAN FOR REAL. I HAVE A PSYCHIATRIST. AND I'M JOURNALING, WHICH HELPS.
WE SHOULDN'T BE LISTENING TO THIS.
WE HAVE TO. WE'RE ON A CASE.
AND YOU'RE HERE. THAT'S A BIG STEP.
YEAH. THANKS. I THINK THIS TIME IT'S GOING TO STICK.
I KNOW. BUT IT STILL FEELS WRONG.

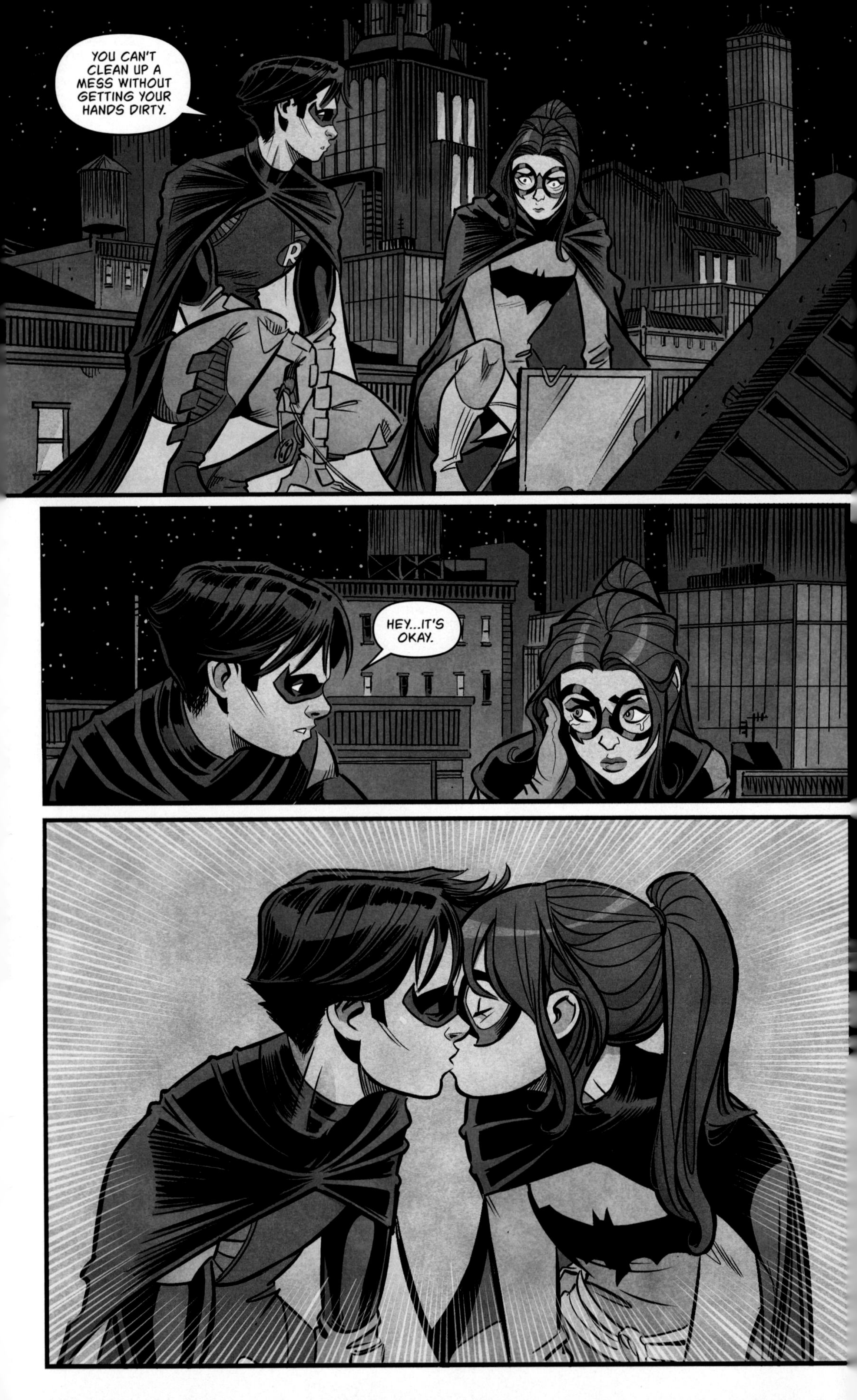
YOU CAN'T CLEAN UP A MESS WITHOUT GETTING YOUR HANDS DIRTY.
HEY...IT'S OKAY.

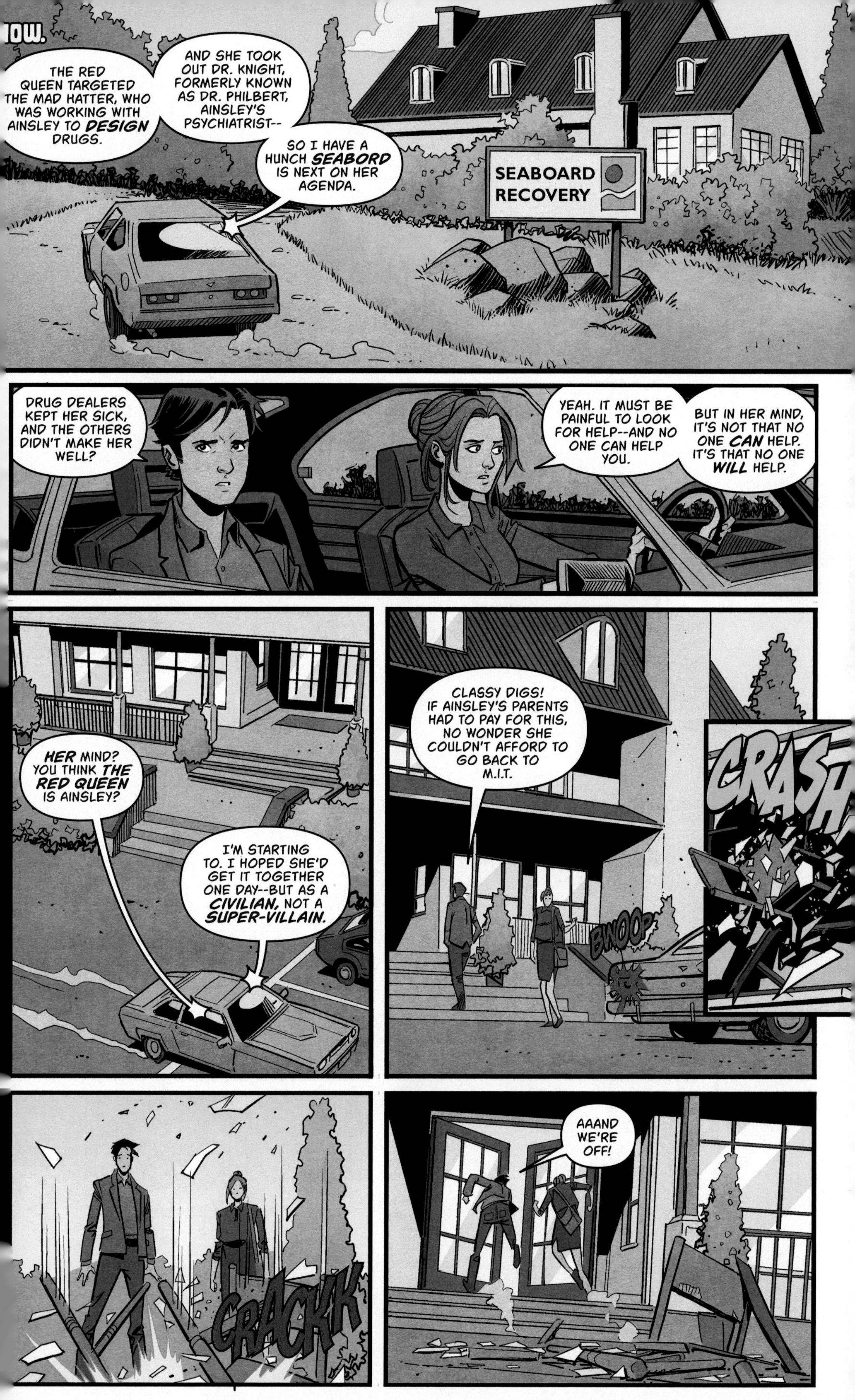

IOW.
THE RED QUEEN TARGETED THE MAD HATTER, WHO WAS WORKING WITH AINSLEY TO DESIGN DRUGS.
AND SHE TOOK OUT DR. KNIGHT, FORMERLY KNOWN AS DR. PHILBERT, AINSLEY'S PSYCHIATRIST--
SO I HAVE A HUNCH SEABORD IS NEXT ON HER AGENDA.
SEABOARD RECOVERY
DRUG DEALERS KEPT HER SICK, AND THE OTHERS DIDN'T MAKE HER WELL?
YEAH. IT MUST BE PAINFUL TO LOOK FOR HELP--AND NO ONE CAN HELP YOU.
BUT IN HER MIND, IT'S NOT THAT NO ONE CAN HELP. IT'S THAT NO ONE WILL HELP.
HER MIND? YOU THINK THE RED QUEEN IS AINSLEY?
I'M STARTING TO. I HOPED SHE'D GET IT TOGETHER ONE DAY--BUT AS A CIVILIAN, NOT A SUPER-VILLAIN.
CLASSY DIGS! IF AINSLEY'S PARENTS HAD TO PAY FOR THIS, NO WONDER SHE COULDN'T AFFORD TO GO BACK TO M.I.T.
BWOOP
CRASH
CRACKK
AAAND WE'RE OFF!

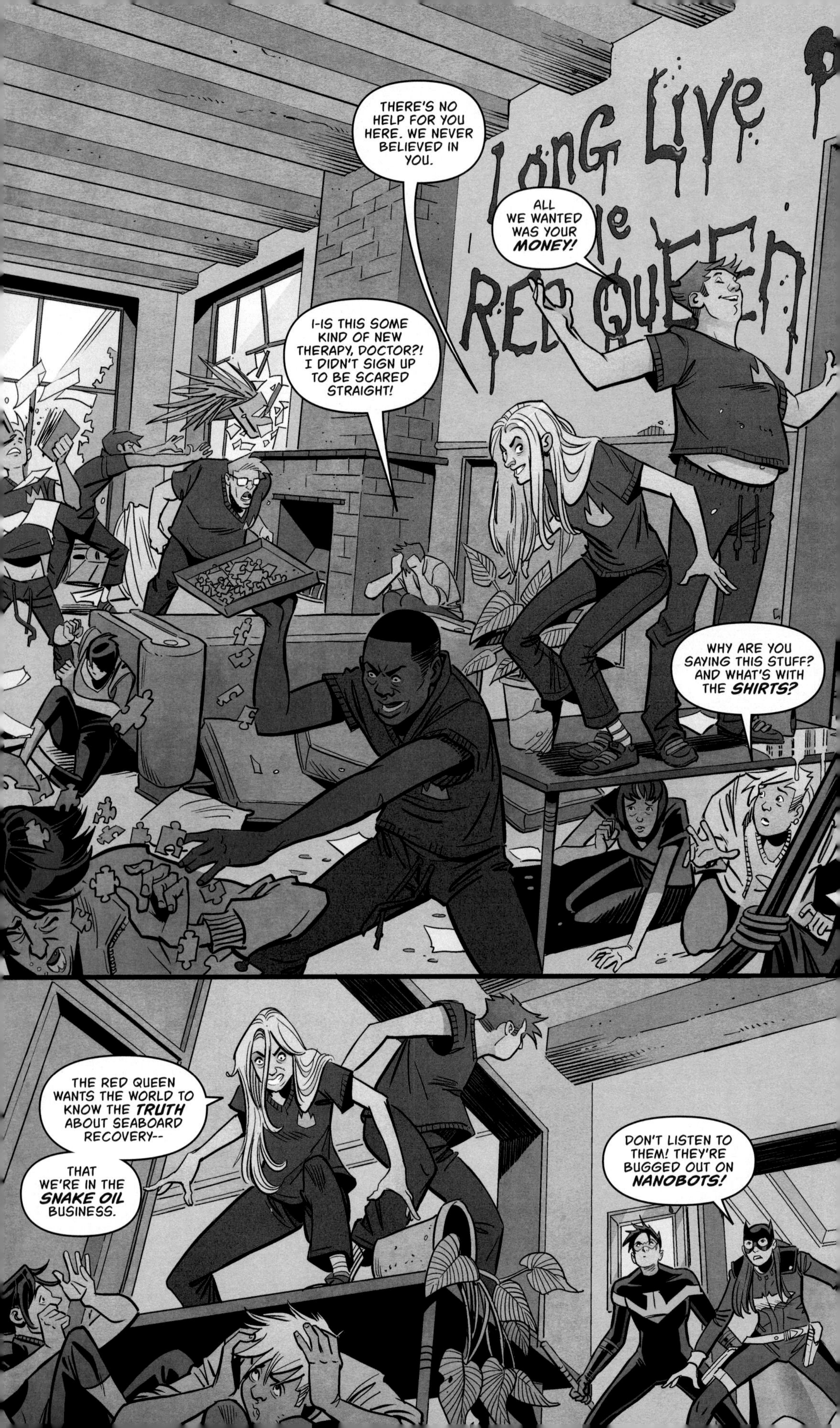
THERE'S NO HELP FOR YOU HERE. WE NEVER BELIEVED IN YOU.
LONG LIVE THE RED QUEEN
ALL WE WANTED WAS YOUR MONEY!
I-IS THIS SOME KIND OF NEW THERAPY, DOCTOR?! I DIDN'T SIGN UP TO BE SCARED STRAIGHT!
WHY ARE YOU SAYING THIS STUFF? AND WHAT'S WITH THE SHIRTS?
THE RED QUEEN WANTS THE WORLD TO KNOW THE TRUTH ABOUT SEABOARD RECOVERY--
THAT WE'RE IN THE SNAKE OIL BUSINESS.
DON'T LISTEN TO THEM! THEY'RE BUGGED OUT ON NANOBOTS!

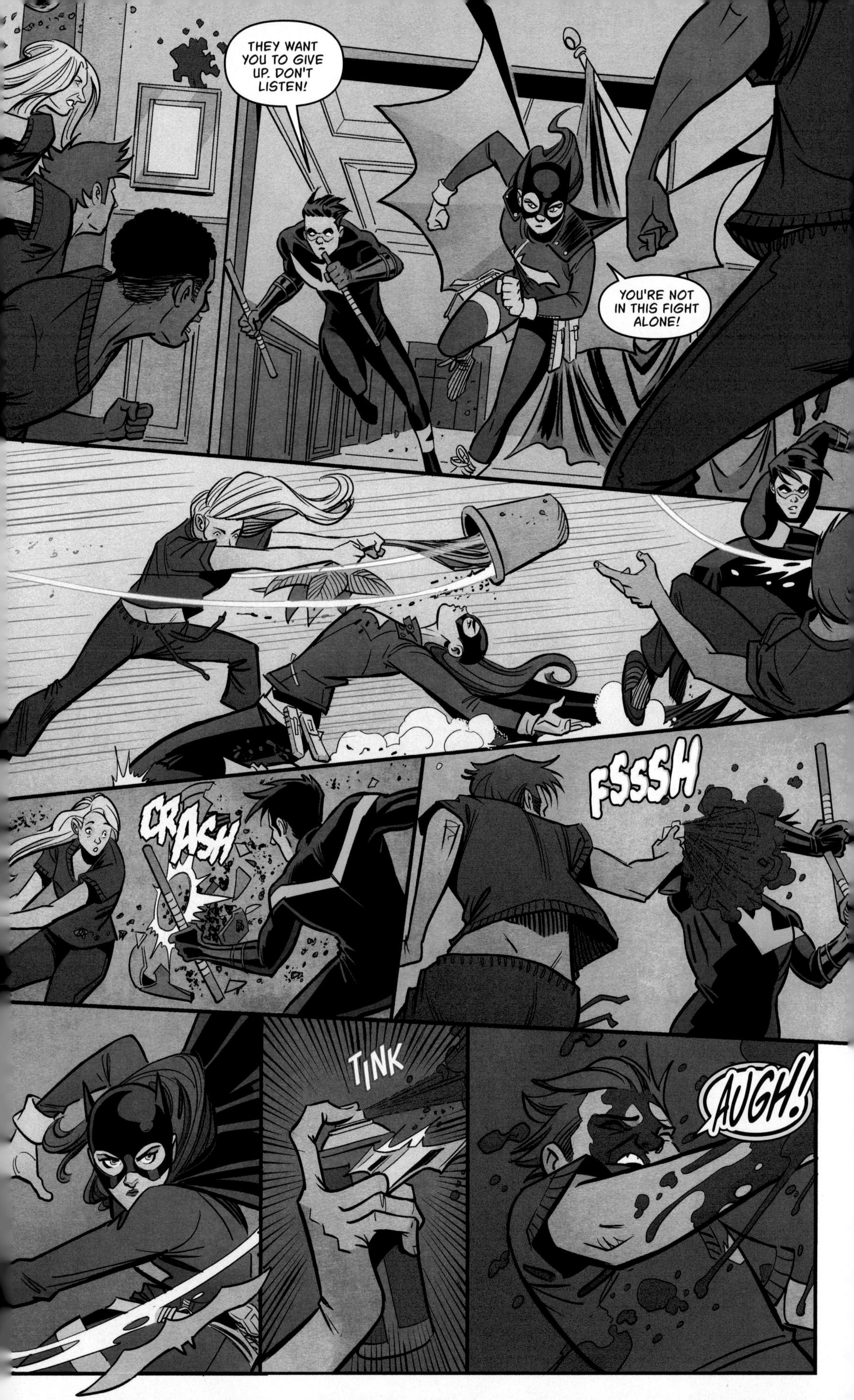
THEY WANT YOU TO GIVE UP. DON'T LISTEN!
YOU'RE NOT IN THIS FIGHT ALONE!
CRASH
FSSSH
TINK
AUGH!

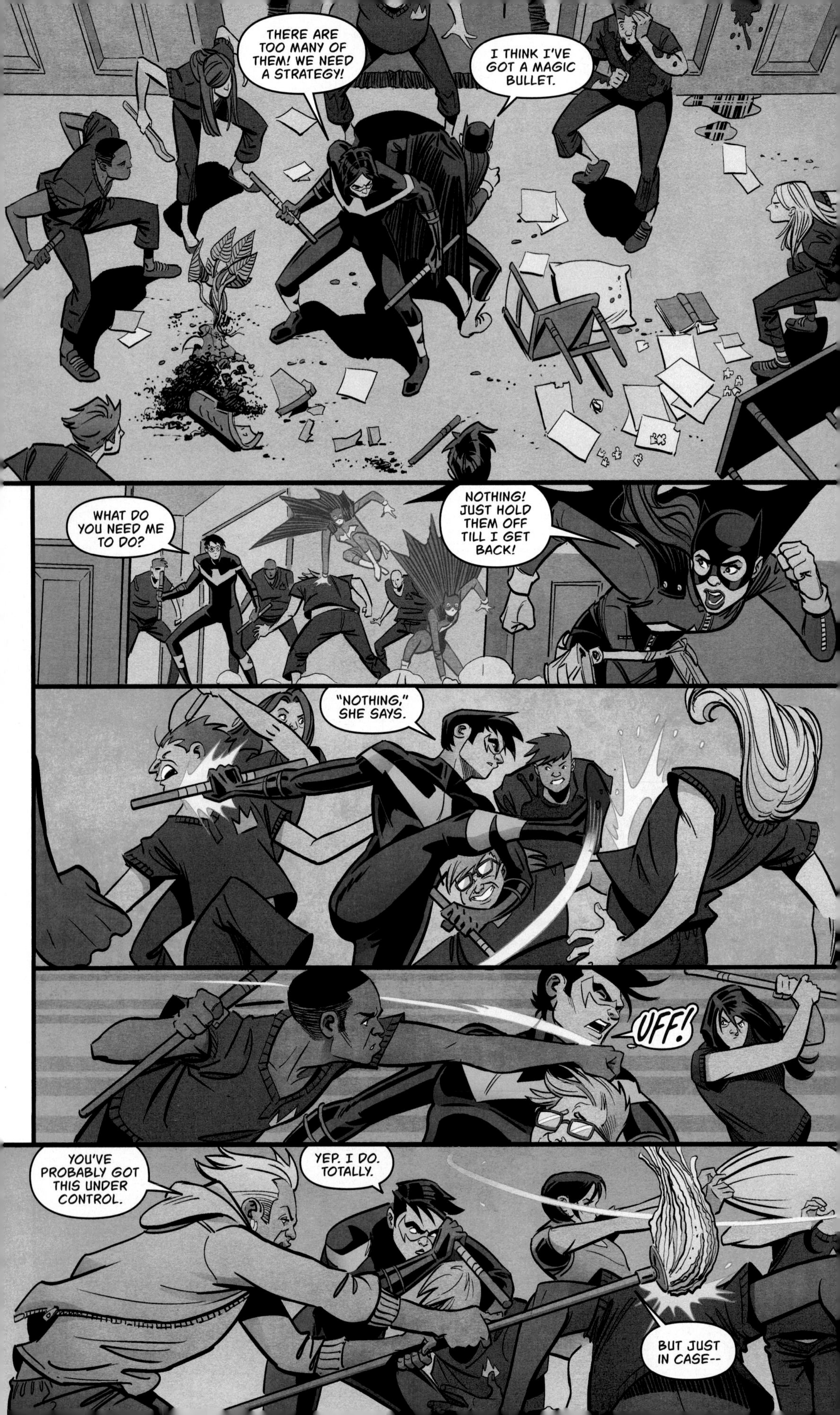
THERE ARE TOO MANY OF THEM! WE NEED A STRATEGY!
I THINK I'VE GOT A MAGIC BULLET.
WHAT DO YOU NEED ME TO DO?
NOTHING! JUST HOLD THEM OFF TILL I GET BACK!
"NOTHING," SHE SAYS.
UFF!
YOU'VE PROBABLY GOT THIS UNDER CONTROL.
YEP. I DO. TOTALLY.
BUT JUST IN CASE--

IF THE RED QUEEN IS **AINSLEY**, SHE PROBABLY BASED THESE NEW 'BOTS ON THE ONES SHE MADE FOR **THE HATTER**.

AND IF SHE RECYCLED HER ORIGINAL **CODE**--

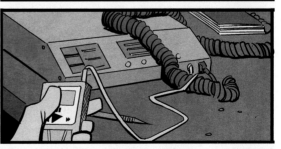

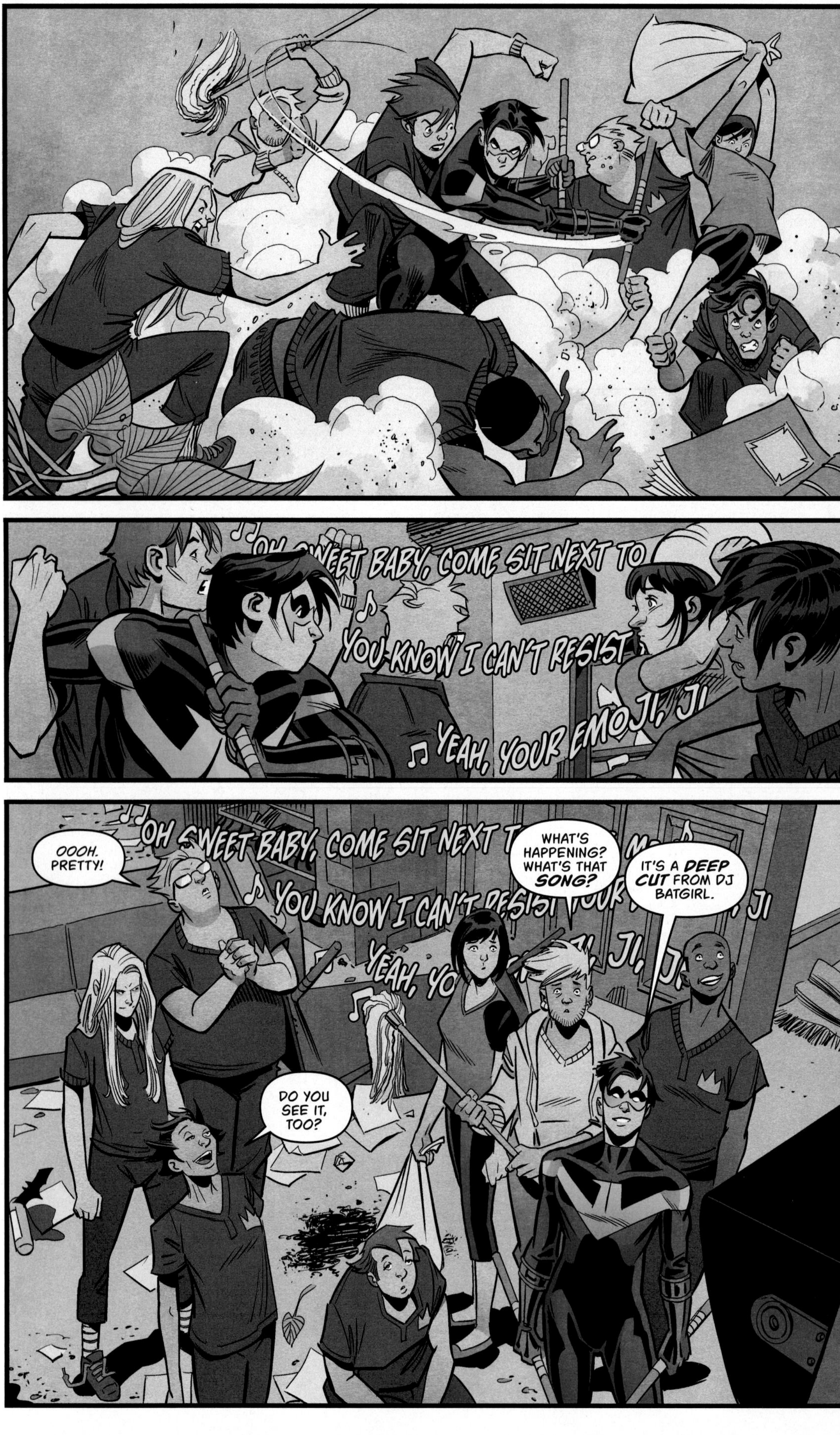
OH SWEET BABY, COME SIT NEXT TO
YOU KNOW I CAN'T RESIST
YEAH, YOUR EMOJI, JI
OOOH. PRETTY!
WHAT'S HAPPENING? WHAT'S THAT **SONG?**
IT'S A **DEEP CUT** FROM DJ BATGIRL.
DO YOU SEE IT, TOO?

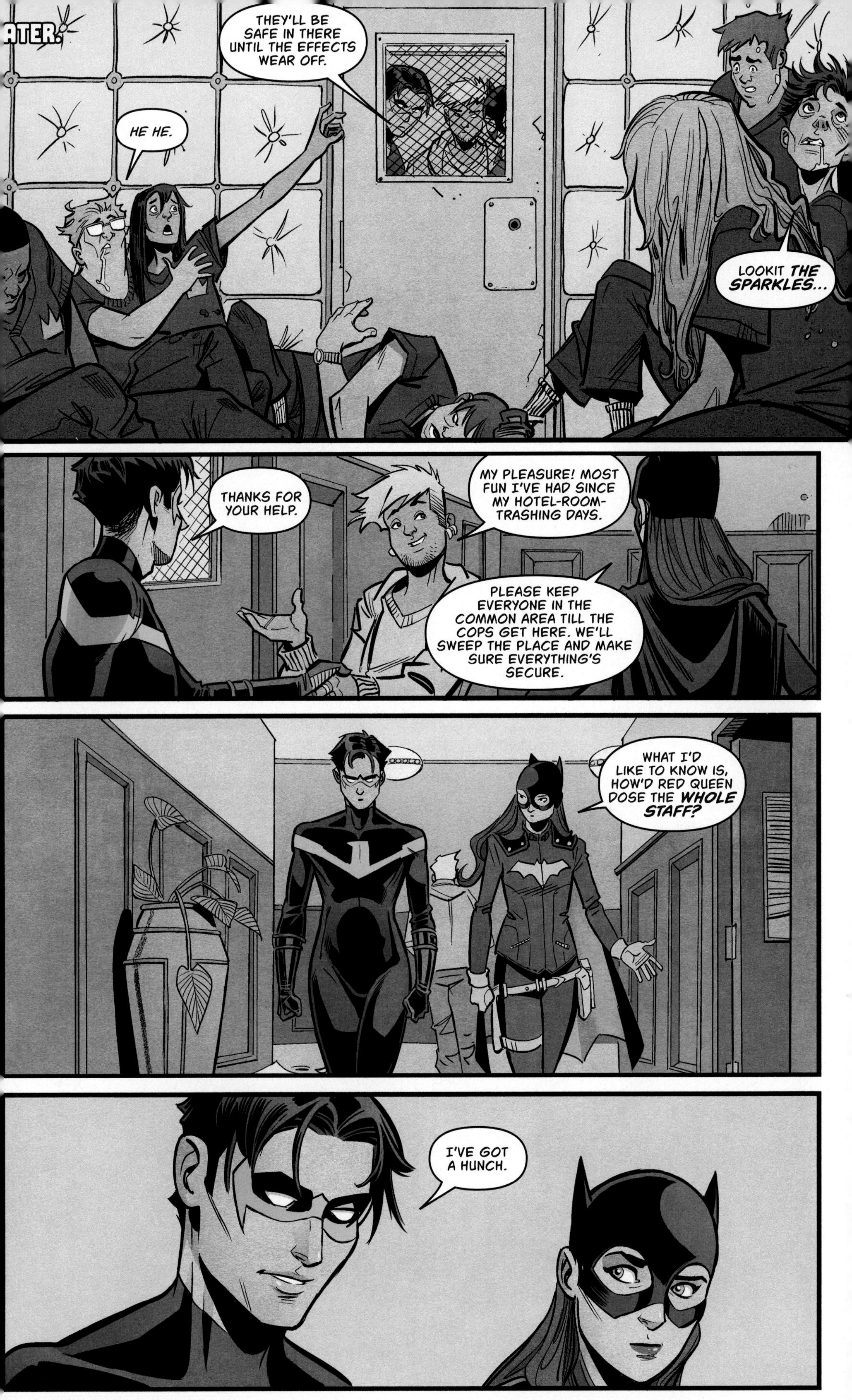

ATER.
THEY'LL BE SAFE IN THERE UNTIL THE EFFECTS WEAR OFF.
HE HE.
LOOKIT THE SPARKLES...
THANKS FOR YOUR HELP.
MY PLEASURE! MOST FUN I'VE HAD SINCE MY HOTEL-ROOM-TRASHING DAYS.
PLEASE KEEP EVERYONE IN THE COMMON AREA TILL THE COPS GET HERE. WE'LL SWEEP THE PLACE AND MAKE SURE EVERYTHING'S SECURE.
WHAT I'D LIKE TO KNOW IS, HOW'D RED QUEEN DOSE THE WHOLE STAFF?
I'VE GOT A HUNCH.

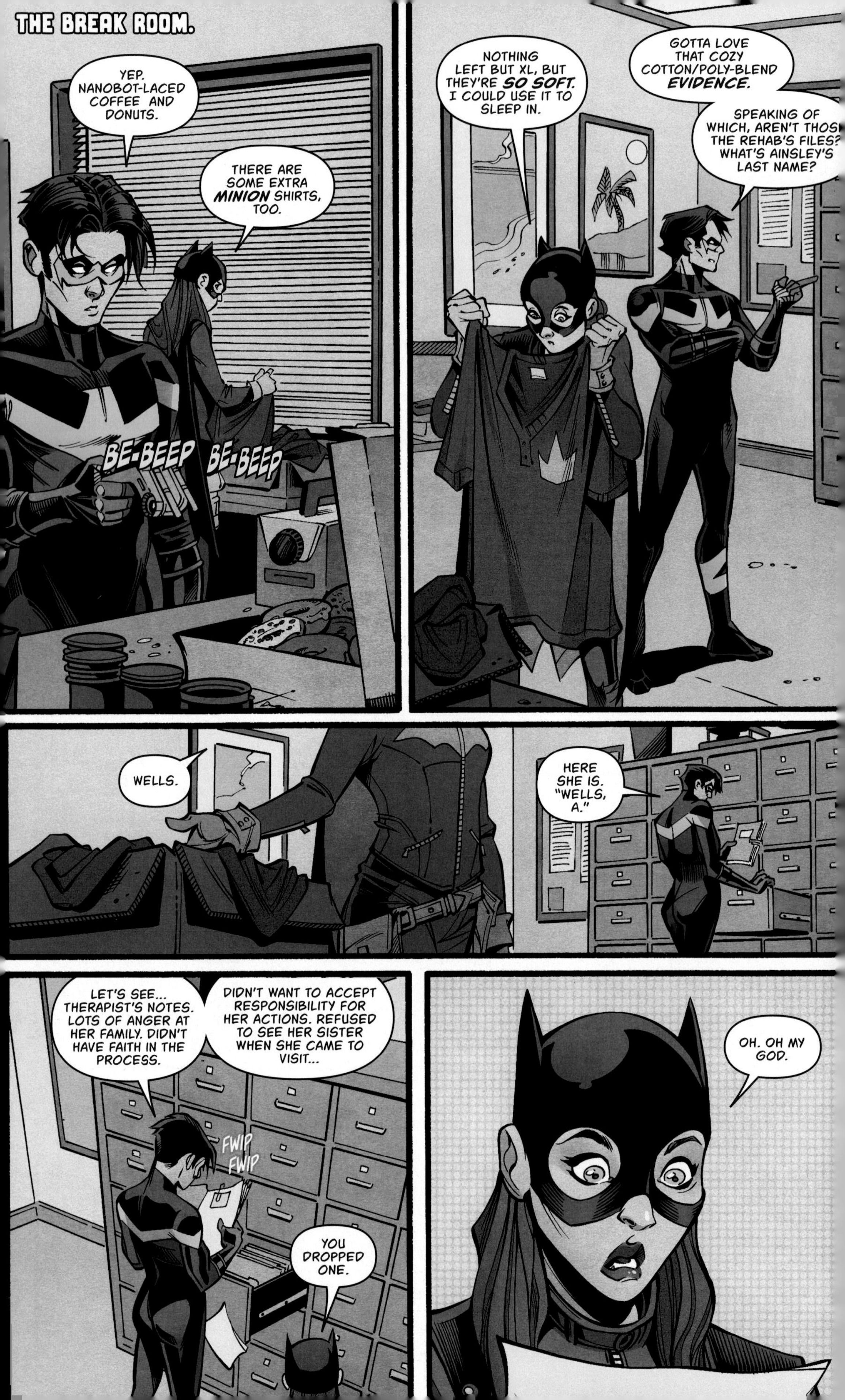
THE BREAK ROOM.
YEP. NANOBOT-LACED COFFEE AND DONUTS.
THERE ARE SOME EXTRA MINION SHIRTS, TOO.
BE-BEEP BE-BEEP
NOTHING LEFT BUT XL, BUT THEY'RE SO SOFT. I COULD USE IT TO SLEEP IN.
GOTTA LOVE THAT COZY COTTON/POLY-BLEND EVIDENCE.
SPEAKING OF WHICH, AREN'T THOS THE REHAB'S FILES? WHAT'S AINSLEY'S LAST NAME?
WELLS.
HERE SHE IS. "WELLS, A."
LET'S SEE... THERAPIST'S NOTES. LOTS OF ANGER AT HER FAMILY. DIDN'T HAVE FAITH IN THE PROCESS.
DIDN'T WANT TO ACCEPT RESPONSIBILITY FOR HER ACTIONS. REFUSED TO SEE HER SISTER WHEN SHE CAME TO VISIT...
FWIP FWIP
YOU DROPPED ONE.
OH. OH MY GOD.

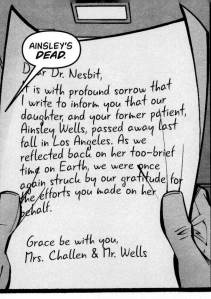

AINSLEY'S *DEAD*.

Dear Dr. Nesbit,

It is with profound sorrow that I write to inform you that our daughter, and your former patient, Ainsley Wells, passed away last fall in Los Angeles. As we reflected back on her too-brief time on Earth, we were once again struck by our gratitude for the efforts you made on her behalf.

Grace be with you,
Mrs. Challen & Mr. Wells

OH NO. I'M SO SORRY. I KNOW YOU WERE HOPING--

SHE OD'D ON THE STREET. SHE'D BEEN HOMELESS FOR MONTHS. SHE WAS ALONE.

THE ONLY THINGS SHE OWNED WERE HER CLOTHES, A COUPLE KNICKKNACKS AND HER JOURNAL.

CLEARWATER, FL, POLICE RECORDS

SHE WAS ALWAYS WRITING IN THAT JOURNAL. I'M SURE SHE WROTE ABOUT US.

IT SAYS HER EFFECTS AND REMAINS WERE PICKED UP BY EDITH WELLS. HER SISTER.

IF AINSLEY DOCUMENTED WHAT WE DID BACK THEN, AND EDITH *READ* ABOUT IT--

DITH IS E RED UEEN.

SHE'S GOT THE EVIDENCE *AND* THE MOTIVE.

SHE LOST HER SISTER.

THAT'S EDITH?

WE WERE JUST FIGHTING HER. SHE'S ONE OF THE STAFF MEMBERS.

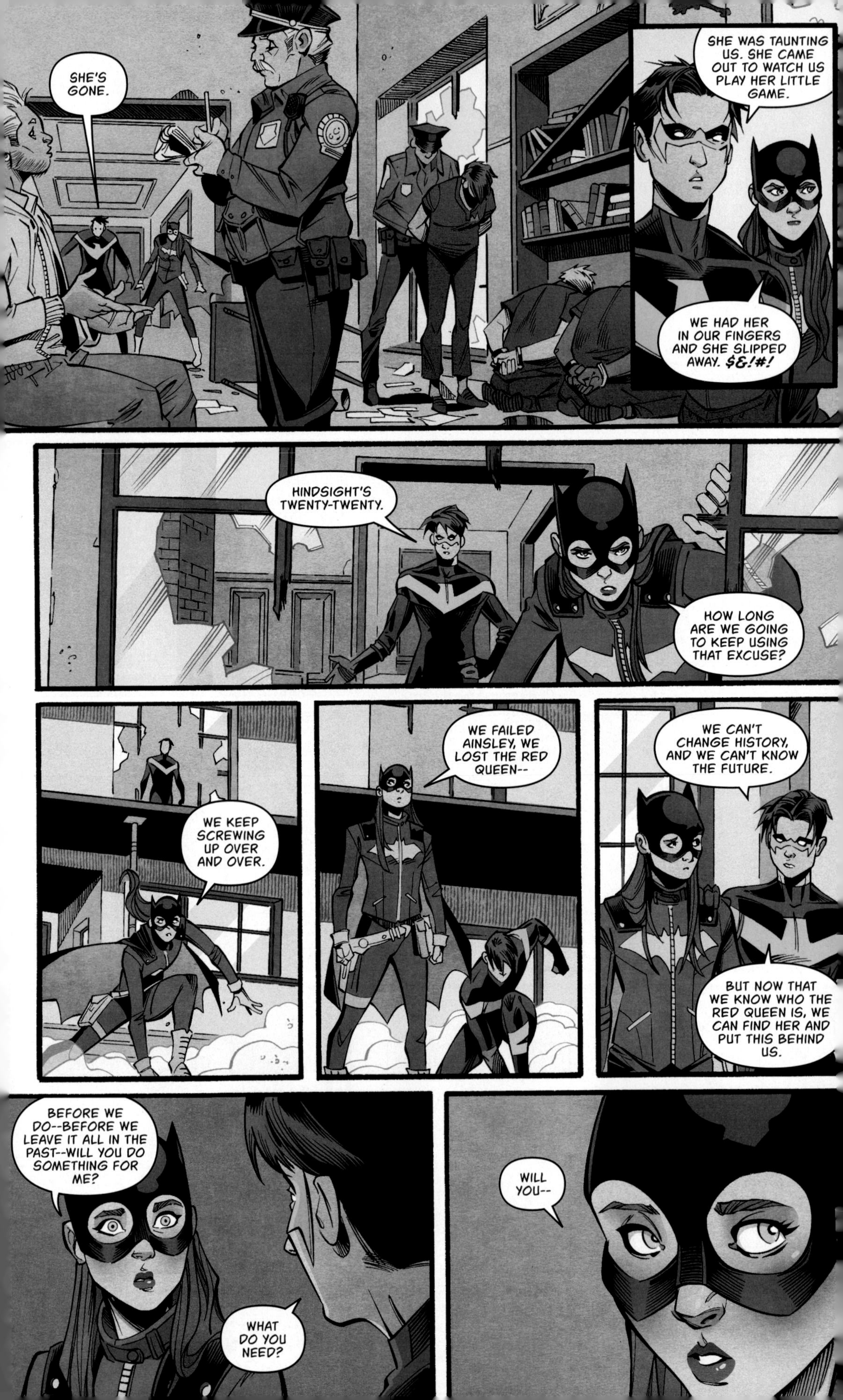
SHE'S GONE.
SHE WAS TAUNTING US. SHE CAME OUT TO WATCH US PLAY HER LITTLE GAME.
WE HAD HER IN OUR FINGERS AND SHE SLIPPED AWAY. $&!#!
HINDSIGHT'S TWENTY-TWENTY.
HOW LONG ARE WE GOING TO KEEP USING THAT EXCUSE?
WE KEEP SCREWING UP OVER AND OVER.
WE FAILED AINSLEY, WE LOST THE RED QUEEN--
WE CAN'T CHANGE HISTORY, AND WE CAN'T KNOW THE FUTURE.
BUT NOW THAT WE KNOW WHO THE RED QUEEN IS, WE CAN FIND HER AND PUT THIS BEHIND US.
BEFORE WE DO--BEFORE WE LEAVE IT ALL IN THE PAST--WILL YOU DO SOMETHING FOR ME?
WHAT DO YOU NEED?
WILL YOU--

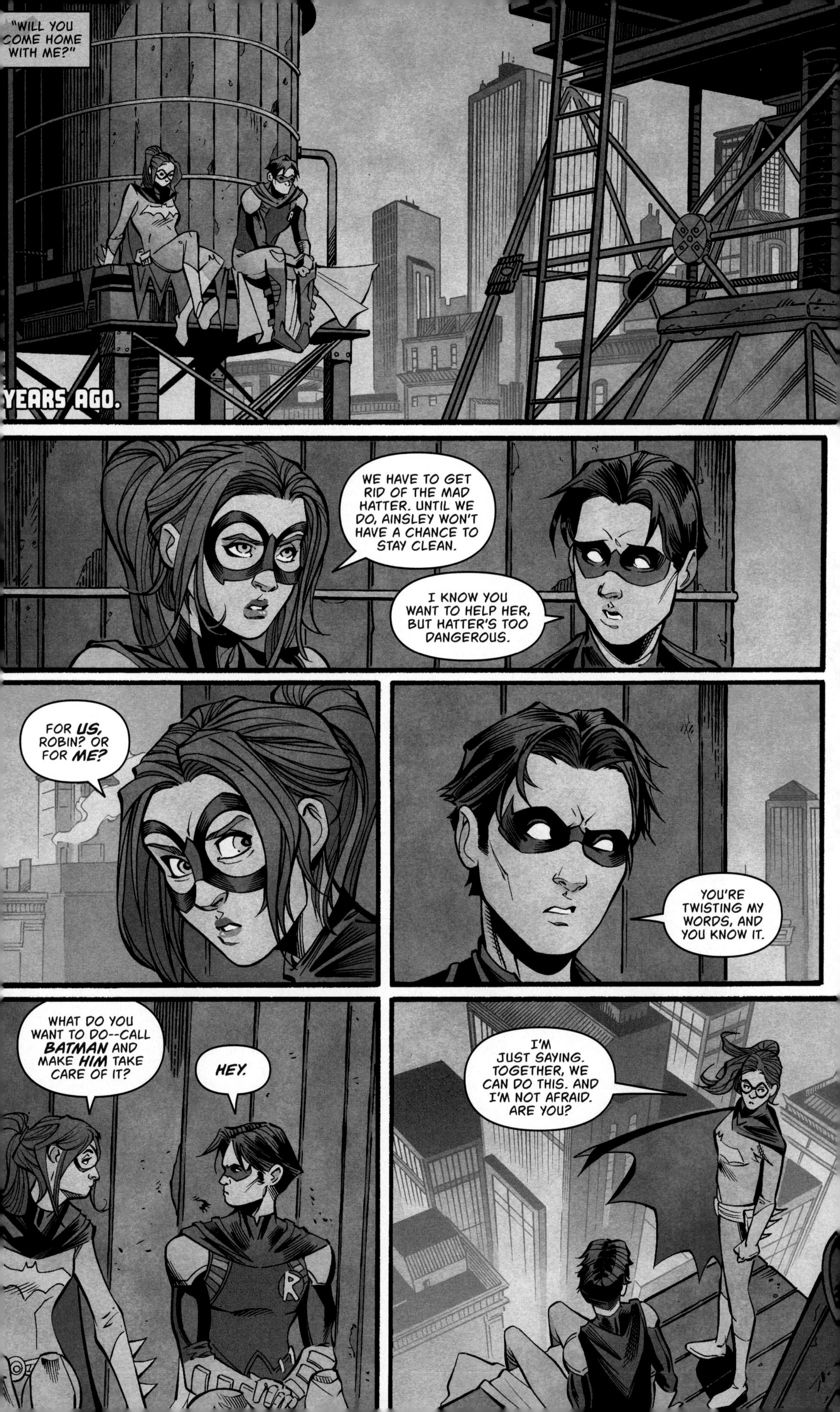
"WILL YOU COME HOME WITH ME?"
YEARS AGO.
WE HAVE TO GET RID OF THE MAD HATTER. UNTIL WE DO, AINSLEY WON'T HAVE A CHANCE TO STAY CLEAN.
I KNOW YOU WANT TO HELP HER, BUT HATTER'S TOO DANGEROUS.
FOR US, ROBIN? OR FOR ME?
YOU'RE TWISTING MY WORDS, AND YOU KNOW IT.
WHAT DO YOU WANT TO DO--CALL BATMAN AND MAKE HIM TAKE CARE OF IT?
HEY.
I'M JUST SAYING. TOGETHER, WE CAN DO THIS. AND I'M NOT AFRAID. ARE YOU?

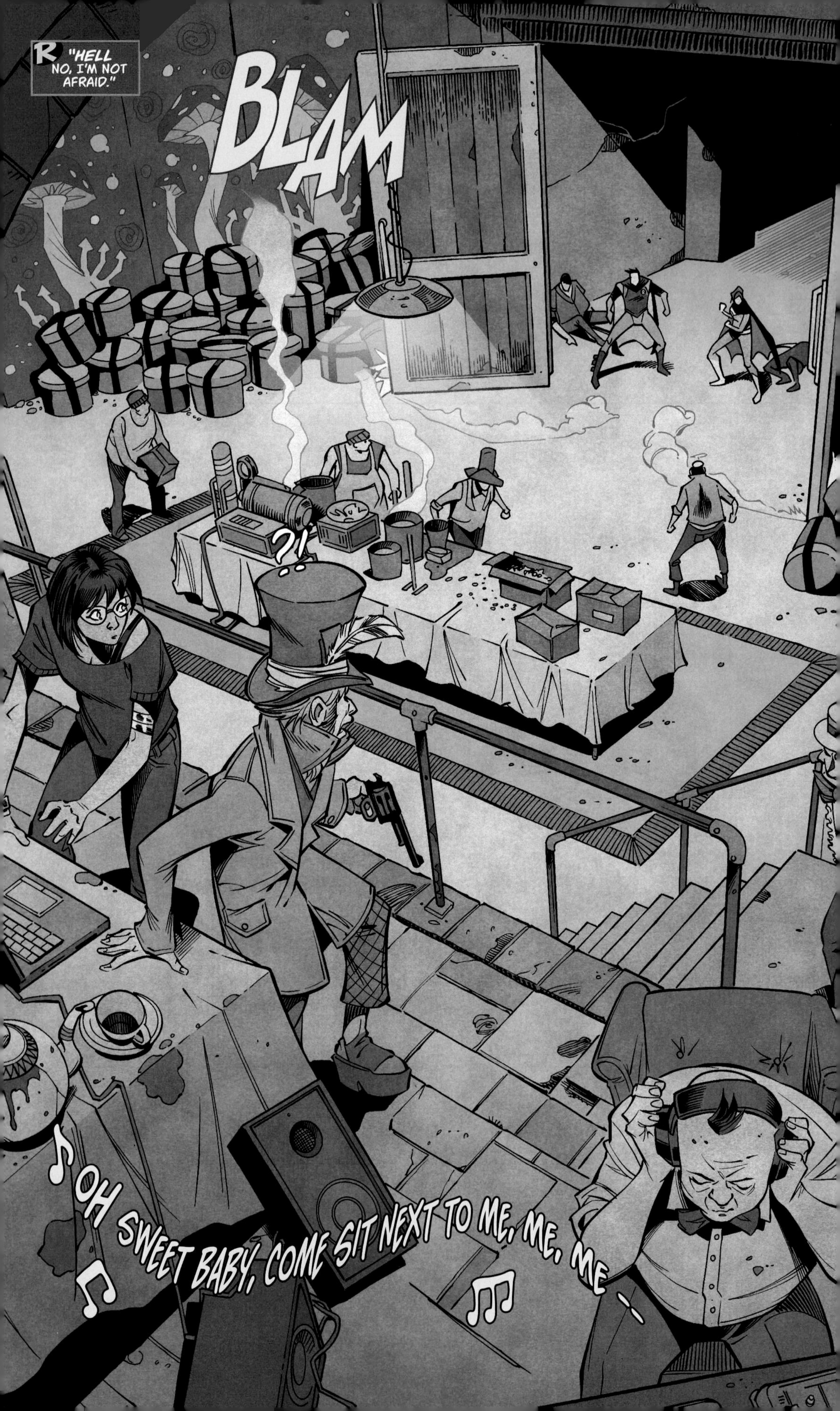
"HELL NO, I'M NOT AFRAID."
BLAM
?!
OH SWEET BABY, COME SIT NEXT TO ME, ME, ME --

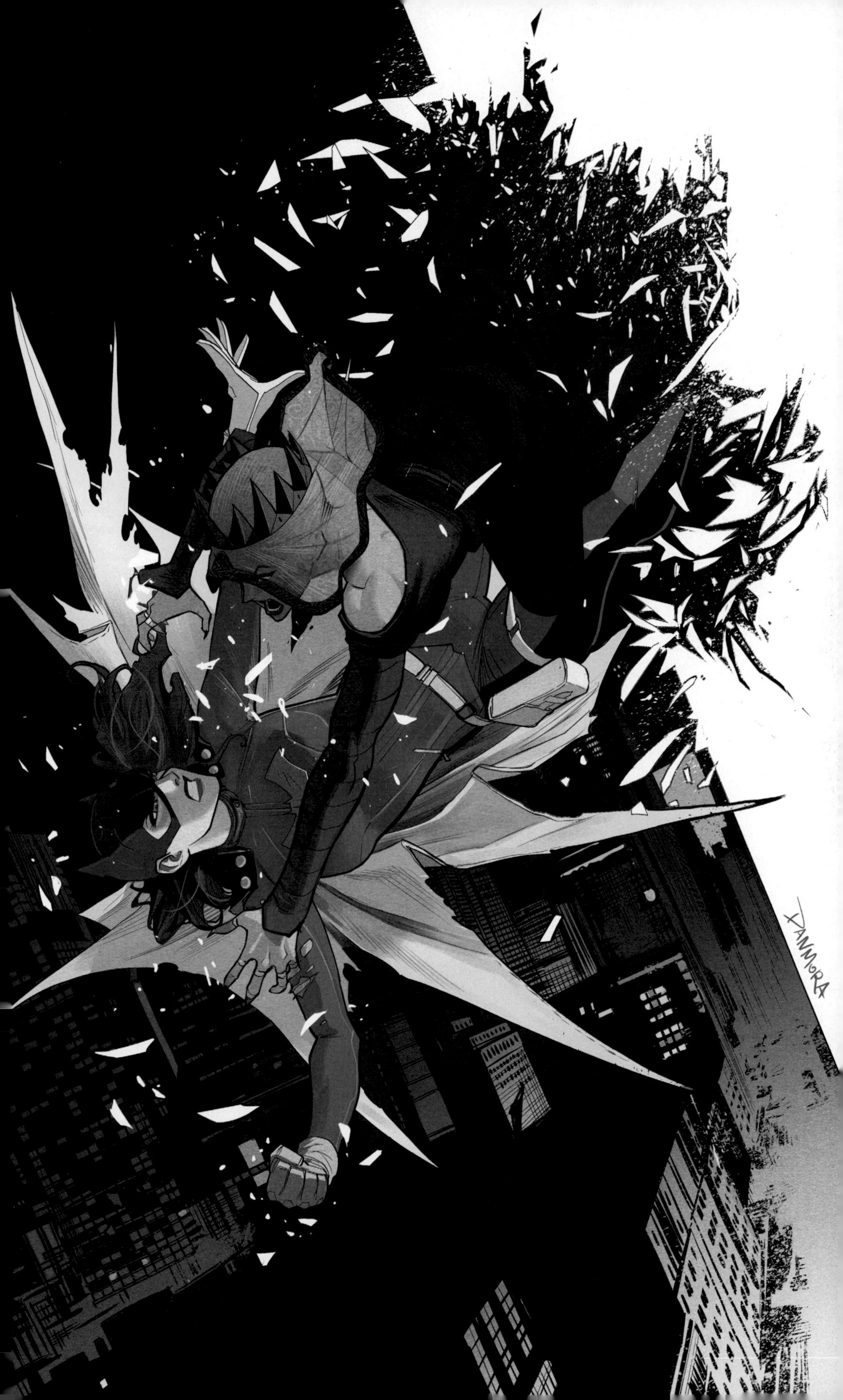
DANMORA

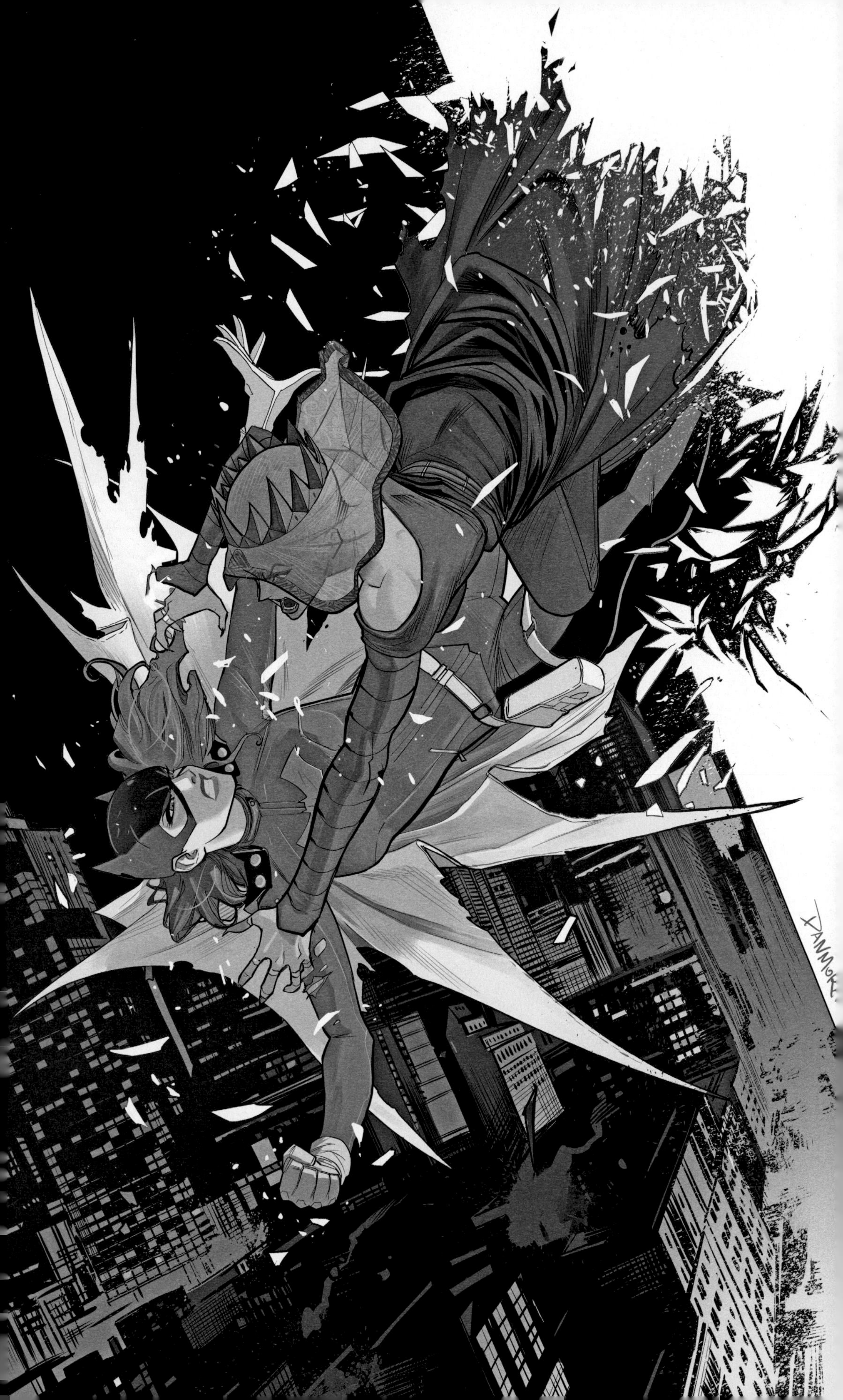

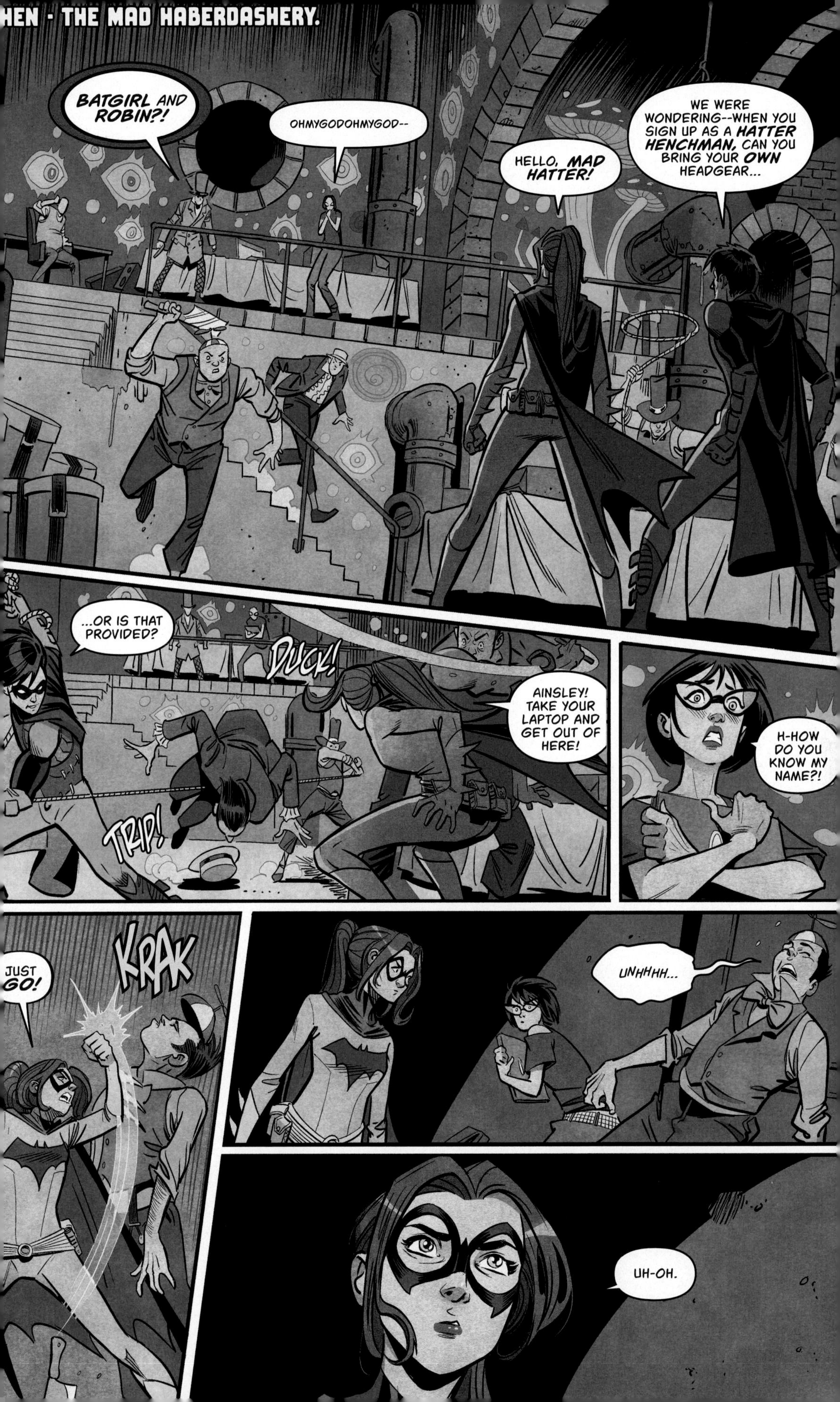
HEN - THE MAD HABERDASHERY.
BATGIRL AND ROBIN?!
OHMYGODOHMYGOD--
HELLO, MAD HATTER!
WE WERE WONDERING--WHEN YOU SIGN UP AS A HATTER HENCHMAN, CAN YOU BRING YOUR OWN HEADGEAR...
...OR IS THAT PROVIDED?
DUCK!
TRIP!
AINSLEY! TAKE YOUR LAPTOP AND GET OUT OF HERE!
H-HOW DO YOU KNOW MY NAME?!
KRAK
JUST GO!
UNHHHH...
UH-OH.

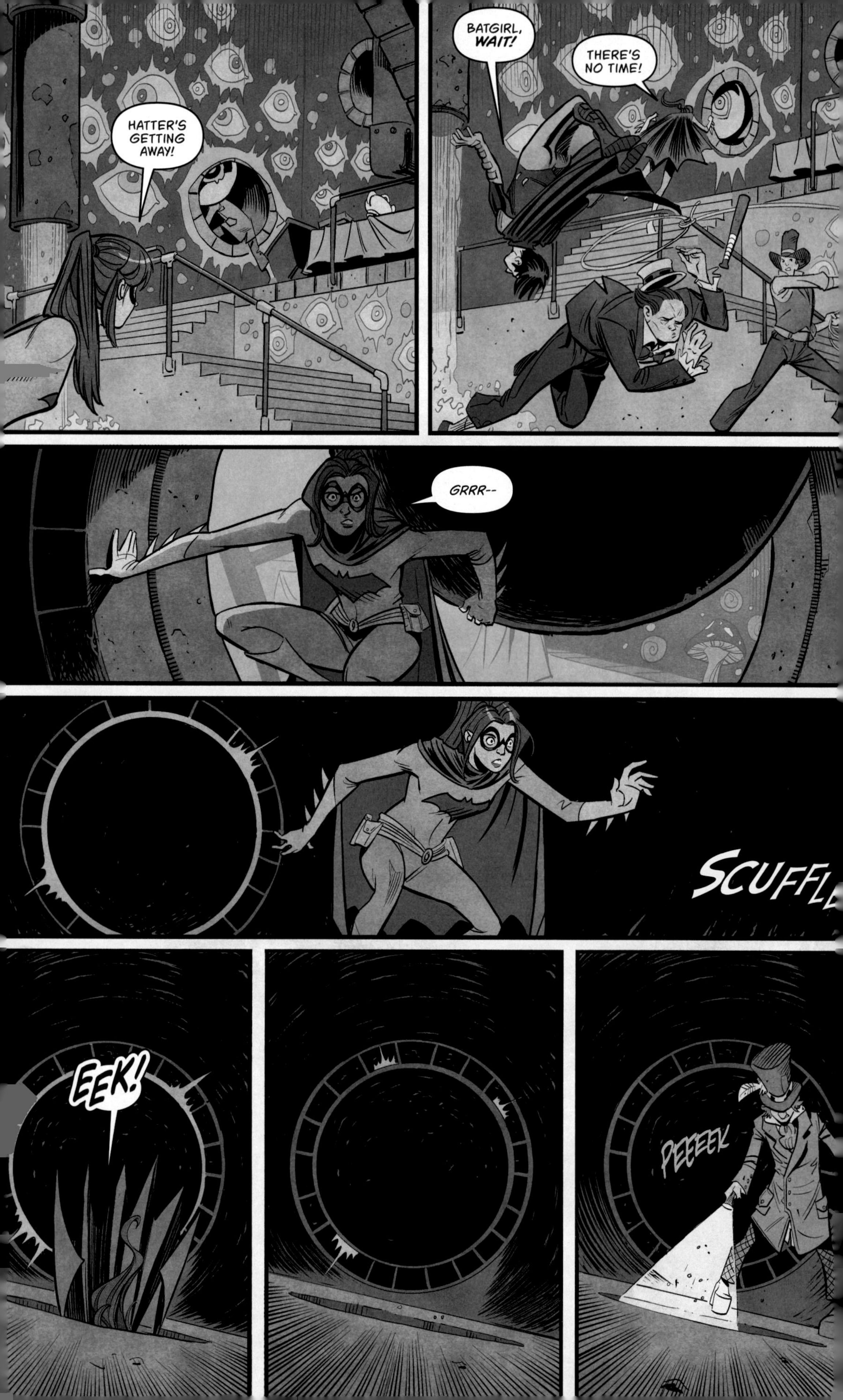
HATTER'S GETTING AWAY!
BATGIRL, WAIT!
THERE'S NO TIME!
GRRR--
SCUFFLE
EEK!
PEEEEK

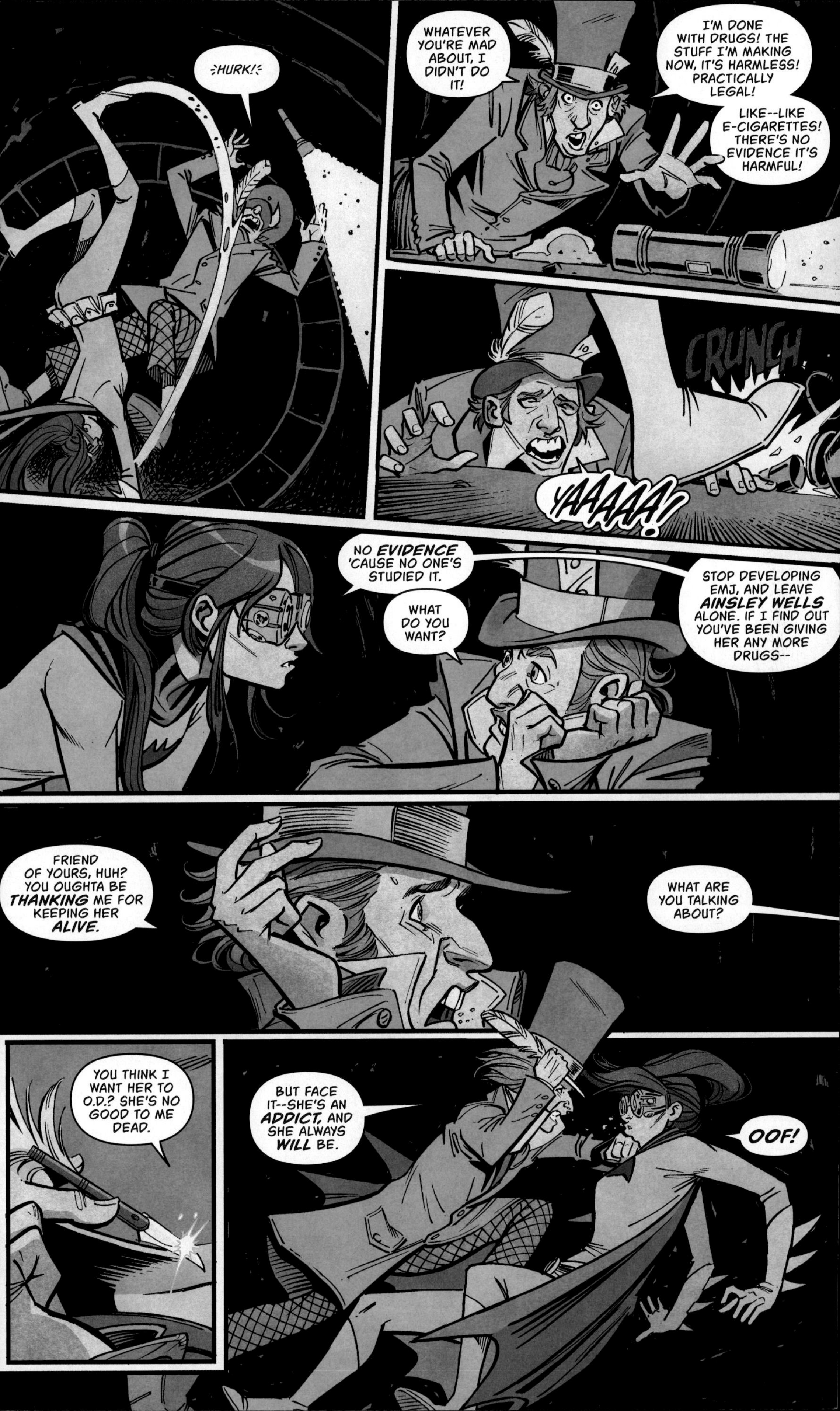

HURK!
WHATEVER YOU'RE MAD ABOUT, I DIDN'T DO IT!
I'M DONE WITH DRUGS! THE STUFF I'M MAKING NOW, IT'S HARMLESS! PRACTICALLY LEGAL!
LIKE--LIKE E-CIGARETTES! THERE'S NO EVIDENCE IT'S HARMFUL!
CRUNCH
YAAAAA!
NO **EVIDENCE** 'CAUSE NO ONE'S STUDIED IT.
WHAT DO YOU WANT?
STOP DEVELOPING EMJ, AND LEAVE **AINSLEY WELLS** ALONE. IF I FIND OUT YOU'VE BEEN GIVING HER ANY MORE DRUGS--
FRIEND OF YOURS, HUH? YOU OUGHTA BE **THANKING** ME FOR KEEPING HER **ALIVE.**
WHAT ARE YOU TALKING ABOUT?
YOU THINK I WANT HER TO O.D.? SHE'S NO GOOD TO ME DEAD.
BUT FACE IT--SHE'S AN **ADDICT,** AND SHE ALWAYS **WILL** BE.
OOF!

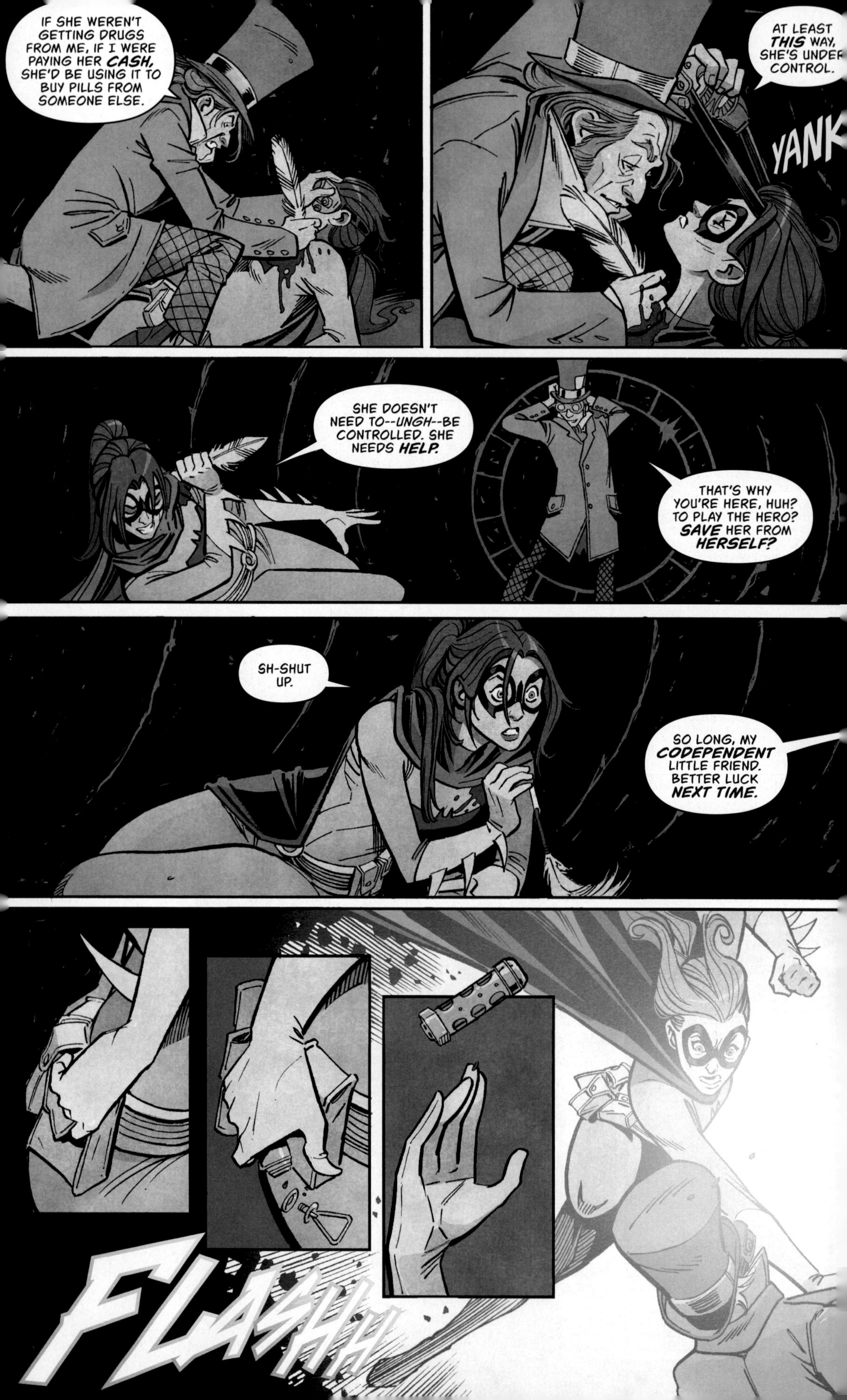
IF SHE WEREN'T GETTING DRUGS FROM ME, IF I WERE PAYING HER CASH, SHE'D BE USING IT TO BUY PILLS FROM SOMEONE ELSE.
AT LEAST THIS WAY, SHE'S UNDER CONTROL.
YANK
SHE DOESN'T NEED TO--UNGH--BE CONTROLLED. SHE NEEDS HELP.
THAT'S WHY YOU'RE HERE, HUH? TO PLAY THE HERO? SAVE HER FROM HERSELF?
SH-SHUT UP.
SO LONG, MY CODEPENDENT LITTLE FRIEND. BETTER LUCK NEXT TIME.
FLASHH

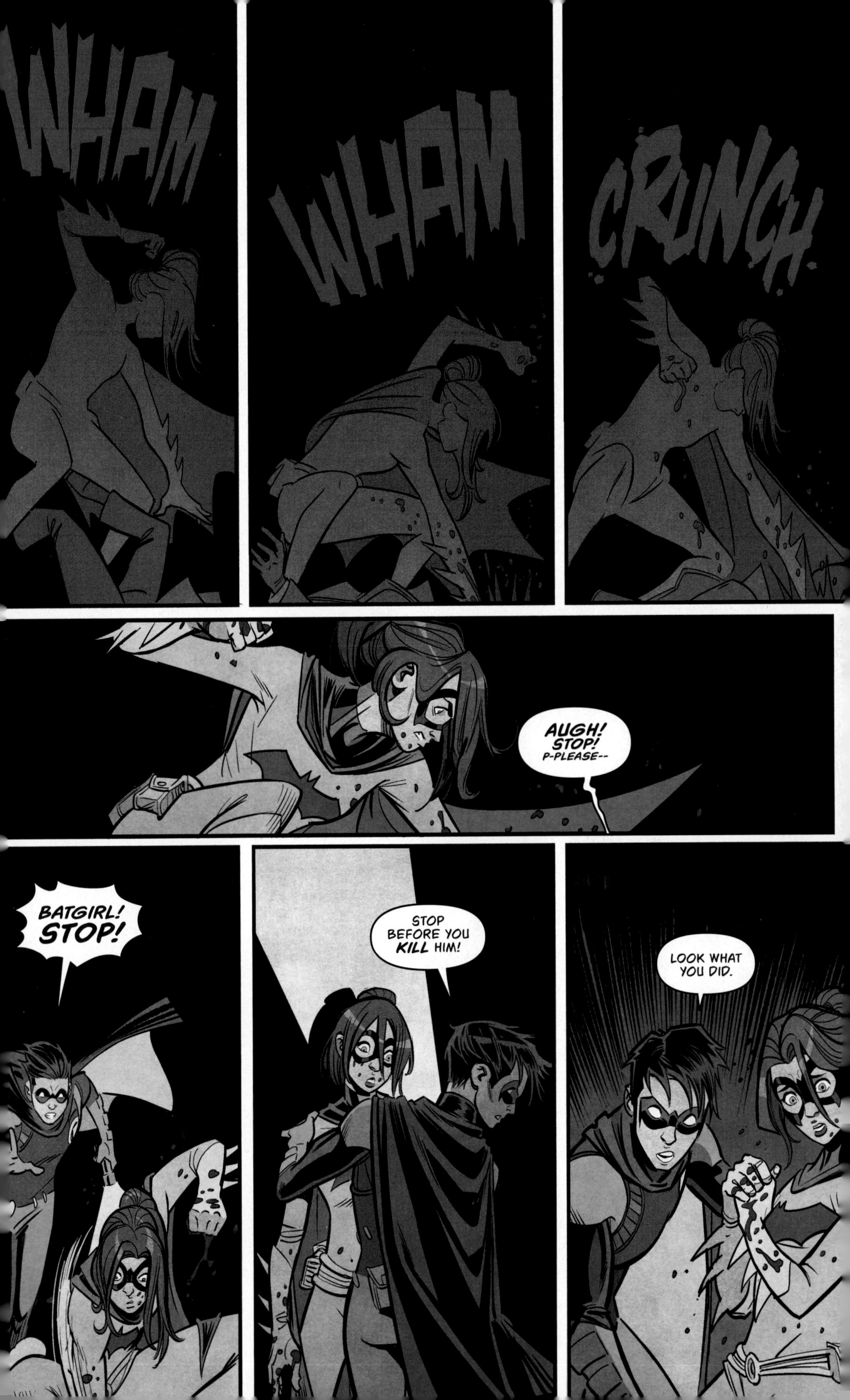
WHAM
WHAM
CRUNCH
AUGH! STOP! P-PLEASE--
BATGIRL! STOP!
STOP BEFORE YOU KILL HIM!
LOOK WHAT YOU DID.

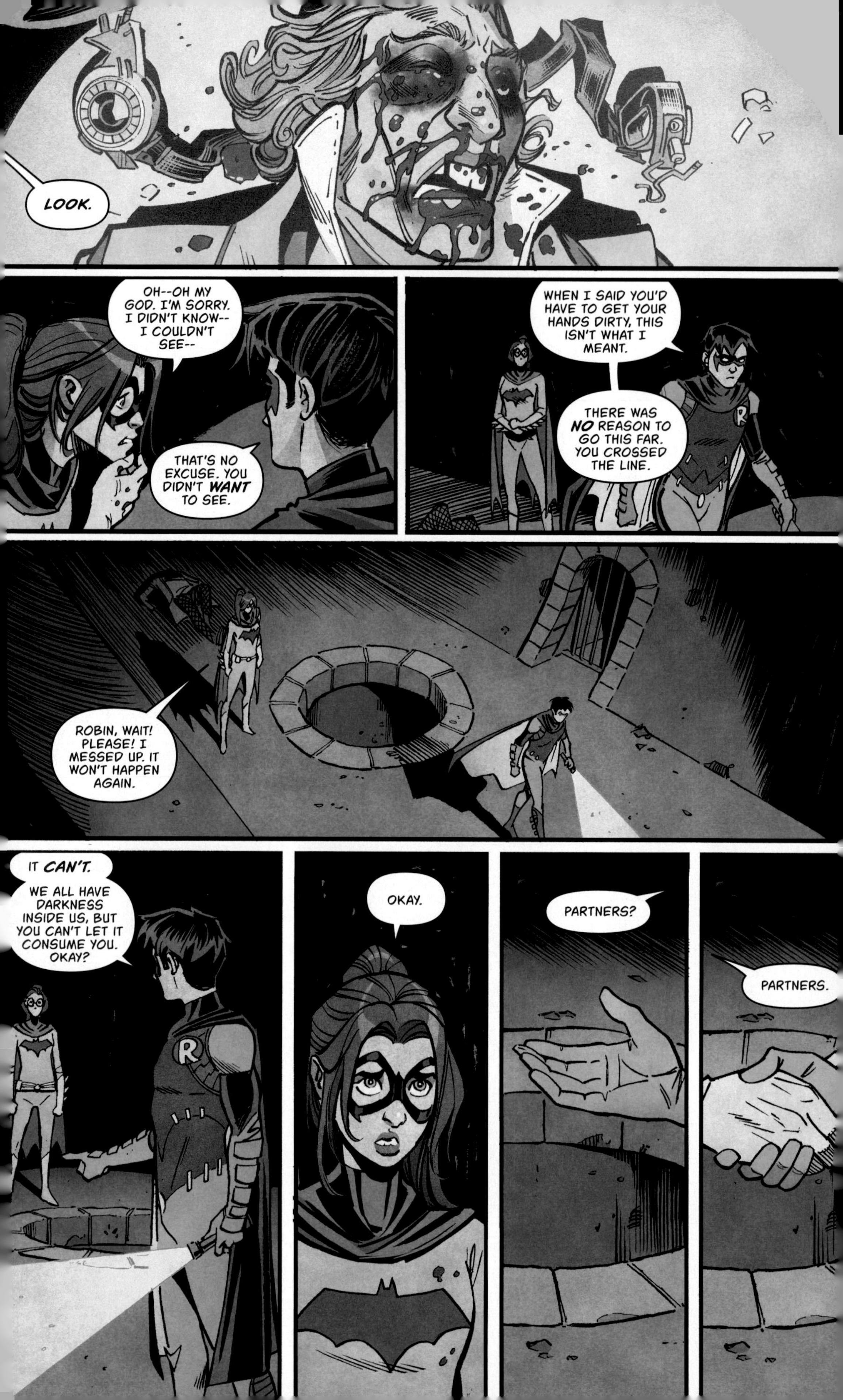
LOOK.
OH--OH MY GOD. I'M SORRY. I DIDN'T KNOW-- I COULDN'T SEE--
THAT'S NO EXCUSE. YOU DIDN'T **WANT** TO SEE.
WHEN I SAID YOU'D HAVE TO GET YOUR HANDS DIRTY, THIS ISN'T WHAT I MEANT.
THERE WAS **NO** REASON TO GO THIS FAR. YOU CROSSED THE LINE.
ROBIN, WAIT! PLEASE! I MESSED UP. IT WON'T HAPPEN AGAIN.
IT **CAN'T.**
WE ALL HAVE DARKNESS INSIDE US, BUT YOU CAN'T LET IT CONSUME YOU. OKAY?
OKAY.
PARTNERS?
PARTNERS.

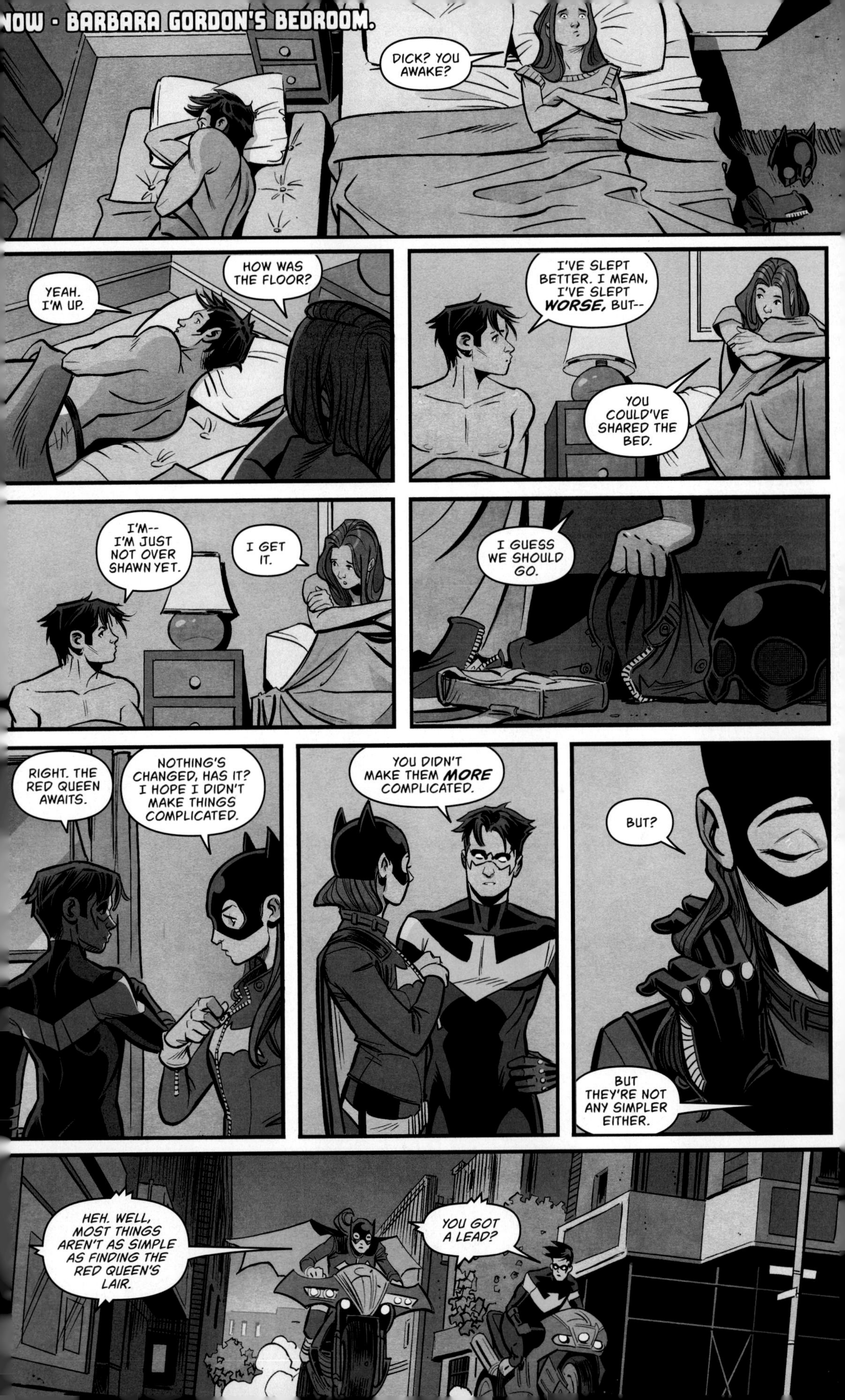
NOW - BARBARA GORDON'S BEDROOM.
DICK? YOU AWAKE?
YEAH. I'M UP.
HOW WAS THE FLOOR?
I'VE SLEPT BETTER. I MEAN, I'VE SLEPT WORSE, BUT--
YOU COULD'VE SHARED THE BED.
I'M-- I'M JUST NOT OVER SHAWN YET.
I GET IT.
I GUESS WE SHOULD GO.
RIGHT. THE RED QUEEN AWAITS.
NOTHING'S CHANGED, HAS IT? I HOPE I DIDN'T MAKE THINGS COMPLICATED.
YOU DIDN'T MAKE THEM MORE COMPLICATED.
BUT?
BUT THEY'RE NOT ANY SIMPLER EITHER.
HEH. WELL, MOST THINGS AREN'T AS SIMPLE AS FINDING THE RED QUEEN'S LAIR.
YOU GOT A LEAD?

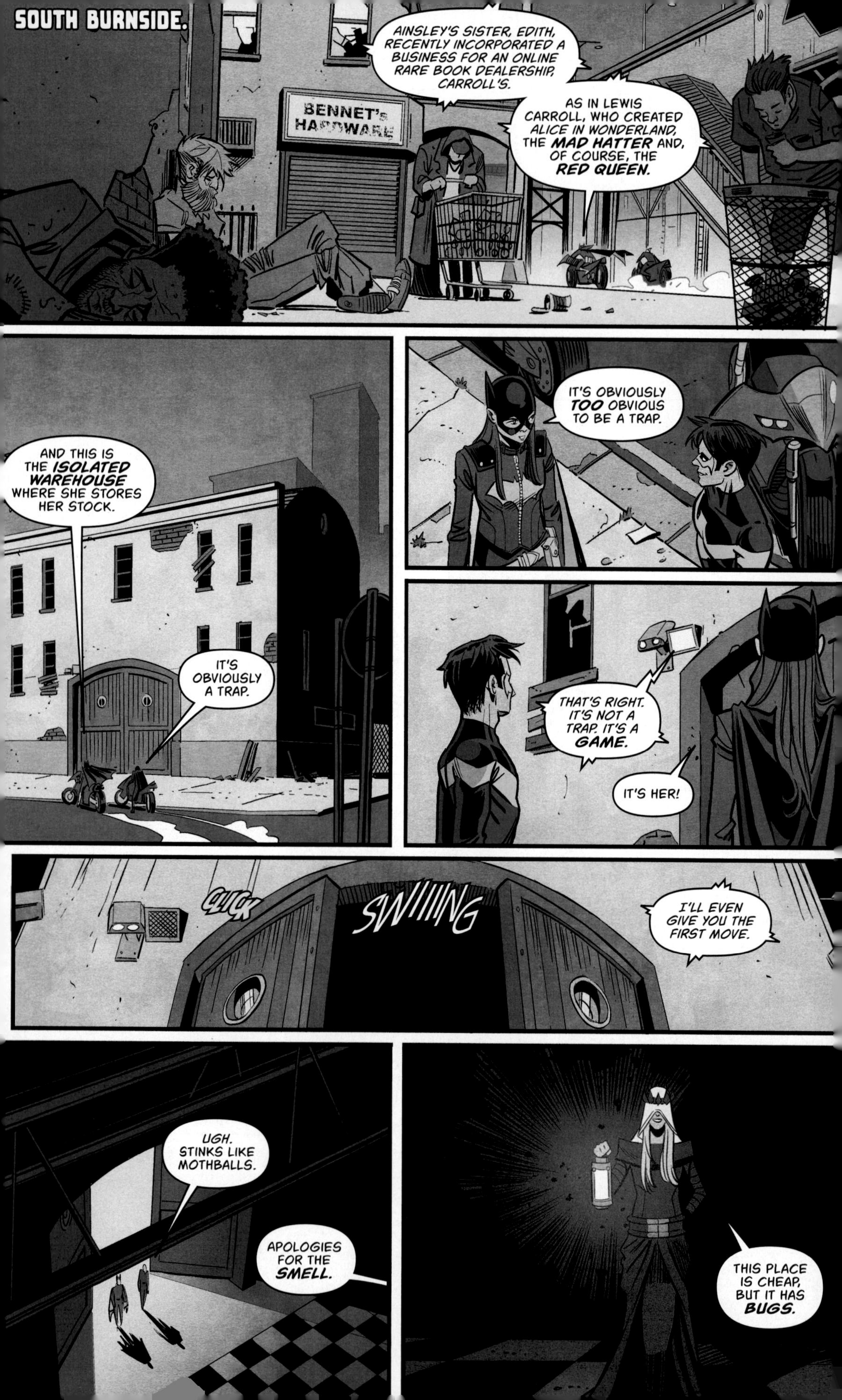
SOUTH BURNSIDE.
BENNET's HARDWARE
AINSLEY'S SISTER, EDITH, RECENTLY INCORPORATED A BUSINESS FOR AN ONLINE RARE BOOK DEALERSHIP, CARROLL'S.
AS IN LEWIS CARROLL, WHO CREATED ALICE IN WONDERLAND, THE MAD HATTER AND, OF COURSE, THE RED QUEEN.
AND THIS IS THE ISOLATED WAREHOUSE WHERE SHE STORES HER STOCK.
IT'S OBVIOUSLY A TRAP.
IT'S OBVIOUSLY TOO OBVIOUS TO BE A TRAP.
THAT'S RIGHT. IT'S NOT A TRAP. IT'S A GAME.
IT'S HER!
CLICK
SWIIIING
I'LL EVEN GIVE YOU THE FIRST MOVE.
UGH. STINKS LIKE MOTHBALLS.
APOLOGIES FOR THE SMELL.
THIS PLACE IS CHEAP, BUT IT HAS BUGS.

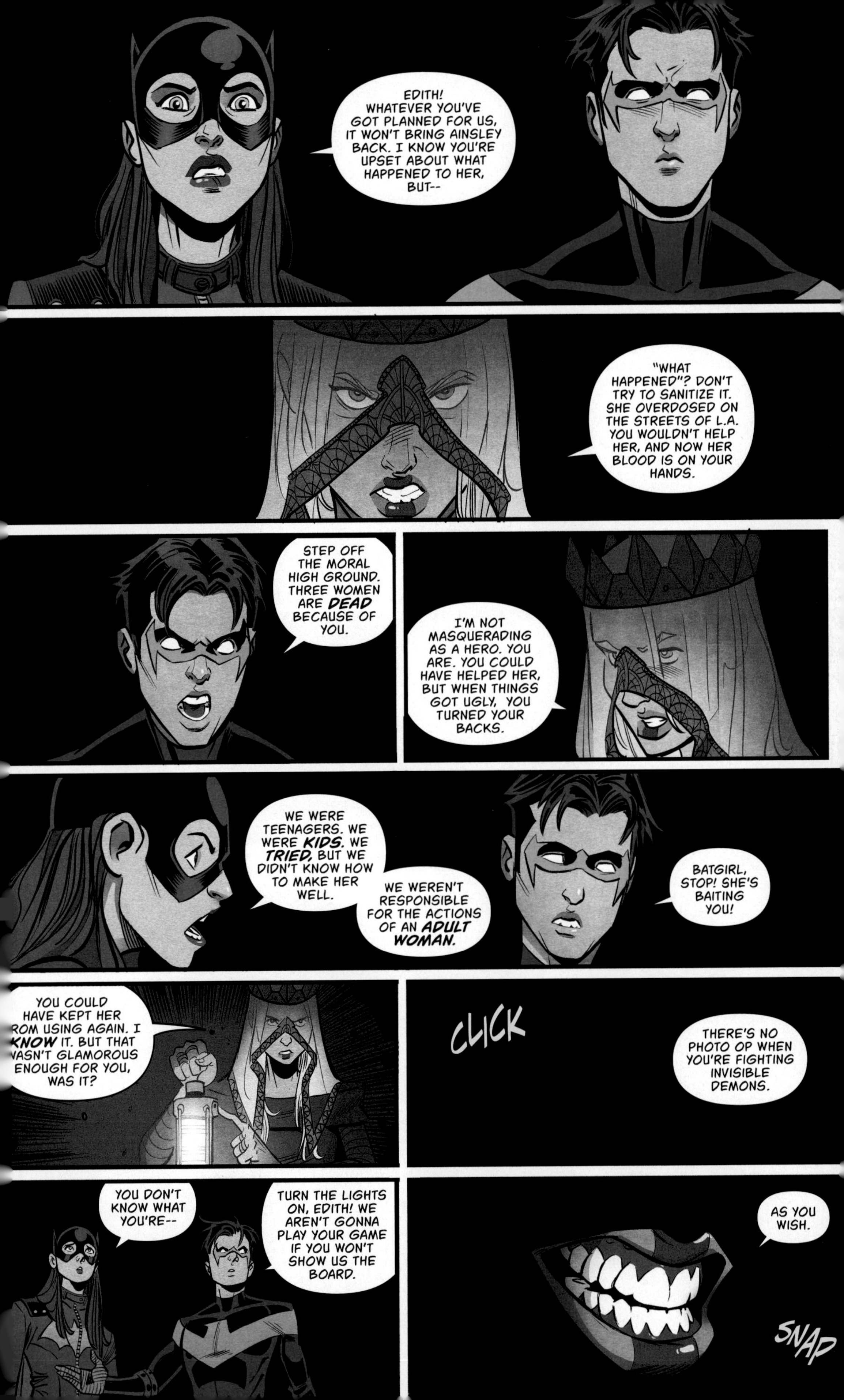
EDITH! WHATEVER YOU'VE GOT PLANNED FOR US, IT WON'T BRING AINSLEY BACK. I KNOW YOU'RE UPSET ABOUT WHAT HAPPENED TO HER, BUT--
"WHAT HAPPENED"? DON'T TRY TO SANITIZE IT. SHE OVERDOSED ON THE STREETS OF L.A. YOU WOULDN'T HELP HER, AND NOW HER BLOOD IS ON YOUR HANDS.
STEP OFF THE MORAL HIGH GROUND. THREE WOMEN ARE DEAD BECAUSE OF YOU.
I'M NOT MASQUERADING AS A HERO. YOU ARE. YOU COULD HAVE HELPED HER, BUT WHEN THINGS GOT UGLY, YOU TURNED YOUR BACKS.
WE WERE TEENAGERS. WE WERE KIDS. WE TRIED, BUT WE DIDN'T KNOW HOW TO MAKE HER WELL.
WE WEREN'T RESPONSIBLE FOR THE ACTIONS OF AN ADULT WOMAN.
BATGIRL, STOP! SHE'S BAITING YOU!
YOU COULD HAVE KEPT HER ROM USING AGAIN. I KNOW IT. BUT THAT VASN'T GLAMOROUS ENOUGH FOR YOU, WAS IT?
CLICK
THERE'S NO PHOTO OP WHEN YOU'RE FIGHTING INVISIBLE DEMONS.
YOU DON'T KNOW WHAT YOU'RE--
TURN THE LIGHTS ON, EDITH! WE AREN'T GONNA PLAY YOUR GAME IF YOU WON'T SHOW US THE BOARD.
AS YOU WISH.
SNAP

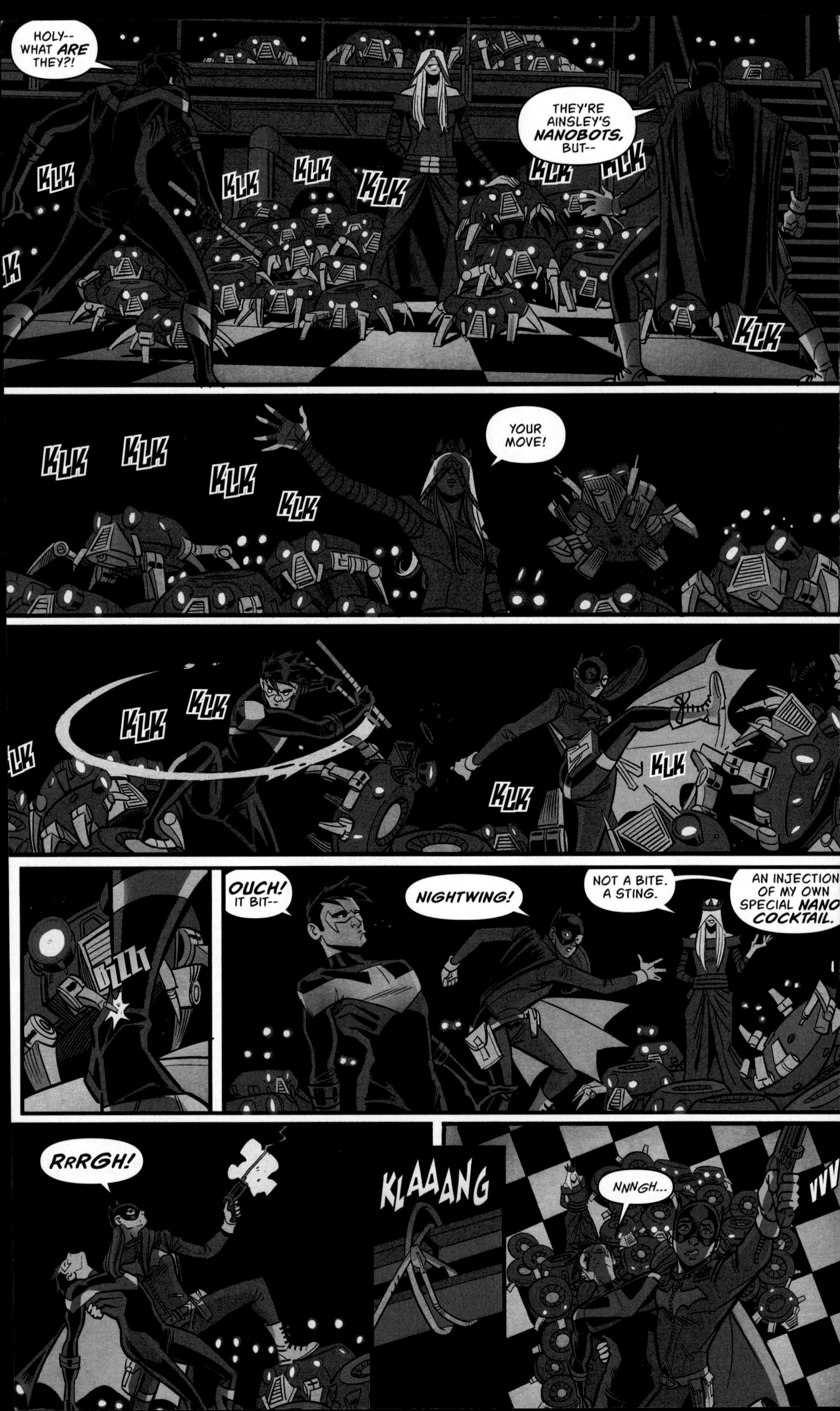
HOLY-- WHAT ARE THEY?!
THEY'RE AINSLEY'S NANOBOTS, BUT--
KLK
KLK
KLK
KLK
KLK
KLK
YOUR MOVE!
KLK
KLK
KLK
KLK
KLK
KLK
KLK
BZZZT
OUCH! IT BIT--
NIGHTWING!
NOT A BITE. A STING.
AN INJECTION OF MY OWN SPECIAL NANO COCKTAIL.
RRRGH!
KLAAANG
NNNGH...

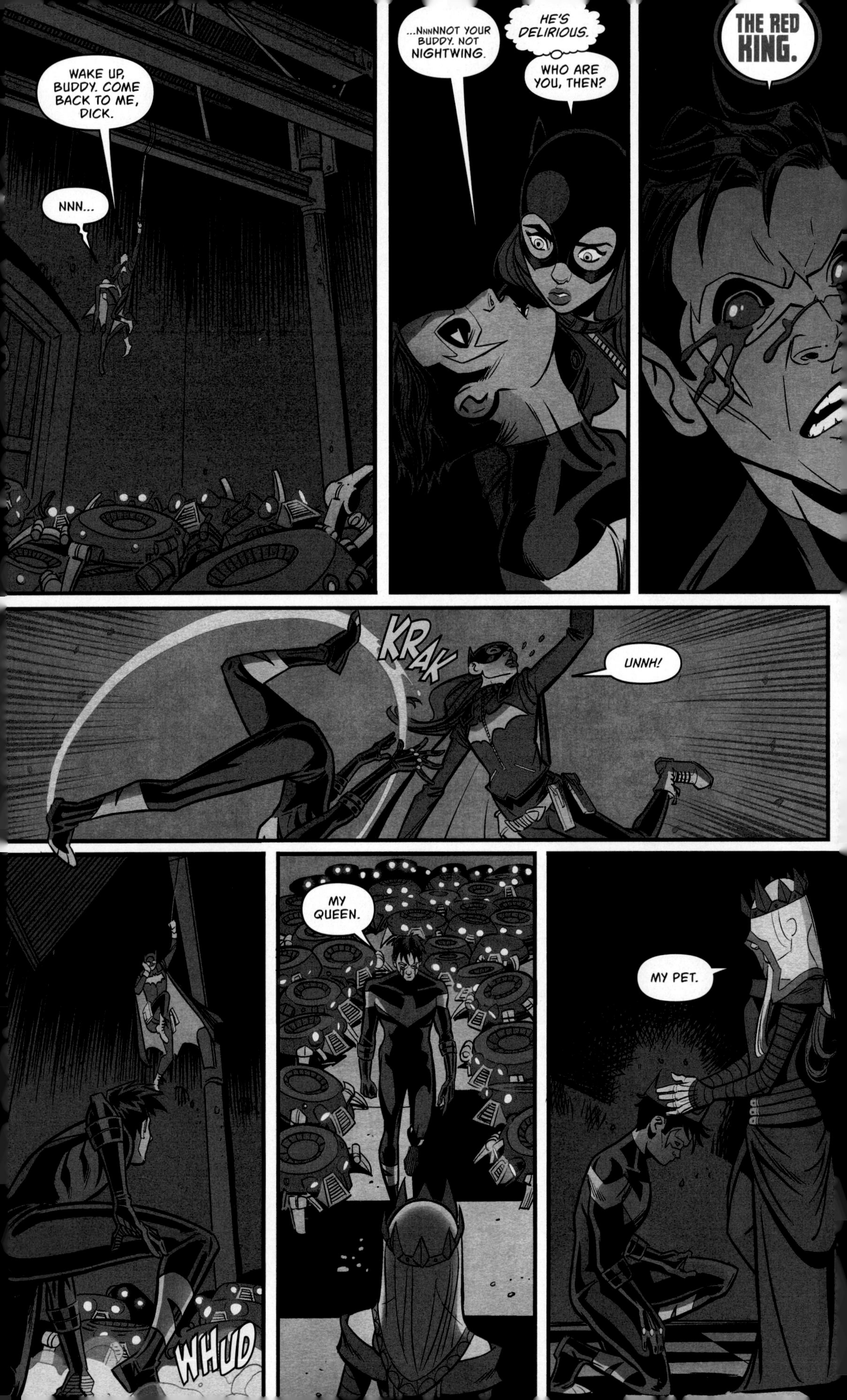
WAKE UP, BUDDY. COME BACK TO ME, DICK.
NNN...
...NNNNNOT YOUR BUDDY. NOT NIGHTWING.
HE'S DELIRIOUS.
WHO ARE YOU, THEN?
THE RED KING.
KRAK
UNNH!
MY QUEEN.
MY PET.
WHUD

STOP THIS, EDITH! HE DOESN'T DESERVE THIS! I WAS THE ONE WHO GOT US MIXED UP WITH AINSLEY!

IF YOU WANT TO HURT SOMEONE, IT'S *ME*, NOT HIM.

YOU WANT TO MAKE A DEAL? *TOO BAD*. QUEENS NEVER MAKE BARGAINS.

BESIDES, I *AM* HURTING YOU.

THERE'S NO HEL LIKE WATCHING SOMEONE YOU LOVE *SLIP AW* FROM YOU.

WATCHING THEM *TURN* ON YOU.

PET--SHE DISGUSTS ME. GET RID OF HER.

YES, MY QUEEN.

I KNOW YOU'RE IN THERE, NIGHTWING! DON'T MAKE ME FIGHT YOU!

IDIOT! HE CAN'T HEAR YOU!

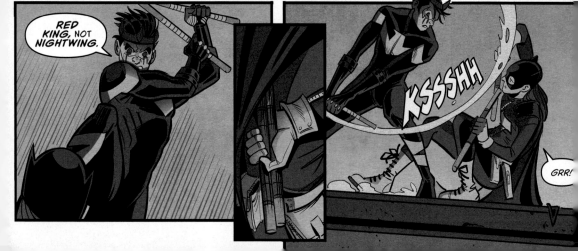

RED KING, NOT NIGHTWING.

KSSSHH

GRR!

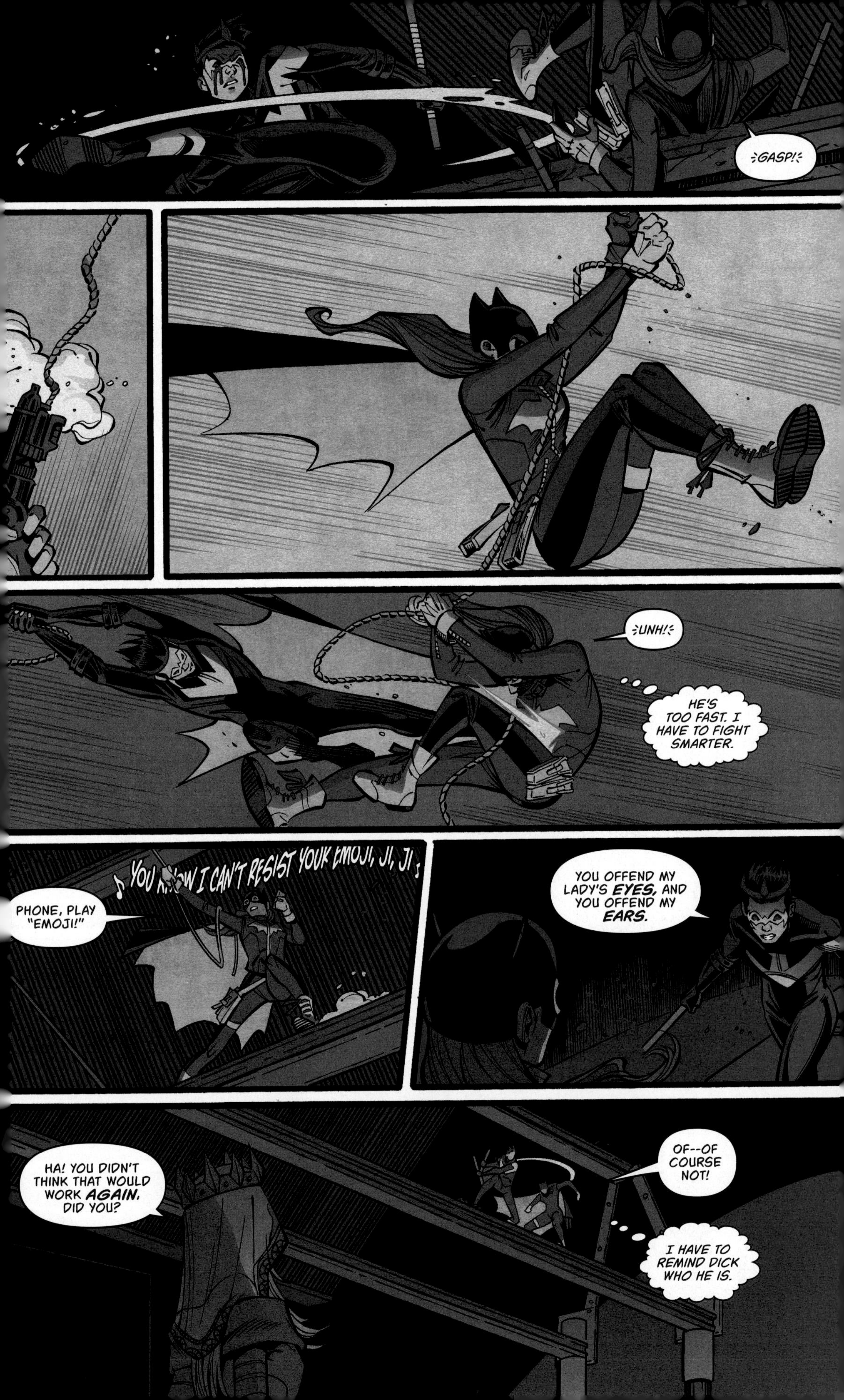
GASP!
UNH!
HE'S TOO FAST. I HAVE TO FIGHT SMARTER.
PHONE, PLAY "EMOJI!"
YOU I CAN'T RESIST YOUR EMOJI, JI, JI
YOU OFFEND MY LADY'S EYES, AND YOU OFFEND MY EARS.
HA! YOU DIDN'T THINK THAT WOULD WORK AGAIN, DID YOU?
OF--OF COURSE NOT!
I HAVE TO REMIND DICK WHO HE IS.

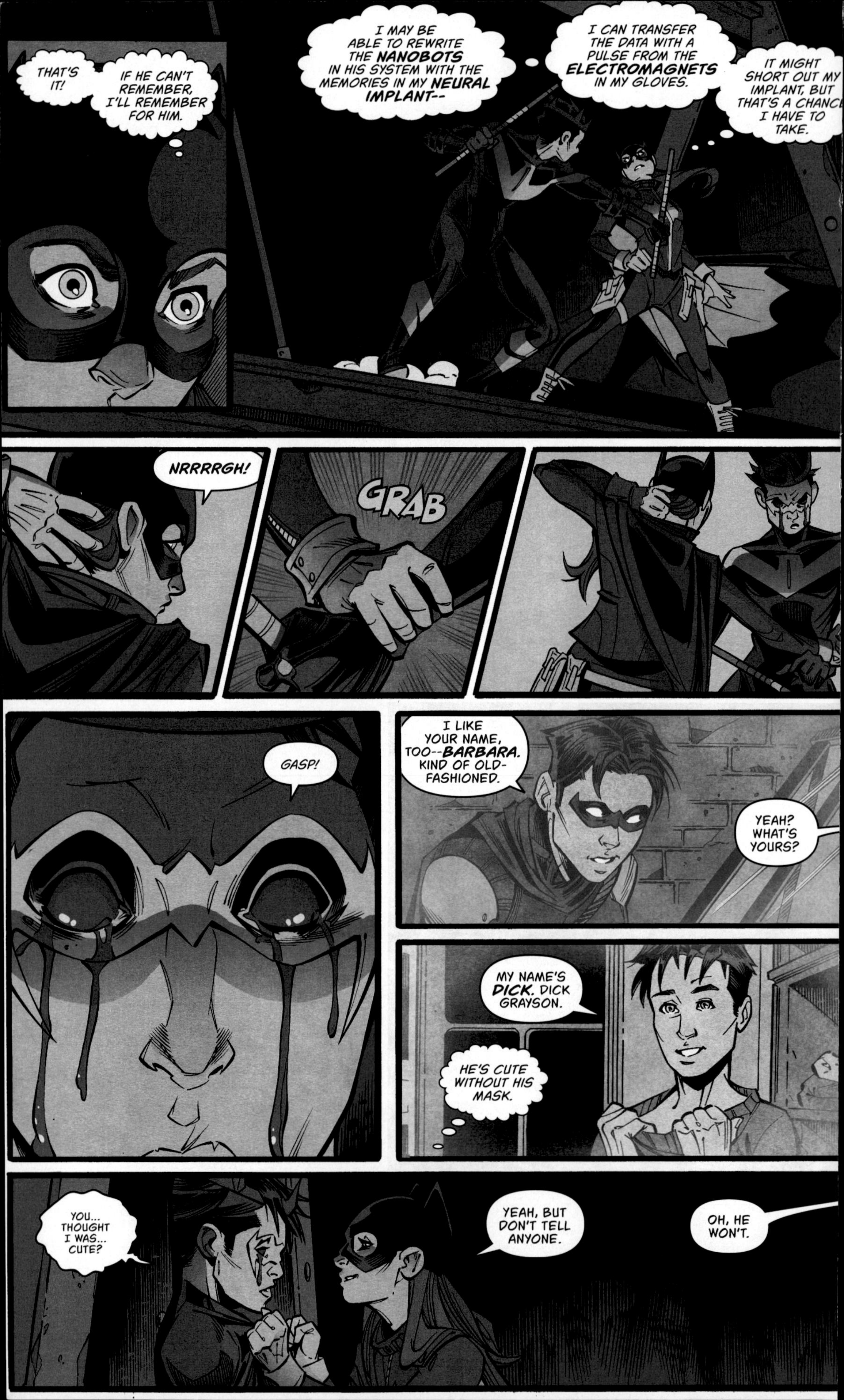
THAT'S IT!
IF HE CAN'T REMEMBER, I'LL REMEMBER FOR HIM.
I MAY BE ABLE TO REWRITE THE NANOBOTS IN HIS SYSTEM WITH THE MEMORIES IN MY NEURAL IMPLANT--
I CAN TRANSFER THE DATA WITH A PULSE FROM THE ELECTROMAGNETS IN MY GLOVES.
IT MIGHT SHORT OUT MY IMPLANT, BUT THAT'S A CHANC I HAVE TO TAKE.
NRRRRGH!
GRAB
GASP!
I LIKE YOUR NAME, TOO--BARBARA. KIND OF OLD-FASHIONED.
YEAH? WHAT'S YOURS?
MY NAME'S DICK. DICK GRAYSON.
HE'S CUTE WITHOUT HIS MASK.
YOU... THOUGHT I WAS... CUTE?
YEAH, BUT DON'T TELL ANYONE.
OH, HE WON'T.

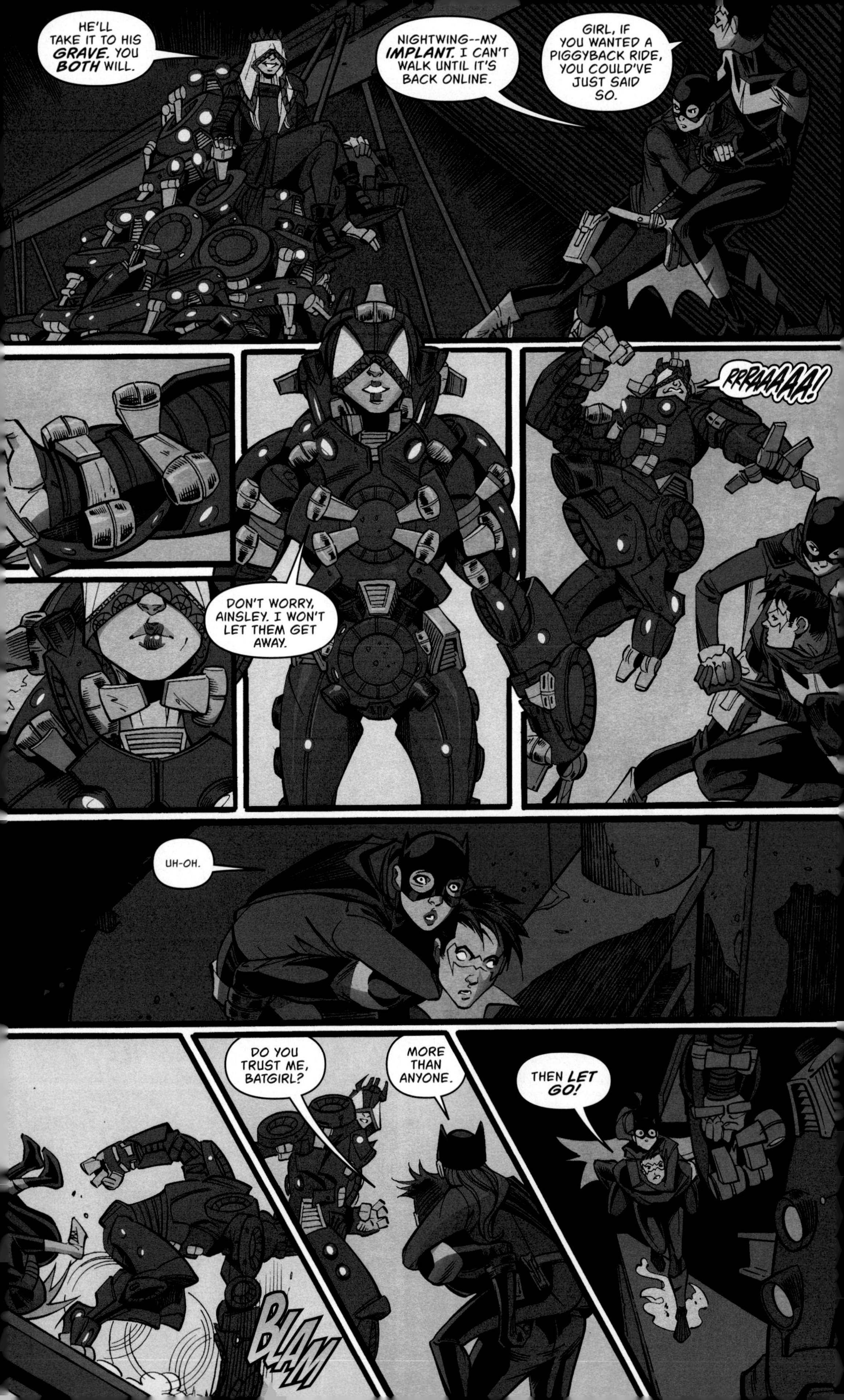
HE'LL TAKE IT TO HIS GRAVE. YOU BOTH WILL.
NIGHTWING--MY IMPLANT. I CAN'T WALK UNTIL IT'S BACK ONLINE.
GIRL, IF YOU WANTED A PIGGYBACK RIDE, YOU COULD'VE JUST SAID SO.
DON'T WORRY, AINSLEY. I WON'T LET THEM GET AWAY.
RRRAAAAA!
UH-OH.
BLAM
DO YOU TRUST ME, BATGIRL?
MORE THAN ANYONE.
THEN LET GO!

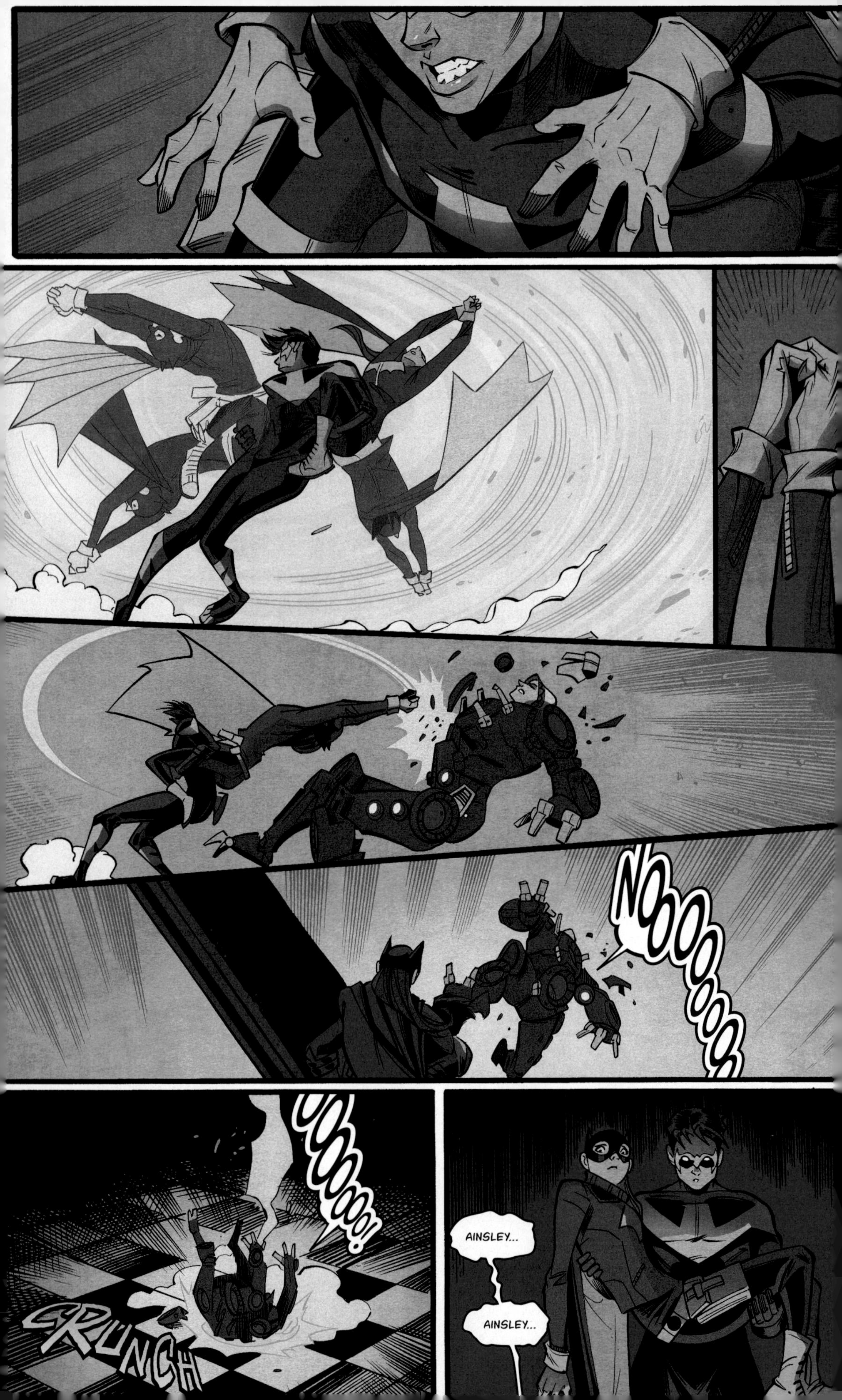
NOOOOOO
OOOOO!
CRUNCH
AINSLEY...
AINSLEY...

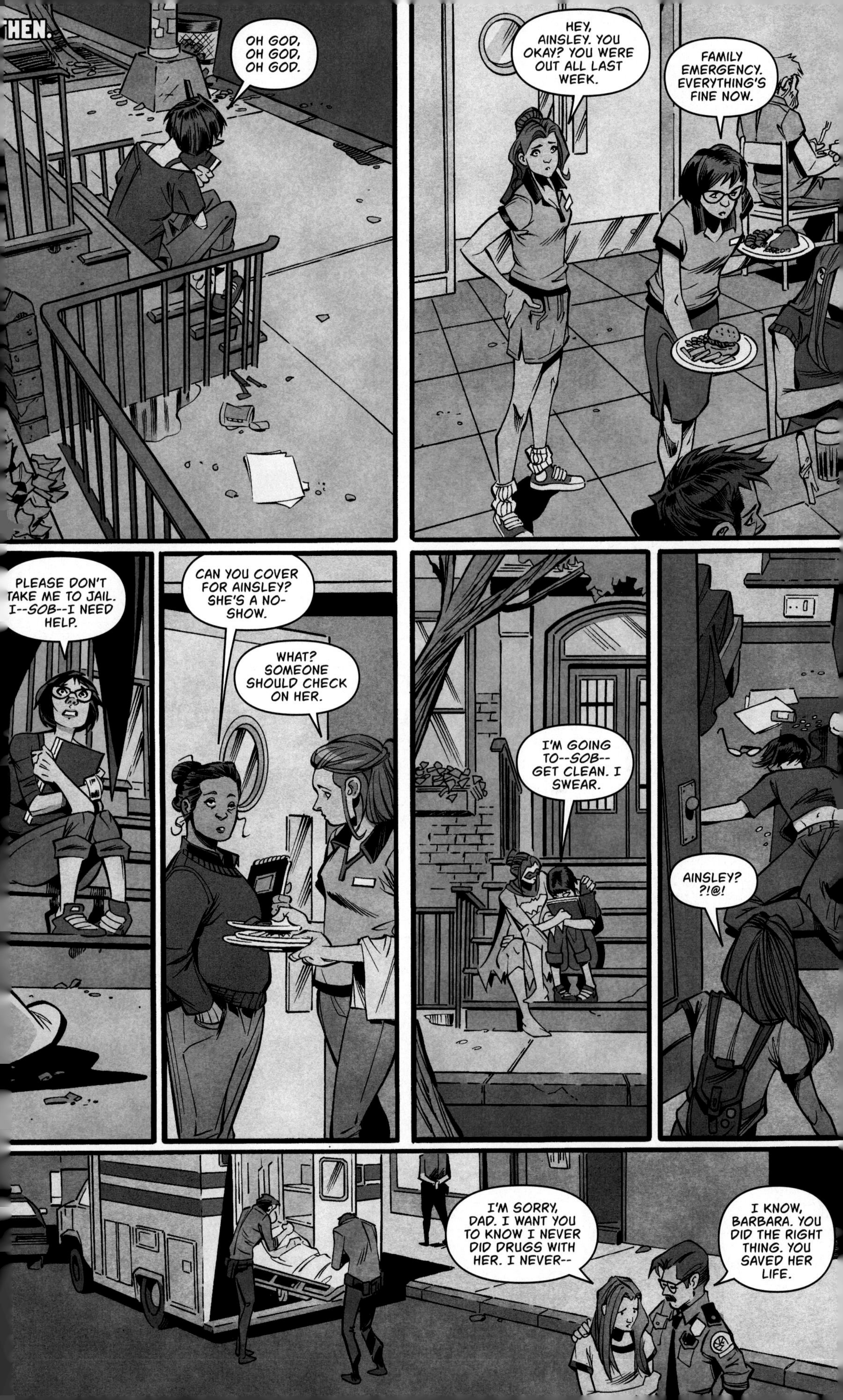
HEN.
OH GOD, OH GOD, OH GOD.
HEY, AINSLEY. YOU OKAY? YOU WERE OUT ALL LAST WEEK.
FAMILY EMERGENCY. EVERYTHING'S FINE NOW.
PLEASE DON'T TAKE ME TO JAIL. I--SOB--I NEED HELP.
CAN YOU COVER FOR AINSLEY? SHE'S A NO-SHOW.
WHAT? SOMEONE SHOULD CHECK ON HER.
I'M GOING TO--SOB--GET CLEAN. I SWEAR.
AINSLEY? ?!@!
I'M SORRY, DAD. I WANT YOU TO KNOW I NEVER DID DRUGS WITH HER. I NEVER--
I KNOW, BARBARA. YOU DID THE RIGHT THING. YOU SAVED HER LIFE.

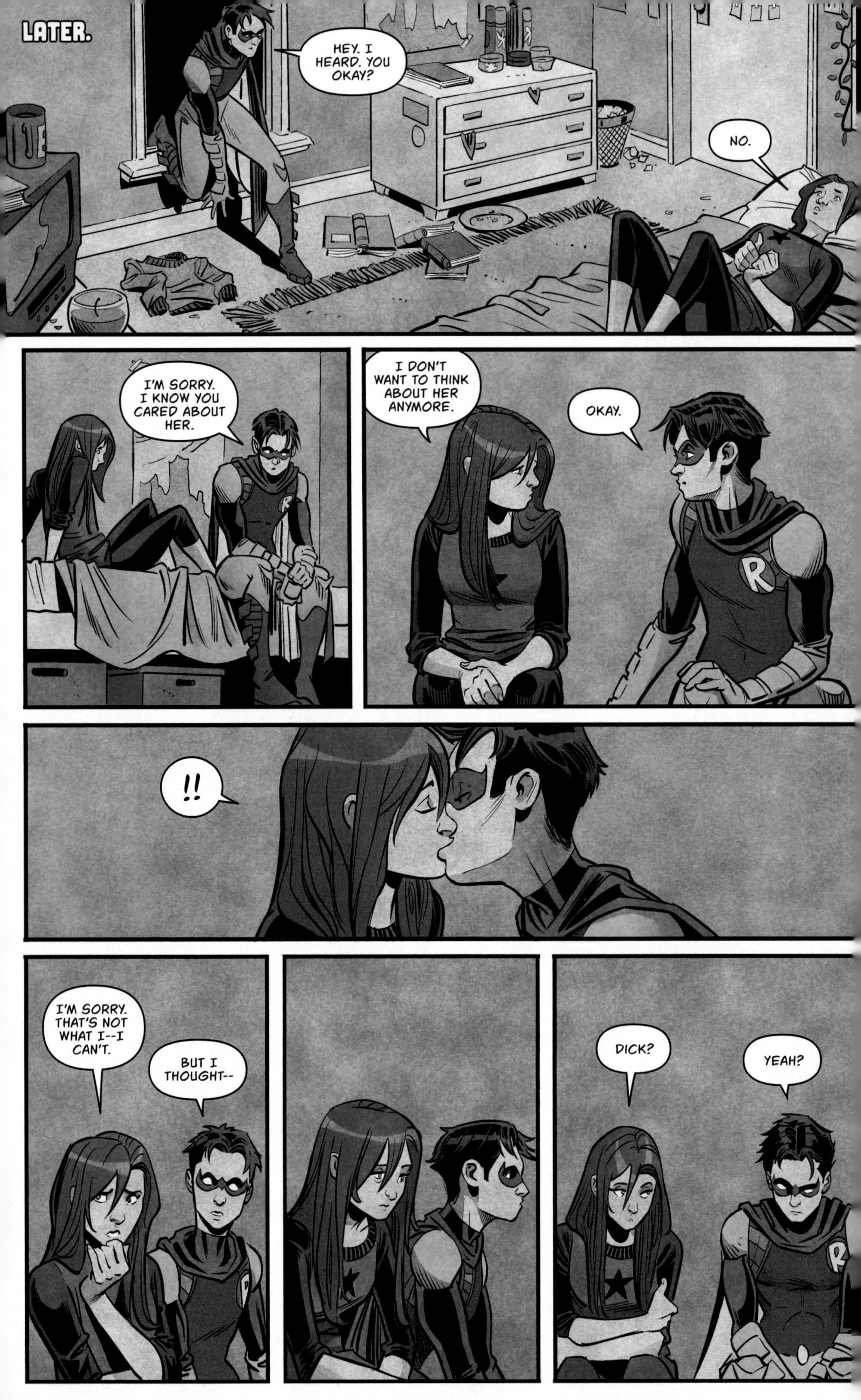
LATER.
HEY. I HEARD. YOU OKAY?
NO.
I'M SORRY. I KNOW YOU CARED ABOUT HER.
I DON'T WANT TO THINK ABOUT HER ANYMORE.
OKAY.
!!
I'M SORRY. THAT'S NOT WHAT I--I CAN'T.
BUT I THOUGHT--
DICK?
YEAH?

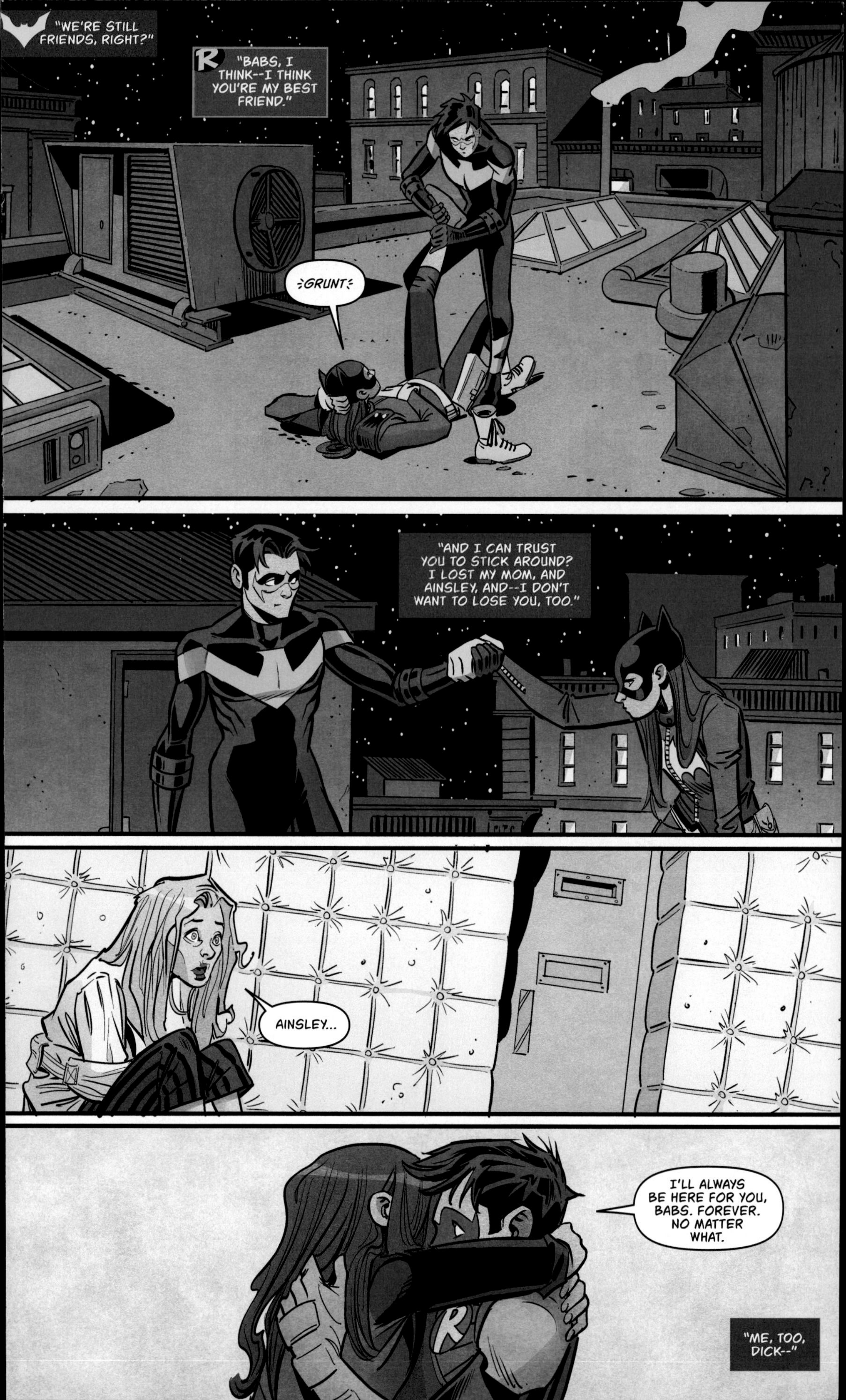
"WE'RE STILL FRIENDS, RIGHT?"
"BABS, I THINK--I THINK YOU'RE MY BEST FRIEND."
GRUNT
"AND I CAN TRUST YOU TO STICK AROUND? I LOST MY MOM, AND AINSLEY, AND--I DON'T WANT TO LOSE YOU, TOO."
AINSLEY...
I'LL ALWAYS BE HERE FOR YOU, BABS. FOREVER. NO MATTER WHAT.
"ME, TOO, DICK--"

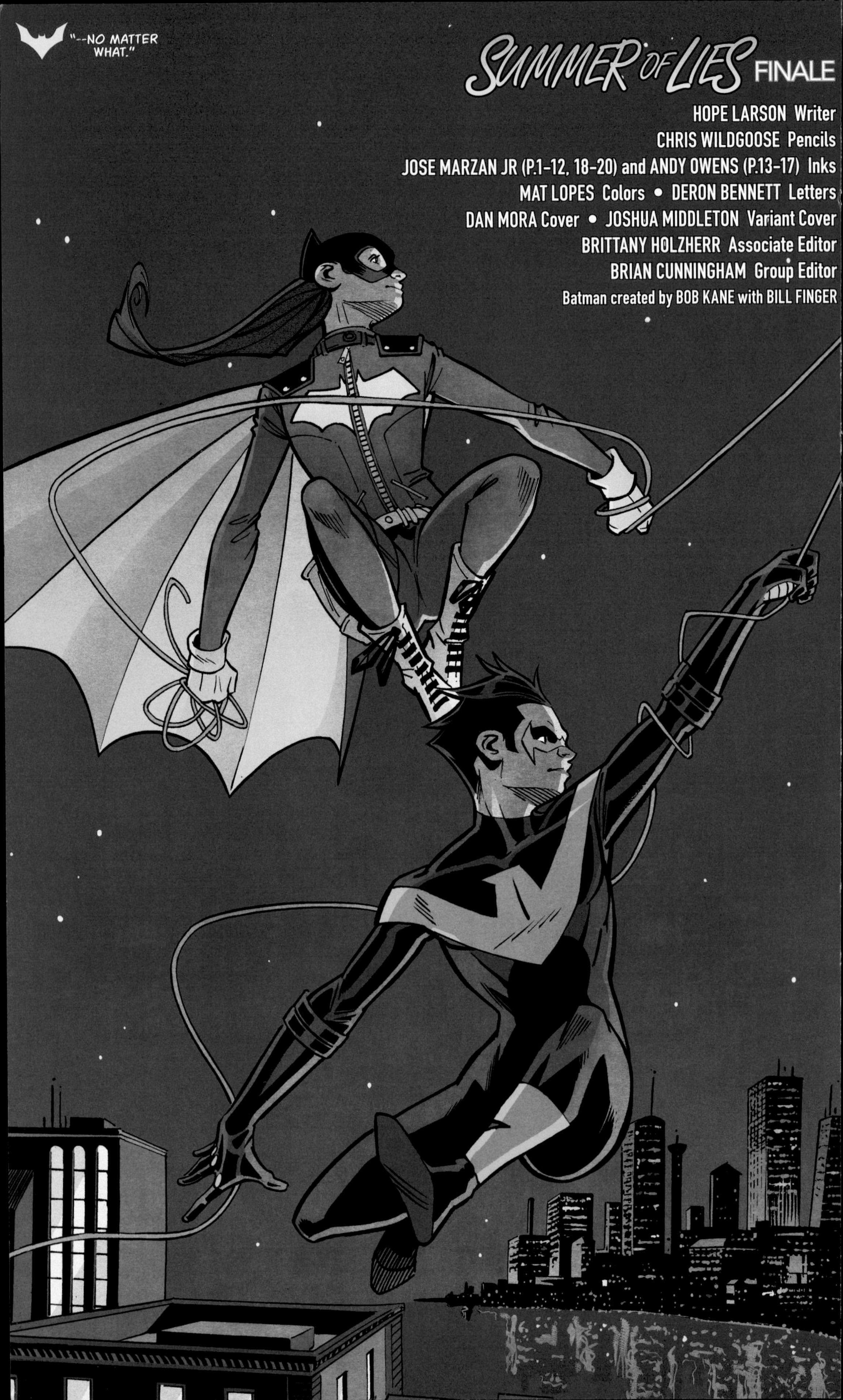
"--NO MATTER WHAT."
SUMMER OF LIES FINALE
HOPE LARSON Writer
CHRIS WILDGOOSE Pencils
JOSE MARZAN JR (P.1-12, 18-20) and ANDY OWENS (P.13-17) Inks
MAT LOPES Colors • DERON BENNETT Letters
DAN MORA Cover • JOSHUA MIDDLETON Variant Cover
BRITTANY HOLZHERR Associate Editor
BRIAN CUNNINGHAM Group Editor
Batman created by BOB KANE with BILL FINGER

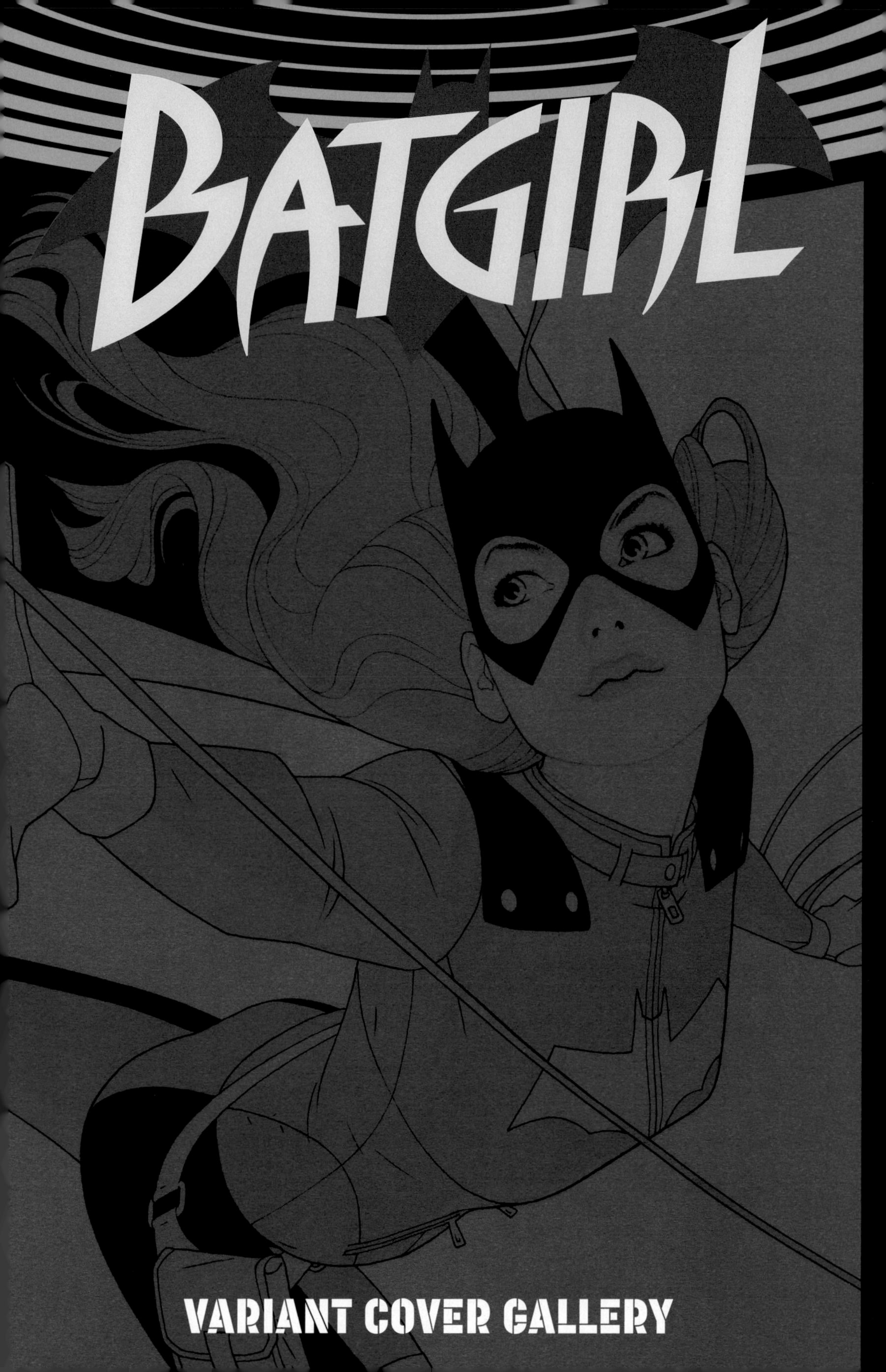
BATGIRL
VARIANT COVER GALLERY

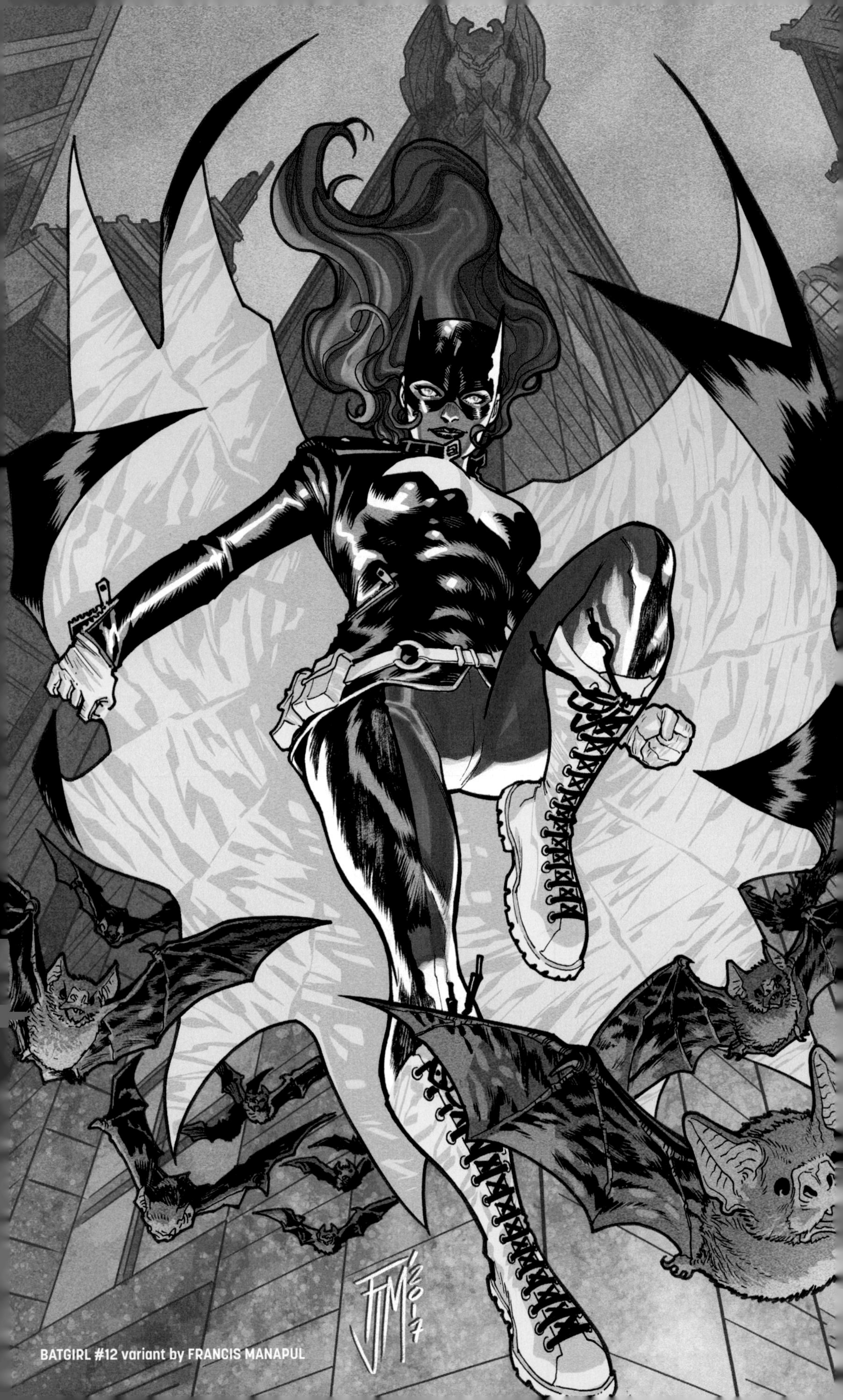
FJM 2017

BATGIRL #12 variant by FRANCIS MANAPUL

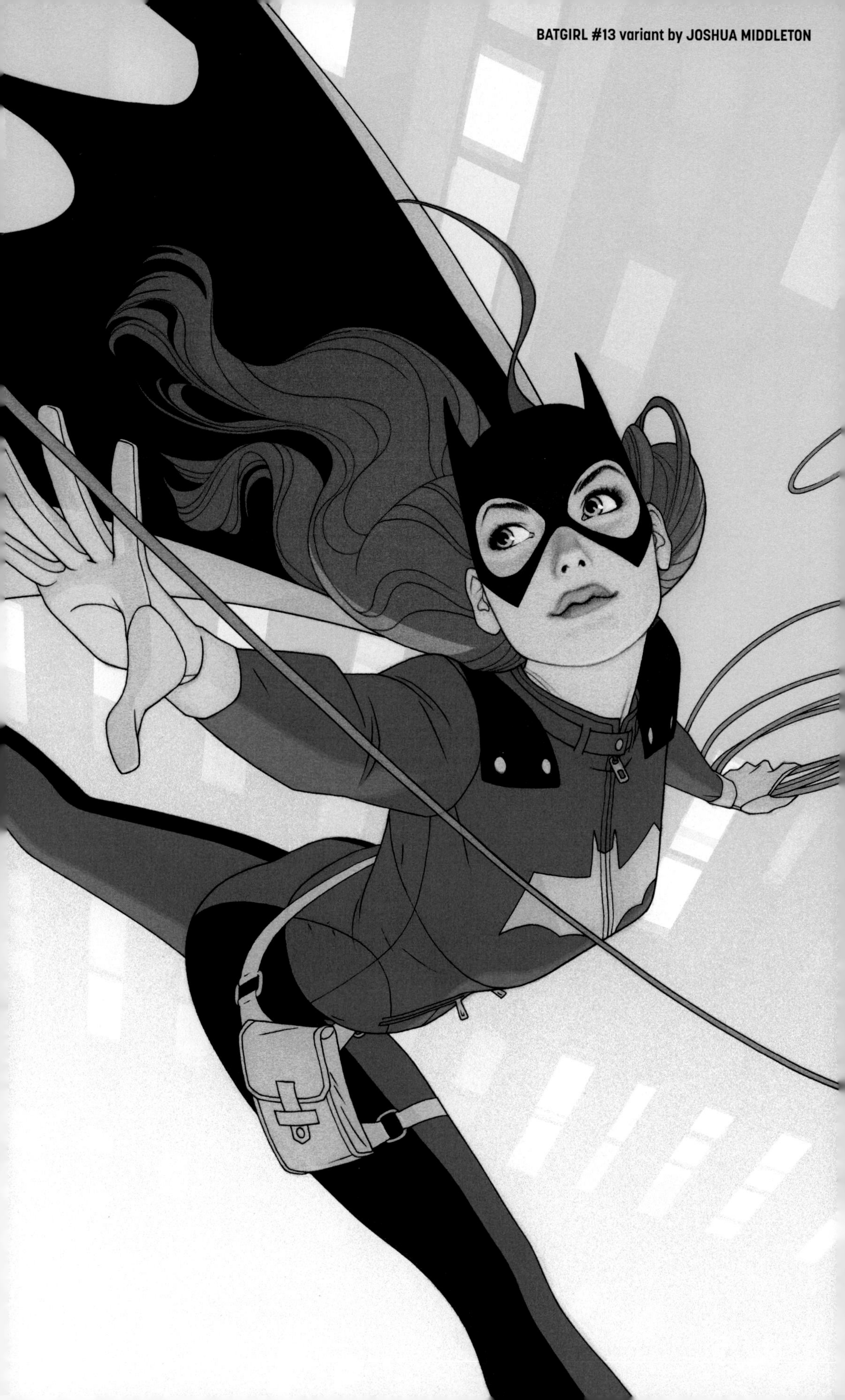

BATGIRL #13 variant by JOSHUA MIDDLETON

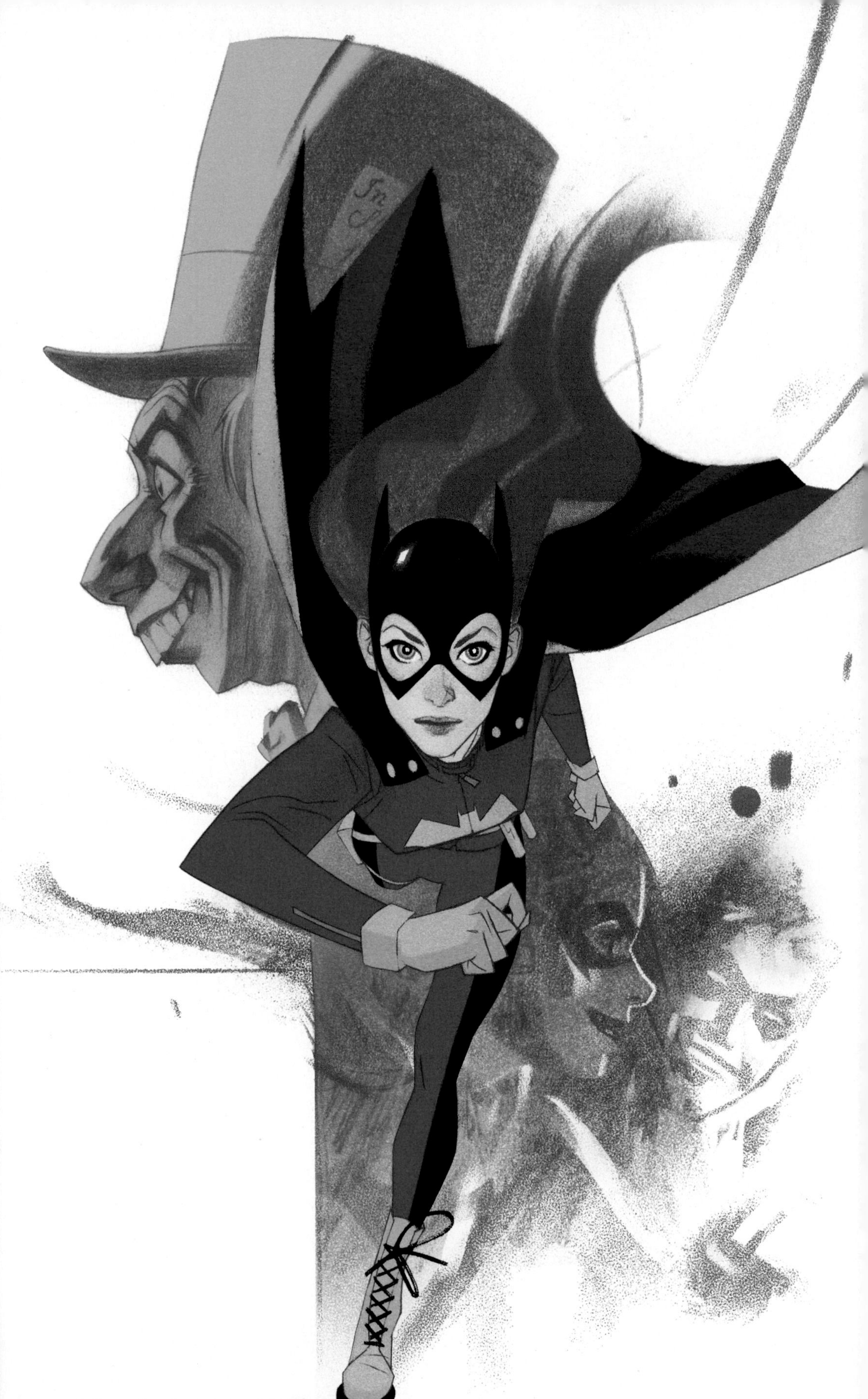

BATGIRL #14 variant by JOSHUA MIDDLETON

BATGIRL #15 variant by JOSHUA MIDDLETON

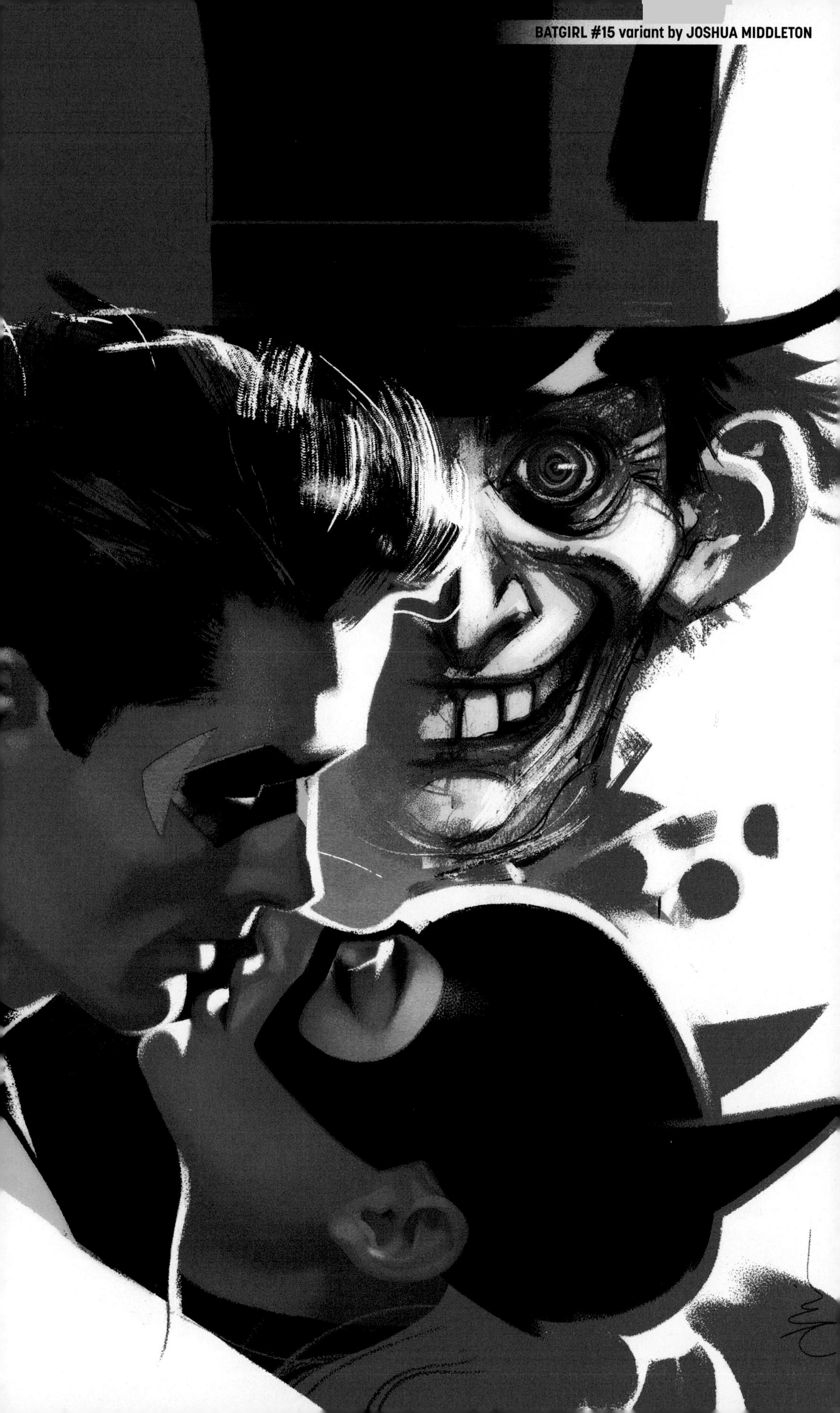

BATGIRL #16 variant by JOSHUA MIDDLETON

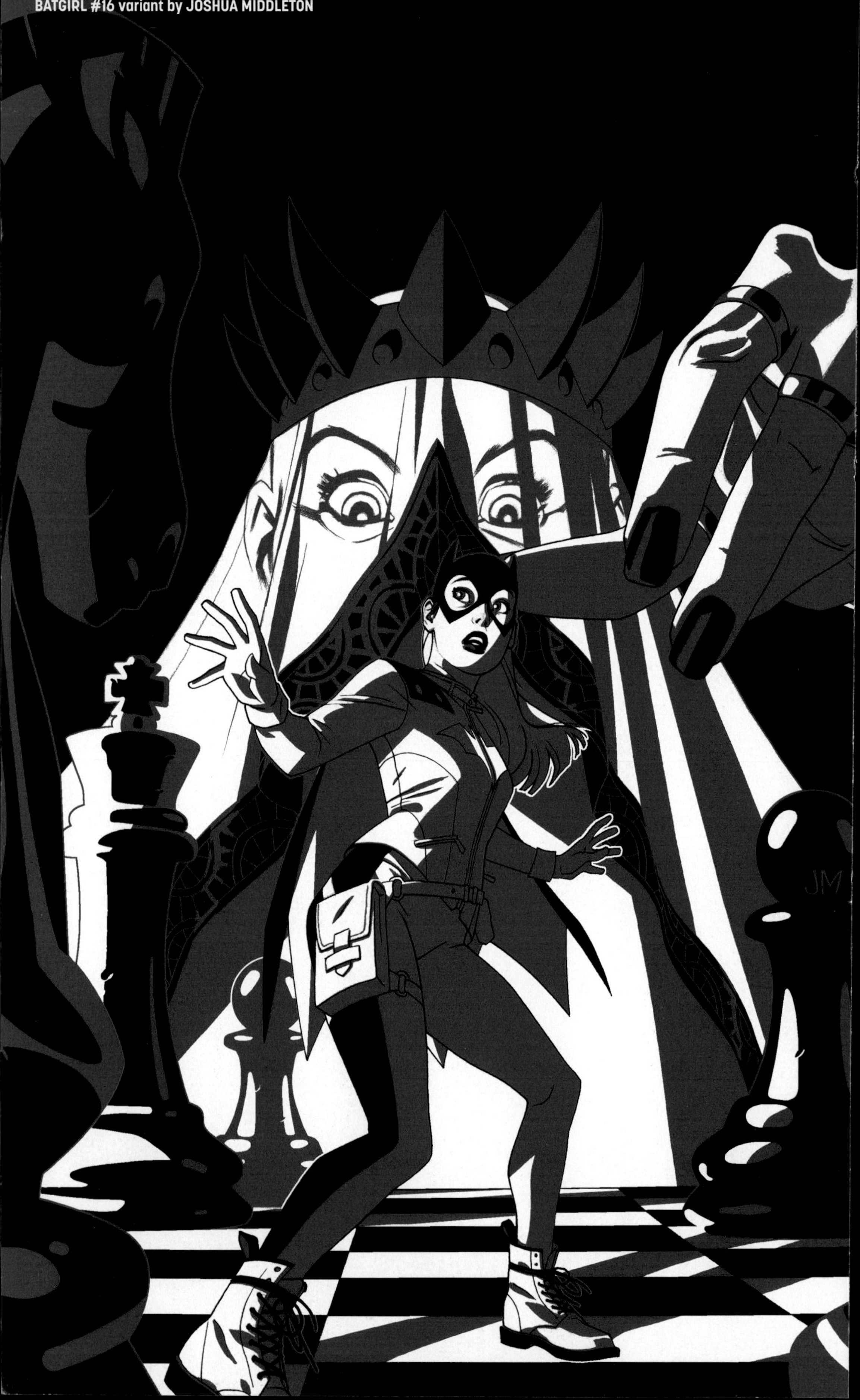
JM

BATGIRL #17 variant by JOSHUA MIDDLETON

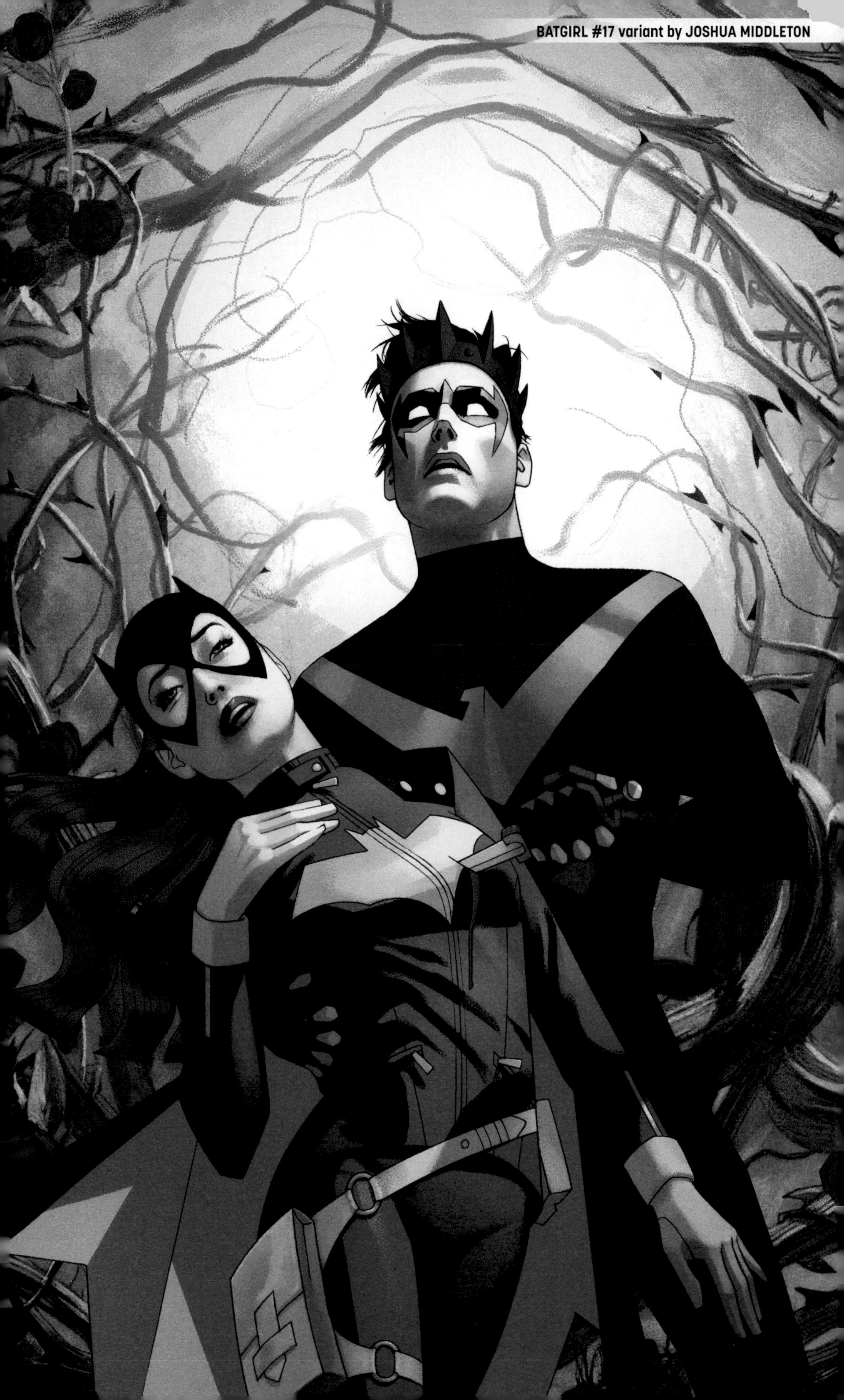

"A brand-new take on a classic, and it looks absolutely, jaw-droppingly fantastic."
– NEWSARAMA

"A whole lot of excitement and killer art."
– COMIC BOOK RESOURCES

BATGIRL
VOL. 1: BATGIRL OF BURNSIDE
CAMERON STEWART &
BRENDEN FLETCHER
with BABS TARR

BATGIRL VOL. 2:
FAMILY BUSINESS

BATGIRL VOL. 3:
MINDFIELDS

BLACK CANARY VOL. 1:
KICKING AND SCREAMING